Faculty Development for
Student Achievement

Faculty Development for Student Achievement

The QUE Project

Ronald J. Henry

Georgia State University

Editor

ANKER PUBLISHING COMPANY, INC.

Bolton, Massachusetts

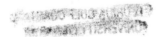

Faculty Development for Student Achievement
The QUE Project

ISBN 1-882982-97-5

Composition by Beverly Jorgensen, Studio J Graphic Design
Cover design by Frederick Schneider/Grafis

Anker Publishing Company, Inc.
563 Main Street
P.O. Box 249
Bolton, MA 01740-0249 USA

www.ankerpub.com

Library of Congress Cataloging-in-Publication Data

Faculty development for student achievement : the QUE Project / Ronald J. Henry, editor.
    p. cm.
  Includes bibliographical references and index.
  ISBN 1-882982-97-5
  1. College teachers—United States. 2. Curriculum enrichment—United States. 3. Academic achievement—United States. I. Henry, Ronald J.

  LB1778.2.F319 2006
  378.1'2—dc22

                        2005035461

Table of Contents

List of Figures ———————————————

About the Authors

The Editor

Ronald J. Henry was a cofounder of the Quality in Undergraduate Education (QUE) project and directed its work throughout the seven years of its existence. He has been provost and vice president for academic affairs at Georgia State University since 1994, and previously served in the same capacity at Miami University of Ohio and Auburn University. He earned degrees in physics from Queens University in Belfast, Northern Ireland, and has published more than 120 refereed articles or book chapters. He received continuous federal funding for his research in physics from 1970 through 1993 from the Office of Naval Research, NASA, and the U.S. Department of Energy.

In Georgia, Dr. Henry has played a prominent role in the development of state standards in the context of education from preschool through the end of college (P–16). He was appointed by Governor Zell Miller to the Georgia P–16 Council and served as the chair of the P–16 Subcommittee on Assessment and Research. At the national level, Dr. Henry was a member of the National Leadership Council of the Southern Regional Education Board, has examined for the Malcolm Baldrige National Quality Award, and was a member of the National Research Council's Committee on Undergraduate Science Education. In 2004, Dr. Henry received the Michael P. Malone Award from the National Association of State Universities and Land-Grant Colleges for his contributions to international education.

The recipient of many foundation grants to improve education, including more than $2 million for the QUE project, Dr. Henry is presently co-principal investigator for a multiyear National Science Foundation grant of $34,700,000 to develop a Partnership for Reform in Science and Mathematics.

The Contributors

Susan Albertine is dean of the School of Culture and Society and professor of English at The College of New Jersey. She specializes in late 19th-century and early 20th-century literature and women's writing. She was project director of QUE from 1999–2004.

Barbara Baumstark is professor of biology at Georgia State University (GSU), where she is also director of instructional programs for the department and director of the Bio-Bus Project. She received her Ph.D. in biology from MIT and has published 31 articles on her research in the areas of molecular genetics and microbial pathogenesis. Dr. Baumstark has received GSU's Instructional Innovation Award and the College of Arts and Sciences Outstanding Teacher Award. She was an original member of QUE at the first national meeting in 1998.

Susan L. Ganter is director of the Centers for Ocean Sciences Education Excellence at the Consortium for Oceanographic Research and Education, on leave from Clemson University where she has been an associate professor of mathematical sciences since 1999. Dr. Ganter is a founding member of the National Numeracy Network, an organization devoted to promoting quantitative literacy for all citizens through proactive education and outreach. She was a QUE consultant in mathematics.

Gloria John taught English at Catonsville Community College (now a campus of The Community College of Baltimore County) for 25 years and then served as associate dean of liberal education and learning services for 5 years, where she worked on student learning outcomes and assessment. She was QUE's communications specialist from 2001–2004.

Tim Keirn teaches in the Department of History and the College of Education at California State University–Long Beach. He studied at the University of California–Los Angeles and at the London School of Economics and Political Science. He is a specialist in British history and history education. He was an original member of QUE in 1998.

Bernard L. Madison is professor of mathematical sciences at the University of Arkansas. Nationally known for his work promoting universal mathematical knowledge (numeracy), he has published in his research field and in mathematics education and policy. He was visiting mathematician at the Mathematical Association of America (MAA) in 2001 and is now co-director of the MAA project Preparing Mathematicians to Educate Teachers. He was a QUE consultant in mathematics.

Ruth Mitchell was a cofounder of the QUE project and principal partner at the Education Trust for more than 10 years. She has a B.A. from Oxford University and a Ph.D. in English from the University of California–Los

Angeles, where she taught writing and editing. She is the author of books and articles on educational assessment and professional development.

Brett Mizelle is assistant professor of history and director of the American Studies Program at California State University–Long Beach. He received his M.A. in history and Ph.D. in American studies from the University of Minnesota. He is the author of a number of articles on the cultural contribution of animal exhibitions in the early American republic. He was a member of the California State University–Long Beach QUE cluster group.

Jerry Sarquis is professor of chemistry and biochemistry at Miami University of Ohio. He has been interested in chemical education throughout his career. He coauthored two high school chemistry textbooks, was secretary of the American Chemical Society's Division of Chemical Education from 1993–2004, and recently served as peer-led team learning coordinator for the National Science Foundation's Multi-Initiative Dissemination Project on active learning methods. He was a QUE consultant in chemistry.

Foreword

Higher education in America has become increasingly fragmented over the past two decades—especially in its undergraduate dimension. Researchers like Clifford Adelman (1999) tell us of incoherent patterns of course-taking and remind us that growing majorities of baccalaureate degree earners attend two or more institutions. Others, like William Massy (Massy, Wilger, & Colbeck, 1994), simultaneously claim that "hollow collegiality" now characterizes faculty life at most of our colleges and universities. Conditions like these, if unaddressed, will severely threaten our ability to create quality undergraduate experiences. The Quality in Undergraduate Education (QUE) project shows us that it doesn't have to be this way. And its implications are profound in at least three areas of practice.

First, QUE focused explicitly on managing student transitions. By pairing two-year and four-year campuses with already-established patterns of mutual migration, it tackled the multi-institutional attendance challenge head-on by aligning important courses and requirements. Multi-institutional attendance is a firmly established feature of the undergraduate landscape. With growing demands to educate ever-greater shares of our young adult population, it does little good to address this challenge by simply restricting admissions or through across-the-board articulation agreements that simply name "acceptable" courses. The faculty-to-faculty dialogues that formed the heart of QUE instead forged coherent pathways centered on agreed-upon academic content and levels of challenge, not administrative fiat. The lessons they teach apply just as well to within-institution transitions like prerequisite sequences and developmental study.

Second, these really *were* dialogues—exchanges that led to faculty development as well as curricular coherence. Characteristically, they were held within disciplines—the settings where faculty actually work and live. Having watched several of these conversations unfold personally, I am convinced that this disciplinary specificity was a powerful key to QUE's success. Too many otherwise admirable faculty development conversations fail because they focus only on broad generalities of student performance about which all can agree. Confining initial discourse to the specifics of a discipline, participants could instead locate precisely where they *disagreed* and, through exchanges that were substantive but difficult, begin to establish common ground.

Perhaps most important of all, QUE's work began to shift higher education's collective attention toward standards for student achievement. Twenty years of experience with assessment has familiarized most faculty with the language of outcomes. But far too many still see such goals as unrelated to their work in the classroom. By concentrating on specific expectations that all students should meet at particular levels of undergraduate study, participating faculty went well beyond assessment as currently practiced. They could instead start to depend upon one another to create assignments and learning experiences that cumulated steadily and consistently—helping to avoid the kind of "teaching rework" that has become so common, and frequently so exasperating, in transfer situations.

"Think globally and act locally" is an aphorism much quoted but rarely practiced. The QUE project was admirably guided by a few important big ideas, but it was relentlessly and effectively grounded in local action. Its lessons deserve all our attention.

Peter T. Ewell, Vice President
National Center for Higher Education Management Systems

References

Adelman, C. (1999). *Answers in the tool box: Academic intensity, attendance patterns, and bachelor's degree attainment.* Washington, DC: U.S. Department of Education, Office of Educational Research and Improvement.

Massy, W. F., Wilger, A. K., & Colbeck, C. (1994, July/August). Overcoming "hollowed" collegiality. *Change 26*(4), 11–20.

Preface

Faculty development at its best invites faculty members to reflect on their professional obligations to their academic disciplines and to their students. This book describes the experiences of faculty in biology, chemistry, English, history, and mathematics as they strove to write clearly the learning outcomes they expect from their students at level 14 (transfer or end of lower division) and level 16 (graduation in the major). The writing of outcomes is a profound intellectual challenge that requires deep understanding of the discipline, and consequently of the essential learning that students must acquire. It can only be accomplished in groups, for outcomes are reached by consensus. Outcomes are followed by rubrics (scoring guides for assignments) and assessments, but products are less important for faculty development than the process—the conversation and expression (occasionally passionate) of ideas and values that form the catalyst for intellectual expansion.

Faculty Development for Student Achievement: The QUE Project describes a seven-year project—Quality in Undergraduate Education—that produced important changes in departments and in the teaching of individual faculty in 21 two- and four-year institutions across four states. The story is told first from the organizational perspective in national and local campus meetings, and then from the point of view of faculty in five chapters, one for each discipline. This description of QUE is intended as a model for administrators and faculty seeking to meet the challenges of increasingly diverse students as well as the increasingly divergent ways to earn a degree.

This book explains the QUE model so that other institutions can use it for similar faculty development. Rather than a blow-by-blow report of the QUE project, it focuses on the problems that led to its development: concern about low levels of student learning in postsecondary institutions and demands by state legislatures that funds for postsecondary institutions be tied to assessment of student learning. The institutions involved were state universities and their feeder community colleges, but the QUE model of faculty development applies to all kinds and sizes of postsecondary institutions. The QUE model will interest administrators—provosts, deans, and department chairs—most concerned with faculty development, as well as faculty themselves. Also offered here is practical guidance on establishing standards (called outcomes in this book, for reasons that will be explained), using outcomes to review and revise departmental courses, and writing rubrics to help students understand how their work is being evaluated.

Contents Overview

Chapter 1. Ronald J. Henry provides an introduction to the book, explaining the theoretical background of QUE, its organization, and its major outcomes.

Chapter 2. Ruth Mitchell describes QUE's national activities, the problems associated with the development of standards (outcomes), the development of rubrics, and attempts at cross-disciplinary syntheses.

Chapter 3. Gloria John and Ruth Mitchell discuss QUE's local activities and how faculty interacted on their campuses and at the national meetings, with a focus on their sometimes-uncomfortable relations.

Chapter 4. Barbara Baumstark shares her intellectual journey through standards for biology from the beginnings of QUE in 1998.

Chapter 5. Jerry Sarquis discusses the situation in chemical education today.

Chapter 6. Susan Albertine offers advice to English department chairs based on her QUE experience on the process of developing and using outcomes.

Chapter 7. Tim Keirn and Brett Mizelle present a case study on the transformation of the history curriculum at California State University–Long Beach as a result of their participation in QUE.

Chapter 8. Bernard L. Madison and Susan L. Ganter place QUE's faculty development activities in the national context of developments in mathematics education and quantitative literacy.

Chapter 9. Ruth Mitchell and Ronald J. Henry offer recommendations for similar faculty development projects, based on positive and negative experiences with QUE, and reflections on the project more than one year after the end of funding.

Appendixes. Appendixes include a brief history of the structure and development of QUE; samples of the outcome or "standards" documents written by QUE participants; information on the construction of rubrics; and QUE consultants and leaders, along with their conference appearances and publications.

Ronald J. Henry
September 2005

Acknowledgments

To acknowledge the contributions of all who made both QUE and this book possible is an editor's pleasure as well as duty.

The ExxonMobil Foundation and The Pew Charitable Trusts funded QUE for five years and supported us with their interest and involvement, as well as money.

Policy Studies Associates were more than just QUE's evaluators for four years: They provided us with information and astute observations so that we could make almost continuous in-course corrections.

Janis Somerville of the National Association of System Heads cofounded QUE and was a source of support and guidance throughout its life and beyond.

Ruth Mitchell, another cofounder of QUE when she was a principal partner at the Education Trust, wrote four of the book's chapters twice (responding to participants' comments) and guided the overall process of the book's production. She pulled together materials from seven years of work, including reports by the QUE leadership to our funders; reports of interviews, focus groups, and observations by Policy Studies Associates; reports from cluster leaders; and a voluminous file of emails.

Gloria John, QUE communications facilitator, designed and administered a survey documenting the results of QUE and contributed to Chapter 3 her knowledge of and sympathy for the concerns of community college faculty.

A first draft of this book was reviewed by an informal editorial committee of 18 cluster leaders and consultants whose names are listed in Appendix E.

We thank everyone mentioned here, as well as all who participated at any time in QUE. Their enthusiasm and willingness to think creatively encouraged us throughout a challenging but immensely rewarding process. This book is for them and for those who will emulate them.

1

Introduction

Ronald J. Henry

> Purposeful change ought to result in better student learning, in more
> inventive research and scholarship. The case for higher education thus
> becomes one of clearly stated outcomes that reflect both the guiding
> values and the processes employed to achieve those ends.
>
> — *Turning Point*, 1997, p. 7

The Quality in Undergraduate Education (QUE) project was a faculty development project that focused on learning outcomes as a means to stimulate
conversation among faculty about the quality of student learning and how to
raise it. The conversations occurred along two dimensions: 1) with colleagues
in the same discipline across institutions, states, and the nation, and 2) within
two- and four-year institutions that operated locally in a cluster feeder relationship, teaching the same students successively.

The QUE project operated for seven years (1997–2004) in state-
supported postsecondary institutions in California, Georgia, Maryland, and
Nevada, bringing together faculty in biology, chemistry, English, history, and
mathematics from 21 institutions in nine partner clusters in the four states.

All the QUE participants met twice a year at national meetings, and between meetings, local two- and four-year partners met together on their campuses. The attraction of thinking about the goals of teaching was such that for the initial two years three clusters from three states met without external funding. QUE was funded from 1999 by the Pew Charitable Trusts and the Exxon-Mobil Foundation. Activity in at least four clusters has continued after funding ended in April 2004.

The Professional Conversation

The Quality in Undergraduate Education project has documented outcomes that will be described later, but it had other perceived benefits for faculty members. They valued the conversations at both the national meetings and in their clusters. For many partici-pants, QUE's most significant results are the insights and reve-lations vital to their professional sense of accomplishment that were produced by considering the aims of undergraduate edu-cation. The writing of learning outcomes was the occasion for faculty development; but for the participants, it was not the ulti-

> The best, most useful, most valuable feature [of QUE] was to bring together enthusiastic faculty so that they could discuss their teaching methodology, their values, problems, etc. concerning the teaching profession in institutions of higher learning.
>
> —*QUE participant survey response*

mate product. That was a professional conversation in which they began to see a new perspective on teaching arise from an emphasis on learning. Many faculty who are committed to their disciplines first and unaccustomed to the language of education reform—those who may never have read Barr and Tagg—may begin to see teaching as part of learning when it is approached as an integral part of their own disciplinary mastery (Barr & Tagg, 1995).

Throughout its life (and beyond, as activities continue despite the cessation of funding), QUE was a faculty-oriented project. The initial planners recognized that no change takes place in postsecondary institutions without the faculty's willing participation. Faculty felt that they owned QUE, that they were a community of scholars thinking together about student learning and their responsibility for it. The exchange of views against the background of a common goal—higher levels of student learning—produced changes in techniques, rethinking of assumptions, and revision of attitudes. The QUE project gave faculty the opportunity and the stimulus for the reflective conversations that enlarged their ideas about learning and what is necessary for learning to take place. Further, they came to realize that the essential purpose of faculty development should be the improvement of student learning, not just the improvement of the faculty member. In this way, QUE was about more than supporting the knowledge and skill development of individual faculty or writing learning outcomes. It became a faculty development project designed to help faculty work collectively on problems of practice within their own institutions and with practitioners from other institutions.

Participants in QUE found that the conversations about learning outcomes, assignments, rubrics, and assessment led them to reflect on their teaching so that they realized in many cases that what they thought they were doing and what was actually happening were two different things. These reflections focused on the intentionality of teaching and learning, because communicating expectations to students is only possible after faculty themselves are clear about them. The discussions involved in writing learning outcomes are a necessary preliminary to learning-centered teaching.

On one occasion, a QUE discussion about teaching critical thinking led to the realization that no one could define it, and so faculty began to question how they tell students what they expect. Some had assumed that college students should know how to produce work at the college level, that understanding expectations was somehow magically provided at admission. Only conversation with their colleagues could help them understand the reality of student bewilderment in the face of frequently incomprehensible demands.

In the experience of many faculty members, assessment is associated with compliance in response to some external agency such as a regional accreditation association or a state system office. In spite of, and sometimes because of, the assessment movement that has flourished since its inception in the late 1980s, many faculty members view assessment with suspicion. However, in our professional conversations, we have learned to approach assessment as a register of each student's progress through the curriculum, not just in a particular course. Thus assessment can be viewed as a commitment to individual student learning that first informs instruction (Doherty, Riordan, & Roth, 2002). Design and implementation of assessment is a central dimension of teaching.

The book's remaining chapters describe the participants' experiences and provide further insight into how QUE faculty perceived the effects of discipline-based conversations on their professional identities. Now we will establish why we saw a need for QUE, the rationale for it, and the design we used.

The Need for QUE

The QUE project arose from a matrix of concern about low levels of student learning in postsecondary institutions. Its founding partners were the Education Trust, Inc., a nonprofit national organization that publishes data-based policy reports and offers programs to promote the educational success of low-income and minority students from kindergarten through college (K–16); the National Association of System Heads (NASH), an association of state university leaders concerned about issues such as low graduation rates among minority students, the poor literacy of some graduates, and the preparation of teachers in state universities; and Georgia State University (GSU), whose leaders were prominently involved in NASH and supportive of the Education Trust's work, especially in what were called K–16 councils—groups formed geographically around a four-year institution with its feeder community colleges and K–12 schools to ensure equitable opportunity for all students.

These three entities shared the concerns of such organizations as the Association of American Colleges and Universities (AAC&U) and the American Association for Higher Education (AAHE) that student learning in U.S. postsecondary institutions is not keeping pace with the demands that society places on graduates (e.g., AAC&U, 2002). Student achievement is measured by retention and graduation rates and by anecdotes from employers about its graduates. The first measure is not reassuring and the second has ominous implications for public support (and hence funding) for postsecondary education. Fewer than two-thirds (63%) of students obtain a bachelor's degree within six years of entry, and only 46% of African-American students and 47% of Latino students graduate within six years (Carey, 2004). Only 37% of students graduate within the traditional four years at a college or university (Carey, 2004). Anecdotal complaints by employers of graduates are supported by literacy surveys showing few students with mature literacy skills after four years of postsecondary education (Carey, 2004).

But poor graduation rates and uneven student achievement are not the only challenges facing public postsecondary institutions. They are striving to maintain quality in the face of budget cuts by legislatures at the national and state levels, who are being challenged to balance budgets while addressing other priorities such as health care, K–12 education, and prisons. Further, legislatures are threatening accountability in terms that seem simplistic to university personnel. The system may be losing its competitive edge internationally: The much-vaunted superiority of U.S. postsecondary education is declining as other countries are increasing college-going rates. Some countries have doubled their degree rate over the past 20 years, while the U.S. rate has not changed (Carey, 2004).

The increasing numbers of low-income and minority students now entering postsecondary education place additional stress on cash-strapped institutions. Accountability requires that institutions be more successful at graduating all admitted students. Low-income and minority students are frequently less well prepared for the rigors of college and thus need more resources to succeed. Failure has serious economic, political, and social consequences for a pluralistic society in which income is closely correlated with educational attainment.

To add to the challenges, the number of possible paths to a baccalaureate degree is growing. Students, especially low-income and minority students, now transfer freely among community

> Few maps exist to help students plan or integrate their learning as they move in and out of separately organized courses, programs, and campuses. In the absence of shared learning goals and clear expectations, a college degree more frequently certifies completion of disconnected fragments than of a coherent plan for student accomplishment.
>
> —AAC&U, 2002, p. 3

colleges, state colleges, and research universities. In addition, the development of online universities implies that degrees must have value and meaning beyond individual campuses. A degree should mean approximately the same no matter whether it is obtained after four years in a single institution, after three or four changes of institutions, or after completing work on a computer without ever meeting an instructor or fellow students in person. As Shulman (2000) stated,

> For-profit providers, distance learning, and other new sources for higher education are creating a market where institutions must be prepared to document and display evidence that they are fostering learning, deep understanding, passionate commitments and civic virtues in the domains in which they educate. (p. 52)

Developments in technology have made U.S. society so complex and fast-paced that just keeping up and maintaining informed participation in this democracy exceeds the capacity of most college graduates. They need not only more learning, but learning of a different quality. Bernard Madison, a QUE mathematics consultant, former vice president of the Mathematical Association of America, and advocate of quantitative literacy for all students, believes that postsecondary education must address interdisciplinary issues and connect education to the real world: "We must stop presenting and studying pre-packaged, neatly bundled information—that's not real. Problems and information come at you in random order in the real world and we must get students to practice dealing with them in this way" (personal communication, October 21, 2004).

Participants in QUE managed to touch all these problems and more in the course of extended conversations that radiated out from the development of written learning outcomes, but the project's major focus was on raising the quality of student learning.

The Rationale for QUE

Attempts to improve student academic achievement must be focused on the learning environment they encounter, which is largely under faculty control, although the class size for which faculty are responsible is determined by administrators and available funding. Faculty at most four-year institutions have traditionally paid less attention to the learning environment they create through their teaching than to their research, because publication counts more heavily than teaching in promotion and tenure decisions. The dilemma is how to help faculty change their teaching so that student learning will improve, while preserving time for research.

> What's different about QUE is that the emphasis is so strongly on what students are supposed to do, to get. That makes all the difference.
>
> —QUE participant survey response

The Quality in Undergraduate Education project brought together two strands in current education reform: It adopted the approach advocated by the Carnegie Academy for the Scholarship of Teaching and Learning (CASTL) for introducing the scholarship of teaching and learning (SoTL) to faculty, and it used as a vehicle the development of learning outcomes for the end of the first two years of college (level 14) and the major (level 16) in five academic disciplines (biology, chemistry, English, history, and mathematics).

The Carnegie approach promotes deeper understanding of academic disciplines at the same time as it shapes teaching more productively. Ernest Boyer, who first articulated the expansion of scholarship to include teaching in his seminal book, *Scholarship Reconsidered,* asserted that excellent teaching is marked by the same habits of mind that characterize other scholarly activities such as research (Boyer, 1990; Hutchings, Babb, & Bjork, 2002). Boyer, and the increasing number of scholars who write on postsecondary teaching, see no intellectual conflict between research and teaching (Glassick, Huber, & Maeroff, 1997). Shulman (2000) writes that faculty are members of two professions, devoted simultaneously to their academic disciplines and to their roles as educators: "In both of these intersecting domains, we bear the responsibilities of scholars—to discover, to connect, to apply, to teach" (p. 49).

However, the proliferation of innovative ways to teach and assess—portfolios, curriculum and course redesigns, and imaginative uses of technology—produced by faculty who work within the SoTL paradigm, did not include explicit statements of expected learning outcomes in 1997 when we embarked on the QUE project. Learning outcomes seem to be chronologically primary in the sequence laid out by Glassick, Huber, and Maeroff (1997, p. 24):

> All works of scholarship, be they discovery, integration, application, or teaching, involve a common sequence of unfolding stages . . . :

> 1. Clear goals

> 2. Adequate preparation

> 3. Appropriate methods

> 4. Significant results

> 5. Effective presentation

> 6. Reflective critique

Yet we did not find the case for "goals" made strongly in the literature on SoTL. Instead, we turned to elementary and secondary education because two of the three QUE founders—the Education Trust and GSU—were intimately involved in the development of K–12 standards at the state and district levels and could see how teachers benefited from thinking about their expectations of students.

Admitting to a K–12 origin for an idea is not easy in postsecondary education, especially because the movement included the dreaded word *standards* in its title, standards-based education.[1] When the preliminary discussions for the proposed QUE project were taking place in 1997, the educational community was focused on academic standards and their effects on K–12 education only. To the leaders of QUE, it seemed logical that standards could be extended to postsecondary education to describe a seamless progression from beginning to graduation and to design assessments in direct relationship to expected learning. Assessment is not possible without statements of what should have been learned.

The QUE initiators thus formulated a policy according to which standards would:

- Be stated clearly and openly so that students, faculty, and the paying public know the expected levels of achievement

- Demonstrate the value of years of study beyond high school

- Be consistent across institutions of comparable mission

- Accommodate sophisticated and broadly understandable assessment

- Be adequate to the demands of professional, personal, and civic life beyond college

Standards (Outcomes) as Tools for Learning

The theory of the efficacy of learning outcomes is based on public knowledge: If everyone knows what learning is expected, then students cannot be left untaught—or blamed for not mastering untaught material. The public nature of learning outcome statements is especially valuable for minority and low-income students who struggle against explicit and implicit assumptions that they cannot learn at the same level as others and who often are not aware of the implicit assumptions that underlie assignments given by faculty from different cultural backgrounds. Learning outcomes make responsibilities clear—the responsibilities of faculty to explain essential material and of students to master it.

Questions that are seldom asked before design and development of an undergraduate course include:

- Why am I teaching this?

- Where does it fit in a student's progress toward the essential knowledge and skills of this academic discipline?

- Should I be teaching other concepts?

- Has someone else in the department already taught them?

- If we look at all our curricula, will we find an incremental progress toward mastery of essential knowledge and skills?

Thinking first about explicit learning outcomes for the course allows us to consider these questions.

Such questions were not always asked when QUE first proposed its approach to reform. The common practice was (and still is, to a large extent) that faculty decided on a set of topics for a course, chose the "best" textbook, and covered the material. Assessments were those suggested as exercises in the book; interim or final exams were designed to query students

> Discourse that encourages a shift from instruction to learning serves to reinforce the idea that the point of teaching is student learning.
>
> —*Doherty, Riordan, and Roth, 2002, p. iii*

on the main ideas covered in each chapter. There was little thought or reflection about learning outcomes.

It is probably too much to expect that colleges and universities would institute universal revision of course structures or even that they can rationalize progress toward the degree. In large institutions students battle availability of courses and are glad to get all their requirements, no matter in what order and how much additional time is necessary.[2] But if learning outcomes are clearly defined, those statements can be used at the department level to examine course content and align courses in terms of their contribution toward the learning goal. Such review and revision of courses at the department level subsequently happened in most QUE participating institutions.

Learning outcomes represent the academic community's values, but writing learning outcomes requires time and space for a group of faculty to work together. Participants in the conversation have to examine their individual values and decide how to modify them if the community is to reach consensus. The conversation brings to the surface implicit judgments that become the inconsistencies students face when they sometimes receive widely different grades from different faculty members for similar work. On the positive side, the conversation can also reveal harmonies of thought that may lead to new combinations of courses.

Following both this theoretical assumption that writing learning outcomes rationalizes teaching and observations from the effects of standards-setting in K–12, the QUE model for faculty development envisions faculty writing explicit statements of learning expected in their disciplines for level 14 and at graduation in the major. These benefits follow:

- Department chairs and department committees can examine course offerings for the contribution each course makes to the program's learning goals.

- Faculty can design each course to cohere with others in the same department.

- Faculty can provide students with rubrics (statements of grading criteria) for each assignment.

- Students receive explicit statements of the learning expected in each course and level.

- A student can pursue a coherent program of educational development toward explicit learning goals.

The intellectual challenge for faculty inheres in the difficulty of rendering explicit what "everybody knows" is expected in a course or major. For example, what is the optimum balance of skill and knowledge in history? Is it possible to describe clearly the difference in writing ability between rising juniors and graduates? What mathematics should be acquired in general education? What habits of mind should be expected in biology and chemistry graduates, no matter what their upper-division concentration?

Answering such questions in conversation with colleagues constitutes the intellectual backbone of QUE. Producing written learning outcomes as the focus of faculty development begins the process outlined by Glassick, Huber, and Maeroff (1997). Although reflection is the sixth step, it runs throughout each step.

Once learning outcomes are written, they can be used as standards (in the sense of a yardstick) to ensure that course content and course assessment are aligned with the learning outcomes, and, at a higher level, that curriculum is aligned with them as well. Figure 1.1 lays out the QUE conceptual framework that drove the agenda.

Figure 1.1
The QUE Conceptual Framework

Stage 1

The development of student learning outcomes: What should students know, understand, and be able to do?

- Level 14

- Level 16

- General education (cross-disciplinary competencies)

Stage 2

Course-level alignment and assessment

- Aligning assignment with learning outcomes

- Developing rubrics

- Scoring student work

Stage 3

Curriculum-level alignment and assessment

- Curriculum mapping

- Gap analysis ("super matrix") to ensure that curriculum provides opportunity to reach the learning outcomes

Stage 4

Designing curriculum to match pedagogy with cognition, as documented in literature on the psychology of learning, such as *How People Learn*.[3]

In addition, drafting learning outcomes and using them to guide instruction contributes to public understanding of postsecondary education. Teaching is rationalized, and published learning outcomes clarify for faculty, administrators, and students—the people inside the academy—as well as legislators, employers, parents, and the general public, what students are expected to learn. Postsecondary education frequently appears to those outside its institutions to be closed and mysterious and therefore subject to hostile criticism and even fear. Openness and clarity about the learning represented by the baccalaureate degree can improve public understanding and support.

The Design of QUE

QUE was organized along two dimensions: national/disciplinary and local/interinstitutional. All three founding partners (the Education Trust, NASH, and GSU) were committed to the inclusion of two-year colleges because of their concern for the education of low-income and minority students, for whom community colleges may be the main access to postsecondary education. Including two-year college faculty means overcoming barriers built by years of separation. Although two- and four-year faculty frequently teach the same students in successive years, factors such as geographical distance, perceived difference in academic challenge, and lack of articulation agreements disturb the pattern, not to mention that the two faculties do not always see their interests as congruent: Two-year faculty are not required to undertake research in order to achieve tenure (although many do research because of their interest in their disciplines). Thus, while the following clusters of institutions did not work perfectly in terms of transferring students, they shared with their partners the experience of being public institutions in the same state, subject to the same mandates and budget exigencies. There were four clusters in Georgia, two each in Maryland and California, and one in Nevada.

- Georgia State University and Georgia Perimeter College (a five-campus institution)

- Armstrong Atlantic State University and Coastal Georgia Community College

- Fort Valley State University (a historically black institution) and Middle Georgia College

- Valdosta State University and Abraham Baldwin Agricultural College

- Salisbury University, Chesapeake College, and Wor-Wic Community College

- Towson University and The Community College of Baltimore County

- California State University–Fullerton, Fullerton College, and Mt. San Antonio College

- California State University–Long Beach, Long Beach City College, and Golden West College

- University of Nevada–Reno and Truckee Meadows Community College

These institutions were recruited through the K–16 partnerships organized by the Education Trust and NASH, which explained the proposed project at meetings and by correspondence in 1997. At that time, QUE had no external funding, so institutions that participated had to fund their faculty to attend meetings and spend time on their campuses developing statements of learning outcomes. Three state institutions and their two-year partners did so (University of Nevada–Reno [UNR], Georgia State University, and California State University–Long Beach [CSULB].) (See Appendix A for a brief history of QUE.)

A number of institutions joined QUE because they were already engaged in related projects and saw QUE as an opportunity to continue and expand them.

- Georgia institutions were involved in a statewide K–16 standards-setting movement.

- GSU and Salisbury University were involved in the Standards-based Teacher Education Project, which scrutinized courses taken by future teachers to ensure that topics in K–12 standards were included in those courses.

- Towson University had an administration that hoped to use student learning outcomes to advance assessment, and its partner, The Community College of Baltimore County, had a new three-campus system with a strategic plan built on the foundation of student learning outcomes.

- Fort Valley State University was deeply involved in setting standards across its departments, including raising entry and exit requirements for education students.[4]

- UNR was faced with a mandate for assessment from the Nevada legislature.

- The biology department at California State University–Fullerton had embarked on a deep restructuring of its courses.

- GSU saw QUE as an opportunity to meet the assessment requirements of an upcoming Southern Association of Colleges and Schools accreditation review.

- CSULB felt pressure from the politics of assessment. "We realized we needed to develop standards before others did it for us," a participant said.

- California State University–Fullerton and Fort Valley State University were also members of the Student Learning Initiative based at Alverno College and funded by the Pew Charitable Trusts (Doherty, Riordan, & Roth, 2002).

A QUE science consultant observed that faculty involved in such projects gained the most from QUE: "The groups that have progressed the most are those which had already been thinking about reform before they joined up with QUE." Private institutions were not approached, but the model of faculty development that has emerged from QUE applies equally well to all postsecondary institutions.

This model was a federal structure. It had a central leadership (based at GSU) that received and controlled the funding from 1999, when the grants from the Pew Charitable Trusts and the ExxonMobil Foundation arrived. Then there was a local leadership that organized the partnerships, called clusters, among the two- and four-year institutions to produce written learning outcomes and other products as the project progressed. Each cluster received an annual grant of $32,000, intended to pay for attendance at the two annual national meetings, released time for a cluster coordinator, and activities related to the production and implementation of learning outcomes and assessments. But local control over the funds was absolute, as long as funds were used to advance QUE purposes: The leaders of one cluster donated their time, using their compensation for faculty released time and local meetings.

Other clusters held faculty retreats to discuss learning outcomes or subsidized the production of handbooks on revised courses.

The functions of the on-campus work and the national meetings were separated so that there was no suspicion that we were trying to impose nation-wide standards or goals on the institutions. National goals for postsecondary education seemed an impossible idea that would dissolve QUE immediately if mentioned because of the disparity of missions among U.S. colleges and universities. However, in practice, statements of learning outcomes were readily exchanged and copied from one cluster to another. It became obvious, for example, that history majors in Maryland should command the same history skills as students in California. Biology learning outcomes originally written in the first QUE national meeting in 1998 became the standard for all the clusters. The learning outcomes statements listed on the QUE web site (www.gsu.edu/que) are similar to each other, even though they carry the names of different clusters.

Each cluster was asked to work with three academic disciplines. For example, the Metro Atlanta cluster of GSU worked in biology, history, and mathematics; the Long Beach cluster worked in biology, English, and history. Some clusters were unable to persuade a third department to participate, so they worked in two disciplines only, and at least one cluster added a fourth discipline as news spread across the campuses.

At its best, QUE's federal structure stimulated on-campus learning outcomes-setting and related activities, such as reviews of curriculum, and initiated mutually satisfying partnerships among two- and four-year institutions. National meetings were theme-focused and developed into arenas for speakers (Austin Doherty, Peter Ewell, Andrea Leskes, Grant Wiggins, Kathleen Yancey) and for introduction of topics such as writing rubrics, interdisciplinary connections, and mapping the curriculum (the super matrix)—all intended to model the work to be completed on the campuses.

The QUE leadership provided the participants with expert advice from consultants in their disciplines. These consultants came to be known as critical friends; that is, they saw QUE from a perspective outside the structure but with sympathy for its goals. They included three CASTL scholars, one in biology and two in history. (See Appendix E for a complete list of QUE personnel.)

Critical friends played a dual role for QUE: They brought their expertise to the participants at the national meetings and sometimes to the clusters, but they also ensured that QUE was known and recognized by national disciplinary organizations.

The QUE leadership enjoyed the support of a communications liaison, who was responsible for the dissemination of news and information about meetings to—and from—the participants. QUE was also evaluated formatively and summatively by Policy Studies Associates, who reported through focus groups, observations in the clusters, and telephone interviews.

National Outcomes of QUE

Although it is difficult to isolate the direct effects of QUE on student achievement—indeed it will not be possible for a number of years—the change of focus from inputs to outcomes, from teaching to learning, could affect thousands of students.[5] Students benefit immediately from the clarification of expectations that results from written learning outcomes and assignments designed to enable students to reach the learning outcomes.

The following were the major achievements at the national level:

- The QUE project managed to complete most of the stages in the conceptual framework, although time ran out on assessments and Stage Four was only mentioned. Statements of expected learning outcomes were written in all the disciplines at both level 14 and level 16.

- Perhaps the most useful written products in addition to the learning outcomes were rubrics, scoring guides for assignments and assessments (see Appendix C for rubrics and their construction). Rubrics list the features of student work in response to an assignment or assessment that will earn a letter grade or a numerical score. Along with specific instructions in assignments, rubrics give students a clear picture of the teacher's expectations. Rubrics were the subject of workshops at the national meetings and were applied in the clusters on site. In final interviews, 15 faculty members (of a subset interviewed) reported either beginning or increasing the use of rubrics in their teaching. One biology faculty member

reported working with colleagues to develop rubrics
for the capstone course so
that the whole department
would agree on the level of
achievement expected.

- It is perhaps easier to work
within a discipline because
the structure of postsecondary education reinforces
boundaries, but neverthe-
less, QUE initiated discussions of the interdisciplinary
and cross-disciplinary issues
that preoccupy Bernard
Madison and others who see

> I also benefited from our national confer-
> ences because there was a sharing of
> ideas and rubrics that took place there
> and I feel it helped me in developing
> assessment tools which were improved
> in conciseness and clarity. . . . One as-
> signment I distribute concerns accessing
> and interpreting a primary source from
> the Internet—I have a greater number of
> students being successful. I also include
> cause and effect examples on my exams
> and have also seen student success
> increase in understanding that concept.
>
> *—QUE participant survey response*

the need to enlarge the areas of congruence between the academy and
the real world. The subject was framed by two questions: What does my
discipline need from your discipline? What strategies does your discipline
use for students to acquire cross-disciplinary competencies, such as empathy, conceptual understanding, problem solving, and so on? Answers
varied:

- A cross-disciplinary capstone course was described by an English faculty member who is teaching a course on the reflections in literature
of the concepts of science, especially evolution.

- Faculty cited the extensive use of portfolios as an assessment tool,
thus requiring more writing.

- Faculty advocated a requirement that all students should take an introductory statistics course before proceeding to their majors.

- Faculty suggested using students in other majors to help students
understand concepts. For example, a biology major might explain
cloning to an English class discussing religious views on human
knowledge.

The conversations made clear that interdisciplinary teaching and learning will need focused attention and support if they are to become major features of postsecondary education. But the door is open.

- QUE also resulted in a tool—the super matrix—of potential value to any department assessing the contribution each course makes to student achievement of learning outcomes. It consists of a chart listing the outcomes for each program vertically, with rows for the courses, which receive scores according to the level of the contribution made (see Figure 1.2).

Figure 1.2
The Super Matrix

Learning Outcomes	Course 1	Course 2	Course 3	Course 4	Course 5	Total
1	1	3	4	0	4	12
2	2	1	2	0	2	7
3	1	2	0	2	0	5

After the course syllabus, assignments, and assessments are thoroughly examined, the courses are scored according to the following scale:

- *Score 4:* The learning outcome is fully introduced, developed, and reinforced throughout the course in lectures, labs, assignments, projects, tests, and assessments. Students are able to apply the learning outcome independently.

- *Score 3:* The learning outcome is introduced, developed, and reinforced in lectures, labs, assignments, projects, tests, and assessments. Students have a working knowledge of the learning outcome but may not be able to apply it independently.

- *Score 2:* The learning outcome is introduced and developed, resulting in a minimal working knowledge of the content and/or skill.

- *Score 1:* The learning outcome is introduced in lectures but not reinforced, so that students have only an awareness of the content and/or
  skill.

- *Score 0:* The learning outcome is not mentioned.

For example, Course 4 in Figure 1.2 would need some revision, and the
content of all the courses might be evaluated to increase command of Outcome 3. These revisions are the point of the super matrix—it is not an end
in itself but a means of beginning dialogue about responsibility for student
learning.

Thus QUE participants took learning outcomes, rubrics, the super matrix, and thoughts about cross-disciplinary learning back to their clusters from
the national meetings and produced results exemplified in the next section.

Local Outcomes of QUE

- In one university, the history department transformed its major curriculum according to level 14 standards they helped to develop at the first
  national meeting of QUE in 1998. (A detailed description of this transformation is the subject of Chapter 7.) Learning outcomes have now
  been written for courses in historical skills and historiography that act
  as gateways to ensure that students have the skills necessary for the major. Learning outcomes have also been written for the capstone course.
  Eight faculty members teach the theory course, but all have agreed on
  uniform assignments. These courses use a portfolio assessment system,
  ensuring that history students have writing skills. This approach has been
  so successful in raising the achievement of history majors that other departments are beginning to pay attention. The history department at the
  four-year institution also produced a handbook for students at level 15
  and above, including all the learning outcomes for the major, so that students, including those at the partner community college contemplating a
  history major, will know what is expected of them.

- At another four-year institution, the English department published its learning outcomes for the English major on its web site so that students can see "with one click of a mouse," as a faculty member put it, the expectations of an English major. The partnership with the community college has produced outcomes and assessment for the composition course, so that faculty from both institutions and K–12 teachers assess student work each semester. The success of this joint assessment has aroused interest in evaluating writing in general education courses, all of which require substantial writing. The QUE partners founded a Faculty Writing Center to support faculty from all disciplines in assigning writing to their students by helping faculty design appropriate assessments, assess student writing, and confront the issues arising from asking students to write in different disciplines.

- The biology department at another four-year university completely redesigned its curriculum. Although the process had begun before the department joined QUE, it gained momentum from participation, especially in discussions about the form and function of learning outcome statements. The redesign represented a triumph of cooperation and negotiation among the 27 full-time faculty who recognized in the late 1990s that their biology curriculum was chaotic: Seniors were still taking core courses, upper-division students had different backgrounds so that a coherent ability level and knowledge base could not be relied on, and the courses most students had taken did not follow a logical sequence. By fall 2003, four new core courses complete with learning outcomes were offered, and in the following year learning outcomes were being developed for the other courses in the major.

- The English department at one four-year institution published a Freshman Year Writing Guide, complete with examples of student papers to illustrate the application of rubrics.

- In one cluster, relations between the two- and four-year partners were initiated and flourished dramatically. Participants remarked on the "sense of family" that developed among the faculty of all three institutions. A community college history participant said that the institutions had been working in isolation for 25 years—"no one knew what the other was doing." As a result of three years of QUE cluster meetings, he and a colleague at another partner college said they know how to prepare their students to do well when they transfer to the university and they have redesigned their course syllabi.

Collaboration extended to administrators. The shift to learning outcomes and performance assessment emphasized the need for more writing in all courses, especially history. History faculty at the community colleges wanted to assign more writing, but the large classes made it impossible. So administrators from the four-year university met with their counterparts in the community college administration and were able to convince the administration to reduce the size of history classes from 50 to 35 students.

In biology, the university biology department used the biology standards developed in QUE as a key document in redesigning the introductory course. A combined lecture/lab one-semester course replaced the former two-semester sequence. The new course, to be delivered in classes with a maximum of 20 students, places emphasis on concepts and relationships in biology and includes a mandatory web-based component. After learning of the new introductory course at QUE cluster meetings, the community college biology departments added a one-credit seminar course covering the concepts and skills in the university course. The cordial relations extended beyond faculty to students: Faculty invited biology students from the community colleges to go on field trips with the university students, thus giving them a taste of what it means to be a biology major.

- One university provost has planned disciplinary teams to work on freshman-to-senior learning outcomes for all the academic majors in which students can earn middle and high school teaching certification.

- Another university is working to have all graduate and undergraduate programs develop learning outcomes, performance standards, and assessments using QUE concepts and materials as examples.

Conclusion

This overview of QUE has explained the form and structure of the project, along with some of its effects on faculty professional thinking. This is only an outline. The book's remaining chapters will demonstrate the richness of the QUE experience for the participants. We offer this book's complete description of QUE as an addition to the scholarship of teaching and learning. The QUE project has demonstrated one way among many to raise the quality of student learning, but it is a vital and basic contribution.

Endnotes

1) Ironically, while *standards* is the preferred term in K–12, *outcomes* (preferred by postsecondary personnel) is viewed with suspicion in K–12 because early advocates were burned by "outcomes education." See Chapter 2 for a discussion of nomenclature.

2) The poor record of on-time graduation at state universities is prompting legislators to offer institutions a bonus for completion of the bachelor's degree in four years and the associate degree in two years (see Arenson, 2005).

3) Throughout QUE, participants were urged to read *How People Learn* (Bransford, Brown, & Cocking, 2000) and *Understanding by Design* (Wiggins & McTighe, 1998). National Academies Press has now published an additional volume, *How Students Learn* (Donovan & Bransford, 2005), available on their web site (www.nap.edu).

4) Fort Valley State University reorganized its education department as the first charter department in order to raise its standards.

5) In the 9 four-year institutions involved in QUE, an approximate count of students yields more than 140,000. The partner two-year institutions likely have twice that number, but many are not enrolled in degree programs.

References

Arenson, K. W. (2005, January 26). Bonus planned for colleges whose students finish on time. *New York Times,* p. B1.

Association of American Colleges and Universities. (2002). *Greater expectations: A new vision for learning as a nation goes to college.* Washington, DC: Author.

Barr, R. B., & Tagg, J. (1995, November/December). From teaching to learning—a new paradigm for undergraduate education. *Change, 27*(6), 12–25.

Boyer, E. L. (1990). *Scholarship reconsidered: Priorities of the professoriate.* Princeton, NJ: Carnegie Foundation for the Advancement of Teaching.

Bransford, J. D., Brown, A. L., & Cocking, R. R. (Eds.). (2000). *How people learn: Brain, mind, experience, and school* (Expanded ed.). Washington, DC: National Academies Press.

Carey, K. (2004). *A matter of degrees: Improving graduation rates in four-year colleges and universities.* Washington, DC: The Education Trust, Inc.

Doherty, A., Riordan, T., & Roth, J. (Eds.). (2002). *Student learning: A central focus for institutions of higher education.* Milwaukee, WI: Alverno College Institute.

Donovan, M. S., & Bransford, J. D. (Eds.). (2005). *How students learn: History, mathematics, and science in the classroom.* Washington, DC: National Academies Press.

Glassick, C. E., Huber, M. T., & Maeroff, G. I. (1997). *Scholarship assessed: Evaluation of the professoriate.* San Francisco, CA: Jossey-Bass.

Hutchings, P., Babb, M., & Bjork, C. (2002). *The scholarship of teaching and learning in higher education: An annotated bibliography* (Rev. and updated ed.). Stanford, CA: Carnegie Foundation for the Advancement of Teaching.

Shulman, L. S. (2000). From Minsk to Pinsk: Why a scholarship of teaching and learning? *Journal of Scholarship of Teaching and Learning, 1*(1), 48–53.

Turning point. (1997, May). *Policy Perspectives, 7*(2), 1–12.

Wiggins, G., & McTighe, J. (1998). *Understanding by design.* Alexandria, VA:

2

The QUE Process at the National Level

Ruth Mitchell

QUE fostered interaction between members of our campus from different departments and between members of our campus and those of the community colleges. It raised awareness of what some of the most innovative instructors are working on and where we might find resources to try innovative strategies in our classrooms.

— *QUE participant survey response*

Faculty experienced the Quality in Undergraduate Education (QUE) project in two settings—the national conferences and their local cluster meetings. According to the design of QUE, most of the work of writing outcomes, performance descriptions, and assessments was to be done on the campuses in the clusters. The national meetings were planned to provide opportunities for reporting progress and introducing topics such as writing rubrics, inter-disciplinary connections, and mapping the curriculum, all intended to model the work to be completed on the campuses. This chapter will describe the development of written outcomes, the writing of rubrics, and the discussion of cross-disciplinary issues at the national meetings.

The national meetings occurred twice a year, in spring and fall, at locations chosen alternately for the convenience of QUE participants traveling from the west coast (California and Nevada) or the east coast (Maryland and Georgia). From 1998 to 2004, there were 10 plenary national meetings, plus 1 meeting each on the east and west coasts after the September 11 attacks canceled the fall 2001 national meeting. Each national meeting began on a Friday evening and ended on Sunday morning, thus interfering as little as possible with teaching schedules.

One English faculty member vividly describes the experience of the national meetings:

> I sometimes felt that the trips to distant locales weren't really necessary—why not just communicate by e-mail?—but I've changed my mind completely. It was very useful—in many ways—to lift people out of their own turf and allow them to experience the grass on the other side of other people's fences. I'm convinced that some of the good, serious work got done not despite, but because of, noisy Saturday night dinners in another town, outings that involved flamenco dancers or sweaty blues bands. . . . QUE encouraged creative digression and that . . . was one of its strengths.

Clusters were required to send teams of three faculty members for each discipline to each of the national meetings. Funding for their travel was mostly supplied by the grants, but the institutions were required to match a portion of it. Since each cluster was expected to work in three academic disciplines, at least nine faculty from the two- and four-year institutions in each cluster were expected at each national meeting.

The national conferences stimulated the conversations that for most participants were the core benefit of QUE. Asked what QUE did best, a participant wrote, "Bring together a variety of institutions to work on a common goal and to fundamentally change the way we all look at university coursework and goals for its students." The conversations occurred in plenary sessions and across the table at meals, but they happened predominantly in the disciplinary workshops that took up most of the scheduled time.

The disciplinary workshops focused first on writing student learning outcomes and then moved to writing rubrics and assessments. They'll be discussed here in that order, not necessarily for reasons of chronology but because rubrics and assessments follow logically from outcomes and indeed cannot be written without them.

Writing Student Learning Outcomes

Some participants used the opportunity that QUE presented to fulfill the demands of a state legislature or a regional accrediting agency to write outcomes; others wrote them as a means of clarifying expectations of student learning. One four-year biology faculty member said of outcomes she now uses:

> Students know precisely the content they must master and they recognize how the assessment tool is to be used. In the past I believe students poorly understood the intended outcomes and assessment. I believe this to be the case because the instructors themselves had not formally delineated what we were trying to accomplish. In other words this project has contributed to both students and faculty. We're on the same page.

Another touched on the issue of academic freedom to choose the topics of a course, but expressed no sense of loss:

> My teaching is much more purposeful than in the past. Now, when I make changes in my course, I do so to address learning outcomes instead of making changes because it looked like it might be fun to teach this topic. I now realize that you can have interesting assignments that support your learning outcomes. [My courses now include] more assignments that reflect learning objectives. More rubrics. More lectures on topics like critical thinking in order to provide students with a deeper understanding and explicitly define our goals.

The process of writing outcomes began at the first national meeting hosted by the University of Nevada–Reno. At that point only biology, history, chemistry, and physics were represented.[1] In addition, QUE was unfunded, so participating institutions (Georgia State University and Georgia Perimeter College; University of Nevada–Reno and Truckee Meadows Community College; California State University–Long Beach and Long Beach City College) supported their faculty and administrators from their own budgets.

The QUE project aimed to establish outcomes at level 14 (after two years of college) and level 16 (at graduation, traditionally after four years of college). *Level 14* is shorthand to denote outcomes at lower division that may be used to facilitate transition to upper division in four-year institutions or to transfer from two- to four-year institutions.

Both levels are abstractions in the sense that only just over a third of today's students follow the traditional pattern: general education courses for two years, transfer or proceed to the junior level, graduate after two years of study in a major (Carey, 2004). In the pattern pursued by the majority of U.S. students—almost two-thirds—obstacles prevent the traditional progression through college (Carey, 2004). Students transfer from one institution to another and find they have to take different courses; they take a reduced course load so that they can work, thus stretching out the number of years to reach both level 14 and level 16; or they find they cannot take courses in the expected sequence because classes fill up too quickly. Level 14 and level 16 therefore mean no more than a midpoint and an endpoint and should not be construed as advocating a pattern that is apparently dissolving for the majority of students.

At the initial meeting in Reno, the major issues in writing outcomes surfaced almost immediately. Some faculty expressed puzzlement about the reasons for writing outcomes—questions still heard on some campuses: "Don't we already have standards?" (meaning SAT and ACT scores necessary for admission); "Doesn't the catalog list what students should know and be able to do?" Other faculty resisted the visionary nature of outcomes: "Why should we write outcomes that we know our students can't reach now?" Some objected to the public nature of outcomes: Quality is known and recognized among faculty, so why describe it publicly? Once faculty were persuaded that both the process of developing outcomes and the products had value, they encountered the issues that make writing outcomes a challenging intellectual exercise.

First among these was the name for what we were writing. When the QUE leadership at the Reno meeting announced that the objective was to write standards for student learning in biology, chemistry, physics, and history after two years of postsecondary study (level 14), the participants balked at the word *standards*. (See Chapter 4 for further explanation.) *Standards* has entirely different connotations for postsecondary faculty than for K–12 personnel. To university and college faculty, standards meant the scores on the ACT or SAT, the admissions *standards*. The Education Trust staff, who had worked with standards at the K–12 level for most of the 1990s, found it ironic that the postsecondary faculty preferred *outcomes,* exactly the reverse from the K–12 personnel who had been burned by the furious controversy over *outcomes education* and who therefore speak only of standards.

A participant from Chesapeake College (not present at the first QUE meeting) sums up the general response to *standards:* "The first thing we did was eliminate the word 'standard' and used 'outcome' instead, since 'standard' was a nasty word."

At the first national meeting, the biology faculty members proposed the expression *ideal learning outcomes.* Although it was not universally accepted, the faculty were able to work with the idea of academic goals or outcomes once they were freed from having to use a word they didn't like. In this book, therefore, we use the word *outcomes* as a synonym for *standards, goals,* and *expectations,* as it was used throughout QUE's discussions.

After deciding the nomenclature issue, the QUE participants faced the major problems that make writing outcomes intellectually challenging: What comes first—the course or the outcomes? How do outcomes affect curricula? What should be the ratio of content to skills in outcomes statements? Are outcomes lists of topics to be covered or should they include cognitive challenges? Are level 14 outcomes intended to cover general education, the major, or both? How the QUE participants resolved these dilemmas is discussed in the following sections, as well as how the faculty now use them in their teaching.

Outcomes: Courses and Curricula

The habits of mind necessary to write outcomes challenge faculty because they are used to thinking in terms of courses and topics to be covered. Statements such as "Upon completion of courses X and Y, students should be able to" have the cart before the horse. Outcomes should be written without regard to courses presently in the catalog. Instead, they should be statements of the learning in terms of knowledge and skills that students will have acquired at level 14 or level 16. Then the outcomes should be used to evaluate courses X and Y to ask—Do the content and pedagogy of these courses get students closer to the essential knowledge and skills listed in the outcomes? Do these courses duplicate material taught in other courses? Are the knowledge and skills listed in the outcomes being taught in any of this department's offerings? The super matrix described in Chapter 1 helps to answer these questions and reveals gaps and overlaps (see also Figure 6.2 in Chapter 6).

Writing outcomes requires a level of abstract thinking beyond designing next semester's or quarter's courses. It requires instead thinking about the core knowledge and skills of the academic discipline, in what stages they should be acquired, and how (perhaps by whom) they can best be taught. Despite its importance to the success of students, such focused thinking about the aims of teaching is undervalued in postsecondary education. Only rarely—as for example in the QUE project—do faculty get the opportunity to think collectively about a coherent whole.

Faculty found the process challenging and valuable. The outcomes written by QUE participants now function as templates for curriculum revision and as guides for courses and syllabi. Faculty say that the QUE outcome statements are now integrated into their course descriptions "at both the survey and upper-division levels"; "I have integrated the five standards the history discipline in our cluster agreed upon"; and "Our learning outcomes are based on the QUE learning outcomes."

At the curriculum level, a history faculty member said:

> History's participation in QUE led to some curriculum restructuring across the entire department, including a "skills template" emphasizing particular aspects of historical thinking, research, and analysis to be emphasized at various course levels. While I had been doing these things in my own courses, we now have a way to coordinate our efforts as an entire faculty, and across system institutions as well, due to our collaboration with [the cluster two-year partner]. It has made our curriculum structure easier to convey to new faculty and part-time instructors, as well as giving us a clear sense of progression toward the final assessment exercise for majors, the required senior thesis.

But this happy ending was not reached without struggling with other issues.

Outcomes: The Content Problem

At the K–12 level it is reasonably simple to write outcomes for history, biology, mathematics—even English—because the content and skills all students must master are circumscribed by consensus among educators about the requirements needed to terminate at high school graduation or proceed to college. In the latter case, the outcomes are specified by organizations such as the College Board and ACT, which publish descriptions of the knowledge and skills expected of students aspiring to college.[2] Conversely, postsecondary education offers an array of content that cannot be mastered by a single student.

Students of biology must choose among animal/plant biology, cell/molecular biology, genetics, or microbiology, to name only a few of the specialties. In history, a student can choose from the histories of every ethnic and national group across all periods recorded in writing. And so on. The questions facing outcomes writers are—What content must any student graduating with a major in biology (or chemistry, history, English, mathematics) have mastered? Is there a body of content sufficiently central to the discipline that all students must know it?

If the same content cannot be expected of all graduates, then surely the same skills can be expected. History students must be able to use primary sources, evaluate secondary sources, and write persuasively. Biologists must be able to use laboratory equipment safely and evaluate the accuracy of journal articles. But focusing on skills raises a different problem, best expressed by a participant in the English workshops:

> Reaching agreement on the list of nouns (generic outcomes) we want to include in standards does not seem to be a major problem. The true issues for discussion have to do with the specific nature of the "deep understandings" that distinguish the various levels. Until we can articulate the difference between the desired "seamless transition" in the writing of a sixth grader and that of a college graduate, we have not completely articulated our expectations. What is the difference between a "convincing argument" at level 14 and one at level 16? When we worked with a specific assignment and moved back and forth across assignments, standards, and performance standards, I had a few glimmerings of where we need to go. How does an outcomes writer make clear the difference between the skills of a sophomore and those of a graduate? A diagnostic question might be: If these outcomes are read out of context, could we discern what level they are intended for?

Success in answering these questions varied by discipline. The biologists set out a list of skills and then presented groups of expected knowledge at each level. The chemists designated content knowledge in 14 areas at the sophomore level. Each area contains a knowledge inventory, where topics are listed, and performance expectations, which are introduced with verbs like *explain* and *determine* to indicate the skills needed. Level 16 has eight outcomes, but specialization forbids an exhaustive list of the topics and performance expectations. The English outcomes are essentially lists of skills—reading, writing, and criticism—because of the notoriously difficult issues involved in specifying expected reading.

The history faculty repudiated content entirely in the first meetings of the workshops writing outcomes. Discussions were often heated. One side said that "historical mindedness" was the primary outcome for students at both level 14 and level 16; the other wanted the outcome documents to mandate that some historical content (e.g., the development of democratic government in the United States, including dates such as 1776 and 1789) should be known by all history graduates. Later discussions solved the content problem by designating themes such as the influence of war or religion on the course of history.

Writing outcomes in mathematics seemed superfluous to many of the mathematicians involved because what students need to know and be able to do seemed obvious and well known. When disciplinary groups met to discuss outcomes, the mathematicians sat perplexed. Mathematics is a field steeped—*locked* might be a defensible word—in tradition embodied in textbooks. But as is explained in more detail in Chapter 8, that's not entirely true. Two developments are beginning very tentatively to open up mathematics. One is the need for applied mathematics in subjects other than engineering. On the whole, mathematics departments teach only "pure" mathematics, so that some departments such as psychology (and education) develop their own mathematics courses for statistical research. At the national QUE meeting when mathematicians first participated, a member of the Georgia State University team led a discussion to design a matrix showing what mathematics was needed in each of the other disciplines and therefore what outcomes would apply at level 14. (The matrix has not survived in the final drafts of the mathematics outcomes.)

The other development is the quantitative literacy movement, which has the support of leading mathematicians in the Mathematical Association of America and other professional organizations. Quantitative literacy acknowledges that not only many professions but also responsible citizenship requires mathematical knowledge, especially of statistics and probability. This movement would develop required courses for general education based on the mathematics needed in other disciplines and for the adequate understanding of financial, medical, and political issues.

Bernard Madison, an author of Chapter 8 and a champion of quantitative literacy, tried to enlarge the vision of the QUE mathematics participants.

He posed questions repeatedly:

> How do you know if your undergraduate mathematics program is any good? Why don't mathematics faculty respond to the declining number of math majors—isn't this a message that something's wrong? Why do mathematics faculty think that everything is OK?

Responses showed some reluctance to encounter the central problems that Madison articulated, but also the beginnings of awareness that new methods, if not new content, are needed to involve students.

One faculty participant reports that he finds outcomes for mathematics extremely important to properly set student and faculty expectations.

> However, in many ways they cannot be properly assessed because they are so broad and open to interpretation by individual faculty. . . . The biggest change [as a result of QUE] for me is how I prepare students for exams. Rather than telling them they must know various things I give them a variety of sample problems. This helps them to focus by example and learn the concepts.

Outcomes: Lists of Topics Versus Statements

It is possible to list content as a series of topics (nouns) to be "covered" in a course, but skills require verbs indicating what students are to do, such as *demonstrate, explain, calculate,* and *show.* These verbs function as pointers to teaching techniques, because if students are required to explain, then faculty are obligated to provide them with the explanatory tools of the discipline. Statements of outcomes should ideally combine the two, as should be clear from the discussion of content and skills. See Figure 2.1 for an example from history outcomes.

Figure 2.1
History Outcomes

Standard 2: Identify economic, political, and social forces that have influenced movements and significant events in the progression of history.

Level 14 (major and non-major):
- Discuss the influence of the major agricultural movements on society.
- Discuss the influence of the major industrial movements on society.
- Discuss the evolution of and the need for government.
- Describe the influence of war on the progress of civilization.
- Illustrate the influence of religion on the development of civilization in the course of history.

Outcomes: General Education or Major?

Of the five QUE disciplines, four are usually required of all students at some level. The question of level arose early in the QUE outcomes-setting discussions. Are these outcomes for majors or for required general education courses?

Level 16 outcomes are intended for majors, but level 14 outcomes could apply to students intending to major in the discipline or to students who need the course as part of their general education requirements. In some disciplines and in some institutions these might be the same.

Graduates in the 21st century need both literacy and quantitative literacy. Training in English composition should lead to competency in writing across the curriculum; mathematics in the form of statistics, data, and probability is necessary for disciplines such as biology, chemistry, history (even English in stylistics), sociology, and psychology. But instead, lower-division mathematics begins with calculus for majors in mathematics, physics, and engineering and continues into specialized studies. In both English and mathematics there is a disconnect between their service functions and what faculty regard as the central business of their discipline.

To solve these problems, some QUE disciplinary groups wrote three sets of outcomes—for level 16 and level 14 majors and level 14 non-majors. (See Appendix B for the three sets of outcomes for biology.)

Using the Outcomes

These written outcomes enabled participants to move to Stage 2 of the QUE Conceptual Framework (shown in Figure 1.1 in Chapter 1), where the outcomes are used at the course level, and to Stage 3, where the outcomes are used at the curriculum level with the super matrix. Most of the clusters in QUE experienced some revision of courses and curriculum in one or more disciplines. The following are examples of applying outcomes at the course level, Stage 2:

- "The learning objectives for the general biology lecture course are much more explicit than in the past and students who do not use these objectives tend to do poorly on exams."

- "My courses and syllabus now include specific learner outcomes, educational goals that we identify and discuss. Some of these goals may be analytical in nature, quantitative or qualitative, and fairly complex, giving the students something tangible to strive for."

- One English faculty member said that the effect of QUE work has been to make his directions to students much more explicit and to connect the goals of the assignment to the outcomes. He believes his students have produced better work and earned higher grades as a result.

The following are examples of applying outcomes at the curriculum level, Stage 3:

- In the context of close professional and personal cooperation among faculty, historians in one California cluster transformed their whole curriculum according to level 14 outcomes developed in QUE. The outcomes are for a gateway course ensuring that history majors all have the same skills as they proceed to the upper division. "QUE has very much influenced how we structure our major. The introduction of our 'gateway course' is perhaps the most tangible manifestation of QUE in the department," said a faculty member. The course is taught at both the two-year and four-year institution with a portfolio assessment system, ensuring that history students have writing skills. The course has been so successful in raising the achievement of history majors that other departments in both institutions are beginning to pay attention. An administrator wrote, "Some faculty have become recognized leaders in their discipline as a result of this work."

- In common with other Georgia institutions involved with the P–16 initiative, one four-year university had an outcomes development process already underway when QUE came along. The English department had already developed outcomes for the traditional English major, so they seized the opportunity presented by QUE to expand writing outcomes to three other majors—journalism, creative writing, and professional writing. With the outcomes for the traditional major approved by the department, the faculty developed a new course intended to make the transition from level 14 to level 15 smoother and to raise the level of student performance in the upper division. The new course will be required of majors at the sophomore level. They also produced a student handbook that helps students understand the sequence of courses and revised the senior capstone course so that it resembles a senior seminar in which students create a portfolio.

- The biology department at a California university completely redesigned its curriculum by focusing on learning outcomes, not courses. In fall 2003, four new core courses complete with learning outcomes were offered, and in 2004, learning outcomes were developed for the other courses in the major.[3]

- At the same university, the four-year and two-year partners cooperated on meshing their two English curricula: The four-year English department changed two of its survey courses from upper to lower level when they realized that the community college offered the same courses. Now students do not have to retake those courses when they transfer.

- The mathematics department at a west coast community college used learning outcomes to review their program systemically. The chair explained that she asked the faculty members to list the required mathematical skills in the course where they belonged and then rationalized them in revised courses. She encountered a good deal of acrimonious opposition, but she insisted that students needed a coherent program.

•   Faculty in one institution attributed success in their accrediting process to QUE because they learned as participants how to write the outcomes and assessments the agency required. The extended, sometimes confrontational, sometimes tedious discussions paid off, not only for institutions facing accreditation, but also for a large number of faculty: "QUE has connected dots for me in the educational process that I had not considered before."

As noted in Chapter 1, QUE never attempted to produce statements of outcomes at the national level. However, the clusters freely copied statements from each other and modified them a little—or not at all. After all, history majors in Maryland should command the same history skills as those in California. The biology learning outcomes formulated by the Georgia State University/Georgia Perimeter College cluster became the standard for all the clusters and others were explicit about adopting them. Learning outcomes statements can be found in Appendix B and on the QUE web site (www.gsu.edu/que), where their similarity will be obvious even though they carry the names of different clusters.

Writing Rubrics

In Stage 2, where outcomes are applied at the course level, rubrics are written to guide the scoring and grading of individual assignments or larger units of assessment such as tests and examinations. Workshops on rubric development were led by consultants—QUE's critical friends—and were regarded by faculty as among the most valuable agenda items at QUE's national meetings. One faculty member wrote, "I have generated rubrics to grade assignments and I find them extremely useful. . . . They make it easier for students to see how their work is evaluated and how grades are assigned." Another thought that

> In terms of tangible outcomes from this project, rubrics were the most useful. Not only do they help me keep focused in my grading and maintain the level of consistency in my grading, I have also found they help the students. I routinely now hand

out copies of the rubrics I use ahead of course assignments so that the students know exactly how their work will be judged. [Consequently,] students are now taking more responsibility for their own performance.

The majority of faculty members who answered the survey now use rubrics, either those they designed themselves or rubrics received in exchanges at QUE. (See Appendix C for information on writing effective rubrics.)

Rubrics were the topic of a national conference in 2002. Describing the workshops will illustrate the faculty experience in learning about rubrics and the role of disciplinary consultants at the national conferences. It will soon become obvious that disciplinary consultants did a great deal of preparation for these workshops, both in designing the activities and collecting materials.

One of the history consultants, Lendol Calder, set the tone for the sessions:

> Here's an agenda for our September QUE meeting. In EdSpeak, our theme is going to be "assessing student learning by means of criterion-referenced rubrics." But I'd rather think of it as "Dr. Rubric, or, How I Learned to Stop Wasting Time and Love Assessment."

The agenda referred to was one of five sent out ahead of time to faculty in biology, chemistry, English, history, and mathematics. Most of the time at the conference was spent in disciplinary workshops, each with a different approach to rubrics and their use. The chemistry and mathematics workshops were concerned with their disciplinary programs at their institutions and only partially (in the case of chemistry) with rubrics.

Mathematics workshops did not discuss rubrics. They focused instead on the role of mathematics in the learning of all graduates, as well as appropriate assessments. However, since QUE ended, one mathematics department has found that using rubrics to score common examinations across multiple sections has had an eye-opening effect on its faculty. As an experiment, students' answers to a section of questions were first scored in the traditional way by all the faculty. For a single answer, scores ranged from 1 to 5 (on a 5-point scale). Then the same answers were scored using a rubric the faculty agreed on. The range in scores was reduced, so that interrater reliability was increased.

To continue with the history agenda, here is how Calder described it:

> At prior QUE meetings, we've talked about what history students should know, understand, and be able to do, and devised standards [sic] to articulate the results we want our programs to achieve. Now we're ready to move to the next logical step in the construction of a coherent curriculum: determining what will constitute acceptable evidence that students have attained desirable understandings and proficiencies. We'll want to talk about the usefulness of papers and exams. We'll want to share ideas for innovative assignments and performances. We'll want to discuss the problems of validity and reliability in our assessment practices. But our central focus for the weekend will be on rubrics, the means by which we link standards [sic] to assignments and the student performances on the assignments.

Calder asked the QUE history participants to read an excerpt from Wiggins and McTighe's (1998) book, *Understanding by Design,* and recommended their procedure for curriculum design. Calder characterized it as follows: "Backward design simply reverses the process: One considers the ends first, then derives the curriculum from the evidence of learning that would demonstrate the ends have been met."

The workshop showed QUE participants how to construct rubrics that would embody the outcomes. The workshops were fast-paced, energetic affairs, full of the laughter exemplified by Calder's title for the session. Calder and Mills Kelly moved participants through sample rubrics with insightful criticism softened by humor. Participants brought rubrics they used, and in many cases they took back to their campuses revised and strengthened rubrics as well as rubrics from their colleagues in other institutions. See Figure 2.2 for an example of a history rubric.

Figure 2.2
History Rubric

	Argument/Analysis	Evidence	Expression
Excellent	Well-defined thesis Exceptional introduction, text, conclusion Convincing argument Great degree of originality Use of theory, chronology, historiography	Sophisticated use of sources Incorporates biases of sources Resolves contradictions in sources Masterful use of quotations Subtle inferences drawn	Seamless transitions Skillful use of language No grammatical problems Correct spelling and punctuation Appropriate citations
Thorough	Strong thesis Uniform introduction, text, conclusion Plausible argument Some degree of originality Places thesis in some context	Judicious use of sources Recognizes biases of sources Notes contradictions in sources Appropriate use of quotations Straightforward analysis	Smooth transitions Appropriate word choice Few grammatical problems Few other problems Appropriate citations
Average	Clear thesis Has introduction, text, conclusion Argument Limited originality Attempts to explain context	Uses adequate sources Treats all sources the same Contradictions avoided Limited use of quotations Limited analysis of sources	Noticeable transitions Imperfect word choice Grammatical problems Other errors Inappropriate citations

	Argument/Analysis	Evidence	Expression
Inadequate	Simplistic thesis Missing introduction, text, or conclusion Lacking in argument Lacking originality No theory, chronology, or historiography	Inadequate use of sources Limited treatment of sources Contradictions ignored Poor use of quotations Weak analysis of sources	Missing transitions Poor word choice Grammatical problems Other errors Lacking citations
Unsatisfactory	No thesis No introduction, text, or conclusion No argument No originality No context identified	Inappropriate use of sources No treatment of sources No contradictions Poor use of quotations No analysis of sources	No transitions Poor word choice Poor grammar Many errors No citations

This rubric can be used for a history essay of fairly extended length. It clearly shows the students what is expected along three dimensions (argument/analysis, evidence, and expression) and where student performance is lacking. It provides students with a guide to improve their performance on similar essays.

The English consultant, Susan Albertine, went about the development of rubrics in a slightly different way. She asked each cluster to bring "one or two big assignments" and the appropriate level 14 or 16 outcomes. She obtained permission from one of the participating institutions to use one of their assignments for a group demonstration of writing a scoring rubric. During the first of three workshops on Saturday, the group worked together to design a rubric for the assignment, with the consultant using a pad and markers to record progress.

Albertine pointed out that rubrics have two components—the benchmarks embodied in the written outcomes and the level of performance required by the assignment, depending on when in the course it is given to the students. Figure 2.3 is an example of an English writing rubric that can be used to recognize a successful freshman composition.

Figure 2.3
English Writing Rubric

The expert essay develops clear, thoughtful, and significant ideas with a keen awareness of audience. In addition,

- It offers fresh, thoughtful, logical, detailed, relevant, and interesting development.
- It possesses coherent and effective organization that enhances the development.
- It employs varied, readable, and skillfully constructed sentences.
- It incorporates fresh, precise, economical, and idiomatic diction.
- It has few or no deviations from the grammar and conventions of standard English.
- It uses correct format.

These statements describe expert proficiency. Minimally acceptable proficiency and non-proficiency have the same level of specificity. Of course, anyone can object that *thoughtful, detailed,* and even *idiomatic* are subjective judgments. One individual's effectiveness may not be another's. Judgment is inescapable in humanities disciplines, but its arbitrariness is reduced by statements that permit discussion of specifics rather than generalities. When students can see these descriptions, they can better understand the instructor's evaluation of their work and are less likely to see grades as subjective.

During the second workshop, the participants broke into small groups to write a rubric for the assignments they brought and then reported to the whole group for discussion and constructive criticism. In the third workshop, participants were divided by two- and four-year institutions. Each group scored sample student essays using the original rubric (collected and made into packages ahead of time by the consultant). Then they discussed how the assignment and/or the rubric could be revised to produce higher achievement from the students. Like the history participants, they returned home with examples of rubrics exchanged with colleagues.

The workshop in biology was less concerned with rubrics than those in history and English, because the discipline provides fewer opportunities for judgments that require the guidance of rubrics. However, when rubrics are appropriate, they provide specific information to students about their performance. Figure 2.4 is an example of a biology rubric for a microbiology course.

Figure 2.4
Biology Rubric

Unknown Identification
This assignment meets Standards 1, 2, 3 (prokaryotic cells), and 4, plus the skills and technique standard.

5) Student isolates both unknown bacteria in pure culture and identifies both bacteria according to acceptable flow chart information. Employs and interprets appropriate diagnostic tests.

4) Student isolates only one microorganism in pure culture and identifies it according to acceptable flow chart information. Employs and interprets appropriate diagnostic tests.

3) Student isolates only one microorganism in pure culture and identifies it according to acceptable flow chart information. Needs assistance in identifying which appropriate diagnostic tests to use.

2) Student isolates only one microorganism in pure culture, needs assistance in identifying and using flow chart information, needs assistance in identifying which diagnostic media to use, and cannot interpret media reactions.

1) Student does not isolate either microorganism in pure culture, does not know how to use a flow chart, and does not know which diagnostic media to use or how to interpret media reactions.

Although "rubric became a household word," according to one biology participant, the biology workshops enlarged the topic to include assessment in general, stimulating gratitude from another biology faculty member:

I knew nothing about assessment before joining QUE. Hiring Gordon Uno and Virginia Anderson as consultants made a huge difference because they were able to bridge the gap between the language and philosophy of assessment [and] our understanding of what we are trying to accomplish in the classroom.[4]

Cross-Disciplinary Discussions

As noted in Chapter 1, Bernard Madison, QUE mathematics consultant, makes a strong case for cross-disciplinary and interdisciplinary education. The QUE participants clearly never shrank from aspects of reform that could be described as on the frontier. Outcomes themselves as a means for approaching the aims and processes of undergraduate education seemed "utopian" and "radical" to some of the QUE participants. Crosscutting competencies could be considered even more threatening because they seem to menace the disciplinary barriers that protect faculty from outside interference.

However, as Bernard Madison pointed out, reality is not partitioned like the postsecondary world. In addition to his passionate plea for interdisciplinary education, he urged speedy change: "QUE's accomplishments will sound revolutionary to some, but the pace is evolutionary."

QUE made an attempt to pick up the pace by focusing on crosscutting competencies in 2001. Plenary sessions led by Susan Albertine listed crosscutting competencies that participants thought were essential in all academic disciplines. The lists coincided, as might be expected. Major items were

- Reading and writing across the disciplines

- Quantitative literacy

- Ethics

- Critical thinking

- Self-reflection

- Metacognition

- Understanding of technology

- Historical thinking

- Awareness of diversity

- Awareness of social context

However, in 2001, participants worried about which disciplines should be responsible for teaching all, or even some, of the competencies. This problem is basic not only to the teaching but even more to the assessment of crosscutting competencies. When some faculty said that competencies appear different in each discipline (writing in science is not the same as writing in history, for example), some found that fact so daunting that they doubted the value of listing crosscutting competencies. The resolution at this point was to ensure that competencies were reflected in the learning outcomes and in culminating (capstone) courses in each discipline. Thus these competencies would be perceived as important because they appeared repeatedly in the outcome statements of a number of disciplines.

By 2003, when crosscutting competencies were on the agenda of the national conference again, the mood had become optimistic. "This was the best QUE meeting so far," reported more than one participant. Comfortable in their discipline groups, QUE participants could think more expansively than when crosscutting competencies were first discussed two years earlier. They were also fresh from a panel discussion titled Learning Across the Disciplines, in which QUE consultants Lendol Calder, Susan Ganter, James Roth, and Gordon Uno discussed the nature of excellent teaching in their disciplines and its commonalities with good teaching in all disciplines.

The session was framed by two questions: What does my discipline need from your discipline? What strategies does your discipline use for cross-disciplinary competencies, such as empathy, conceptual understanding, problem solving, and so on? The first question elicited the comment that faculty in one discipline do not necessarily know what another discipline's major concepts are, and that this mutual ignorance makes it difficult for students to understand their general education courses. Conversations among faculty are needed to make connections across disciplines clear to students.

The participants' responses to this discussion of crosscutting competencies were overwhelmingly positive: "What really worked," said one participant, "was the cross-discipline session about what each of us wants. We had an eager, dynamic group"; the cross-discipline sessions "stimulated conversation about communality within academia (and difference)," said another. "What QUE did best was to bring people of different disciplines together to talk about teaching and learning," wrote a chemist. But the grip of the disciplines was reflected in another comment: "The cross-disciplinary discussions were good. However, there will be limits on the amount of time these will be productive." One mathematician was specific about the gains from cross-disciplinary discussions:

> The discussion across disciplines was extremely valuable, although this was so in a general way and not in a specific product-oriented way. For example, an understanding of how biology approaches critical thinking by having students study the literature was very enlightening. By critiquing the scientific approaches in certain papers students can get detailed knowledge about why research comes out the way it does and why this may or may not have a lot to do with the truth that is being sought. Studying history by asking hypothetical "what if this had happened" questions is absolutely outstanding! . . . I have thought about learning in a much deeper way. I can't wait to step down from being chair and actually do more teaching!

In summary, QUE raised the issue that Bernard Madison described so urgently, but participants were ultimately unable to do more than suggest improvements on the margin. But if faculty members are aware that interdisciplinary conversations must take place if students are to learn successfully, then progress has been made.

Conclusion

This chapter described the QUE experience at the national level, in the twice-yearly national meetings. Chapter 3 will focus on QUE activities on the campuses, including a discussion of the relations between community colleges and four-year universities, a vital but sometimes frustrating feature of QUE.

Endnotes

1) Physics later faded from QUE and chemistry became the least represented discipline.

2) The College Board has developed SpringBoard™, a curriculum that incorporates®standards in each academic discipline. ACT's Standards for Transition show the level of expected skills and knowledge in English and mathematics.

3) The biology department's curriculum redesign has been documented in an unpublished article by Joyce Ono, a participant in the process, titled "Highlights and Lessons Learned in a Curriculum Reform Process."

4) Professor Anderson provided QUE participants with a summary of her book on assessment in biology, *Effective Grading* (Walvoord & Anderson, 1998).

References

Carey, K. (2004). *A matter of degrees: Improving graduation rates in four-year colleges and universities.* Washington, DC: The Education Trust, Inc.

Walvoord, B. E., & Anderson, V. J. (1998). *Effective grading: A tool for learning and assessment.* San Francisco, CA: Jossey-Bass.

Wiggins, G., & McTighe, J. (1998). *Understanding by design.* Alexandria, VA: Association for Supervision and Curriculum Development.

3

The QUE Process at the Local Level

Gloria John, Ruth Mitchell

What did QUE do best? Working through curricular issues with two- [and] four-year institutions—this got us together and that is worth plenty!

— QUE participant survey response

As noted in Chapter 2, most of the work of QUE was intended to happen in the local clusters; that is, the partnerships between two- and four-year institutions on their campuses. The cluster coordinators were expected to call meetings, either plenary or within academic disciplines, in order to write outcomes, align courses and curriculum, write rubrics, and make suggestions for the agenda at the national meetings. The clusters were expected to share the outcomes statements with their non-QUE faculty colleagues and respond constructively to criticism. Then a representative team of at least three members from each academic discipline would report on their work at the national meetings.

There was no necessary mix of two- and four-year faculty, although representation from each was expected. Most teams consisted of a majority of either four-year or two-year faculty. For example, Fort Valley State University only had one representative from its two-year partner, Middle Georgia College, a stalwart but unique participant at all the national meetings after Fort Valley joined QUE. Others had more two-year than four-year participants (Georgia State University in March 2002), or maintained an equal representation (Salisbury University, Chesapeake College, and Wor-Wic Community College at all meetings).

About one-third of the participants at national meetings were community college faculty, although two-year participation reached 41% at the March 2001 meeting in Long Beach and 39% for the March 2002 meeting in Reno and both of the 2003 national meetings. At the coastal meetings in 2001, 40% of the participants at the Atlanta meeting were from community colleges, but at the Los Angeles meeting only 19% were. This wide discrepancy confirms the observation of our evaluators, Policy Studies Associates, that east coast QUE participants had stronger partnerships than those on the west coast.

For reasons to be discussed later, the cluster design worked fitfully most of the time, but the faculty experience in a notably successful cluster offers a clear picture of the design's potential and provides a springboard for examples of both successful and unsuccessful onsite work. After the spring 2002 national meeting of history faculty, Mills Kelly, QUE history consultant, said of this cluster's work: "This report offered a picture of exactly how the QUE collaboration was designed to work." The cluster consisted of a four-year university and two community colleges within easy driving distance of each other. The three institutions share students and understand both the opportunities and the barriers facing them. Students who transfer from the two community colleges go to the university. At a recent graduation, 47% of the graduates began as transfer students.

A Smart Start

This cluster of two community colleges and one four-year university was recruited into QUE in summer 2000, when funding from the Pew Charitable Trusts and the ExxonMobil Foundation was confirmed and QUE expanded to nine clusters (see Appendix A for a short chronological history of QUE).

Ron Henry and the QUE project director visited the university during their summer trips to explain QUE to the newly recruited clusters. Henry had met representatives of the university at meetings of the Standards-based Teacher Education Project. The university's new president shared Henry's interest in promoting the scholarship of teaching by establishing outcomes and assessments and therefore welcomed the invitation to join QUE. At the same time, the university and the two community colleges were part of a statewide initiative to establish an Associate of Arts in Teaching degree that would allow students to begin their teacher training in the community colleges and continue at the university. This required close cooperation among the institutions, and QUE provided a structured opportunity.

The university president invited the presidents of the community colleges to join the partnership and asked them to recommend faculty members to be involved. The partnership initially fielded teams in history, biology, and mathematics and added chemistry when it resurfaced in QUE in 2002.

The associate provost and associate dean at the university became joint cluster coordinators. They issued a formal written invitation to a September 2000 dinner to the recommended history, mathematics, and biology faculty at all three institutions, thus establishing from the beginning a cordial social atmosphere. The overture to community colleges was greatly appreciated. A history faculty member at one of the community colleges said, "Although this is driven by the university, they don't dictate policy to us. They made a sincere gesture: They wanted our opinions, advice, and participation."

This partnership began well for a number of reasons. Of great importance was the fact that high-level administrators were involved from the beginning. Not only did administrators in the three institutions speak collegially to each, but the two co-coordinators were administrators at the university. Department chairs were selected to be members of the cluster teams. Wherever QUE has been successful, administrators at the institutional and department levels have been leaders, providing support through their words and their presence where possible.

The university administration gave the cluster co-coordinators authority over the disbursement of QUE funds from the beginning. This proved to be important in the success of the clusters. Another cluster came close to catastrophe because the funds were controlled by an administrator who was not connected with QUE, and another spent a year wrestling with their administration before the cluster coordinator could control the QUE funds.

The two QUE co-coordinators decided to forgo the stipends they could have claimed from the $32,000 annual QUE funds, and instead they shared the resources with everyone in the cluster. This option was more available to them as administrators than it would be to faculty members who acted as cluster coordinators. The administrators demonstrated how much they valued the project and how much they appreciated participants' time and efforts. They also highlighted the importance of their two-year partners by holding meetings on their campuses and by making presentations at the state's two-year faculty conference.

The administration of this cluster remained stable throughout QUE's life. Changes in campus leadership can disrupt projects like QUE.[1] By 2002, many of QUE's cluster coordinators reported changes in key administrators. In five years of QUE, three coordinators from four-year institutions said they had new presidents, and another reported that one of the cluster's two-year partners had a new president. In institutions where these changes occur, fear causes turmoil and distraction. At a Georgia university, the coming of a new president meant that the vice president who wholeheartedly supported QUE reverted to her position as a mathematics faculty member, thus losing institutional support for QUE (although retaining her participation in the mathematics department). The history department at another Georgia university had two chairs in two years. At a Maryland university, the president, the provost, and two deans of the College of Liberal Arts—all supporters of QUE—left their positions. Plans for work on assessment were "stalled during these major changes in top-level administration" in summer 2002.

In the cluster we are focusing on, the administration and department leadership welcomed QUE because it coincided with projects they were already involved in. In addition to the Associate of Arts in Teaching degree in the community colleges, the university was working on assessment because of legislative action and accreditation requirements. The campus was in the process of establishing an assessment committee to create an assessment handbook for the university, although each department was expected to develop an assessment plan. The departments were also expected to establish benchmarks and percentages of students who would reach the benchmarks on the proposed assessments. QUE unified these efforts and gave them a national context for a major faculty development project.

Cluster Meetings

The cluster met twice as a whole between national meetings both as a cluster and in discipline groups led by the university faculty in history, biology, and mathematics. A chemistry group was added in 2002. The cluster meetings followed up the national QUE meetings with discussions and actions—exactly as they were supposed to do. Participants reported on progress toward the development of learning outcomes and also discussed and exchanged course objectives, tests, and teaching ideas.

Their discussions led to changes in academic substance and in the conditions of teaching. For example, the shift to outcomes and performance assessment emphasized the need for more writing in all courses, especially history. History faculty at the community colleges wanted to assign more writing, but the large classes made it impossible. The QUE history coordinator and university administrators met with their counterparts in the community college administration and were able to reduce the size of history classes from 50 to about 35 students.

Participants remarked on the "sense of family" that developed among the faculty of all three institutions. A community college history participant said that the institutions had been working in isolation for 25 years: "No one knew what the other was doing." But as a result of three years of cluster meetings, he and a colleague at the college said they now know how to prepare their students to do well when they transfer to the university. For example, the university history department is developing World Civilization as an introductory survey, replacing Western Civilization, so the community college's history department is changing the course in parallel. Another faculty member said that she perceived that QUE was helping the clusters to develop a "seamless transition" between the colleges and the university.

A mathematics faculty member at one community college learned from a colleague in the other college how to actively engage students in the learning process by being sensitive to their learning styles. The mathematics faculty are raising performance expectations in their classes because they found at cluster meetings that the other community college was offering classes at a more advanced level. All three mathematics departments offer an introductory statistics course, so the faculty who teach this course adapted the QUE mathematics outcomes to it, thus aligning the courses at all three campuses. One of these outcomes requires the students to define variables in writing, a breakthrough in mathematics.

The university biology department used the biology outcomes developed in QUE as a key document in redesigning the introductory course. A combined lecture/lab one-semester course replaced the former two-semester sequence. The new course, to be delivered in classes with a maximum of 20 students, emphasized concepts and relationships in biology and includes a mandatory web-based component. The biology departments at the community colleges, both aware of the new introductory course at the university, looked for ways to provide students a course that would transfer as the equivalent to the university course. They decided to add a one-credit seminar course to deliver the concepts and skills covered in the university course but not in the college curriculum.

The cordial relations extended beyond faculty to students. University faculty invited biology students from the community colleges to go on field trips with the university students, thus giving them a taste of what it means to be a biology major.

It would be misleading to represent all activities in this cluster as successful. A member of the chemistry faculty at the university saw the outcomes developed in QUE as important tools for student learning. But he was disappointed when he presented the idea at a chemistry faculty meeting to find that the department chair expressed no enthusiasm and the department in general did not want to discuss outcomes. He thinks that "the average faculty member has little interest in doing anything other than what they've been doing all along." But, undeterred, he remained an active participant in QUE because he could provide a better learning environment for his students. This is an example of a missed opportunity by the department chair, who could have disseminated the QUE work throughout the department.

In addition to their internal work among the three campuses, the cluster proselytized for QUE. Faculty members discussed outcomes as a means to improve undergraduate education at a meeting of the Association of Faculties for the Advancement of Community College Teaching in 2001 (and again in 2003) and at a joint meeting of the Mathematical Association of America and the American Mathematical Society. (These and other conference presentations by QUE participants and leaders are listed in Appendix D.) They held a joint meeting on assessment with the Standards-based Teacher Education Project in 2001 and gave a workshop on assessment to non-QUE faculty in 2002. In 2003, the cluster competed for the state's Distinguished Program Awards. The partnership did not win, but competing required the compilation of a dossier so there is now a record of the cluster's development and accomplishments.

As a consequence of their work onsite, the cluster faculty were stars at the national meetings when they reported either as a cluster or within their discipline groups. They routinely discussed their progress with using outcomes to align courses and design assessments, the articulation among the two- and four-year institutions, revising courses, and communicating with colleagues. By the September 2003 national meeting, members of the cluster thought they had reached Stage 3—curriculum-level alignment and assessment—almost uniformly across all their four disciplines (see Figure 1.1 in Chapter 1 for the QUE Conceptual Framework). They were the only cluster to do so.

The cluster was thus a nexus of ideas from QUE's national meetings and local interaction at all levels from the institutional and departmental to the personal. A mathematics faculty member from a community college reflected on his own development: "I would have classified myself in the immovable area until I got into QUE," meaning that he is now thinking deeply about the place of mathematics in higher education reform. A university history faculty member is editing a reader on history and the cinema "that is learner centered, thanks to QUE." A biology faculty member at the community college valued the conversation: "The chaos, the turmoil had to be there to get to the 'aha' moments. It takes more time than you think, but the process has merit in itself."

Relations With Community Colleges

Perhaps the most successful achievement of this cluster was the collegial and cordial relationship between the community college and university faculty. Undoubtedly, the high rate of transfer between them motivated the relationship, but other factors—mutual respect and far-seeing leadership among them—contributed immensely. In most other cases, collaboration among two- and four-year institutions presented a challenge that QUE struggled with throughout its duration. In at least one case, community college reluctance to join QUE seemed impossible to overcome. The coordinator of that cluster lamented that "I've tried bottom-up and top-down approaches and the two-year faculty just don't bite. I don't understand why they're not interested."

> The most beneficial aspect of QUE, from my perspective, was the conversation that it facilitated with colleagues from the nearby two-year campus. . . . The discipline-specific nature of this conversation was wonderful. It facilitated a swift focus on determining the relevant histori-cal skills that we wanted our students to attain, rather than discussions of parti-cular content.
>
> —*QUE participant survey response*

Some community college participants, on the other hand, felt that faculty from four-year institutions who worked primarily with students who would either major or minor in a discipline were not sensitive to the complexities presented by a classroom of students in which few of whom would major in the discipline, many of whom would never take more than one course in the discipline, and most of whom would not transfer to four-year institutions. The problem is not unique to QUE and has proved an obstacle in similar reform initiatives that attempt to unite university and community college faculty in a common endeavor.

Two- and four-year institutions have different missions—so different that forcing them together may seem liked a shotgun marriage. The common point of contact is transfer students, but the percentage varies enormously with the communities where the institutions are located. Across the U.S., some community colleges have so few transfer students that their academic departments cannot focus on discipline majors but rather must see many of their courses as "service courses," requirements within trade and vocational curricula. Many community colleges have large numbers of non-credit or credit-free offerings such as English as a second language, remedial courses, and computer courses, most of which fill a community need. Other community colleges exist mainly as gateways to four-year institutions, providing a less expensive alternative for the first two years of college so that students can live at home and perhaps work to pay for upper-level college.[2] Historically, community colleges have struggled to maintain a balance between transfer education and what used to be called technical education. Community college faculty confront students who have a tremendous range in both abilities and expectations. From the perspective of those in the two-year institutions, faculty in four-year institutions have students who are all working toward a four-year degree. Finally, much more so than four-year institutions, community colleges have responsibilities to local constituencies. The values of the community are not always the same as the values of the academic community. Often local educational politics have a greater influence on curricular matters than do academic disciplines. Standards must be framed to respond to the needs of the community as well as the demands of the discipline.

For many years, community colleges have been seen as the poor stepchild of higher education, the place students go when they cannot gain admission anywhere else. Since many community colleges were parented by institutions called junior colleges or technical colleges, they have been labeled (and sometimes, in fact, were) less demanding than four-year institutions. Since most community colleges maintain an open-door admissions policy, the fact that some students enter less prepared for college work than their counterparts in four-year institutions has led to the erroneous assumption that they also leave less educated than those who have completed two years at a four-year institution. The faculty at community colleges have often been labeled "less than" as well.

Inevitably a social hierarchy has developed between community colleges and universities. Although almost 15% of community college faculty have doctorates, because the focus in the community college is on teaching rather than on scholarship within a discipline, faculty are not expected to engage in research (though many do because of their interest in their specialty) and have heavier teaching loads than university faculty (Forrest Cataldi, Fahimi, & Bradburn, 2005). They perceive themselves as looked down upon by their university colleagues: "Before QUE, they would not have even considered us!" said a community college faculty member, joining a chorus of complaints about being dictated to by four-year faculty. A biology faculty member said, "[My work with the QUE cluster] was the first time I felt valued, viewed as an expert in an area, an equal, contributing member." Because two- and four-year institutions traditionally have not met to discuss curricular issues, two-year institutions (and their transfer curricula) have been ruled by the transfer policies of the four-year institutions, policies which are often administered by an admissions person. When discipline leadership at the transfer institution has influenced transfer decisions, they have often demanded more extensive verification of the worthiness of the courses of the two-year institution than they ask of themselves. Thus the notion of four-year institutions dictating the curriculum of two-year institutions has a basis in practice. In the past, meeting as discipline colleagues to discuss the curriculum has rarely occurred across the two-year/four-year divide.

At the QUE national meetings, "they [four-year institutions] have to be constantly reminded that there are community college people at the meeting." The sin here is perhaps one of omission. Little opportunity for two- and four-year partnerships has created a sort of discourse vacuum. Faculty from four-year institutions talk about curricular matters the ways they always have, forgetting to extend their remarks to include community colleges. Meanwhile, the community college faculty are assuming exclusion and are uncertain of where they fit into the discussion. Perhaps the most virulent expression of this sense of inferiority occurred when one cluster explained why their community college partners stopped attending national meetings: "Our two-year people felt dissed, marginalized by the way QUE was being run. They were accused of dumbing everything down in some of the initial discipline-based meetings. That may have been blown out of proportion, but it was there."

Two-year faculty believe that four-year faculty cannot understand the difficulty of helping a large number of underprepared and nontraditional students achieve high standards. Their negative perception of four-year faculty has been heightened by careers replete with discipline colleagues who have asked them, "Why couldn't you get a job at a four-year institution?" Two-year faculty perceive themselves as teachers willing to bring students into the academic community instead of erecting barriers to keep the students out. The community college perception of the four-year faculty is that their attitude toward students is, "If you can't do it, too bad for you!" An interesting reinforcement of this perception occurred when the leadership of one of the two-year partners publicized the institution's strategic plan with a slogan that included the word *learning*. When a new president at the cluster's four-year institution announced an emphasis on "student learning," many of the faculty rejected it as the stuff of the inferior institution across town.

Other issues distancing two- and four-year faculty included the time and funding needed to attend meetings. Because of their heavier teaching loads, community college faculty cannot easily travel to meetings, either locally or nationally, and they usually have no department travel budgets. A California community college faculty member pointed out that "community college faculty have to put in 25 hours of classroom and office time. That's pretty substantial compared to other faculty." The decision by the co-coordinators of the cluster we described in depth to forgo QUE stipends in order to facilitate meeting attendance (local and national) clearly helped to eliminate one obstacle to collegiality. This cluster also maintained equality between the two- and four-year faculty in the teams sent to the national meetings: They mostly consisted of six of each.

Some partnerships between community colleges and universities were a mismatch, despite their geographical proximity. In Southern California, it was difficult to match up one or two colleges with a California State University campus because students transfer to universities all over the region, and, conversely, each university receives transfer students from many different colleges. California State University–Fullerton (CSUF) alone has about eight feeder community colleges. At various times, representatives of Cerritos College, Mt. San Antonio College, and Golden West College joined national meetings in attempts to promote partnerships with CSUF and Long Beach. In Georgia, the college partnered with Valdosta State University, Abraham Baldwin Agricultural College, looked like a logical choice given its proximity, but it provides only 1% of Valdosta's students. Fort Valley State University, a historically black university, was partnered with Middle Georgia College, a largely white institution that did not send more than a handful of students to

Fort Valley. Georgia State University was partnered with Georgia Perimeter College, but the college's five campuses meant that partnership was spread thinly. In some clusters, relations between members of one discipline were closer than relations between the institutions. An English faculty member at a California community college praised her colleagues at the university as "gracious and respectful at meshing their curriculum with ours," but there were no similar relations with the history and biology departments.

By 2002, some community college faculty were no longer sure where they fit in QUE because they do not deal with upper-division students. When level 14 outcomes were written and the disciplinary teams moved on to level 16 outcomes, community college faculty weren't sure it was worth their time to continue in the discussions. A history faculty member at a Maryland community college summed up the problem:

> We've polished the level 14 outcomes, but for level 16 we're deferring to [the university]. I'm somewhere in the middle of the debate about community colleges participating in the development of level 16 outcomes. I think we should participate in the discussion, but ultimately [the university] makes the final decision because they have to live with it.

Nevertheless, some community college faculty continued to attend national meetings because the discussions were not exclusively concerned with outcomes but covered topics emanating from them in Stages 2 and 3. Level 16 was not a universal turn-off for community college faculty. A history faculty member said she enjoyed the level 16 discussions because the continuity from level 14 to 16 made her feel part of a complete program. Because the goal is to develop learning outcomes for graduation, all faculty at all levels need to know where level 14 fits in with and leads to level 16. The most successful partnerships were those that acknowledged the importance of the expertise of the two-year faculty. The four-year faculty have more experience teaching the specialized courses of the major, but the two-year faculty have the experience of teaching more diverse learners. Those QUE participants who actively participated in the discussions of level 16 outcomes were most likely to see learning and assessment as a continuum and to struggle to find ways to help students learn as they progressed through the curriculum rather than continuing to focus on learning and assessment within a course.

Community college faculty find it difficult to maintain high standards because they share teaching with large numbers of adjunct or part-time faculty, paid by the course. (Four-year institutions also hire adjuncts, but not to the same extent. Their situation is complicated by the use of graduate teaching assistants.) The need for adjuncts at community colleges is due to inadequate budgets and fluctuating enrollments. In some departments there may be more part-time and temporary teachers than tenured faculty. Most adjuncts teach remedial courses in mathematics and English, but some are also hired to teach history and other subjects (see Chapter 6). Some adjuncts become "circuit riders," as they teach a course in one institution and then drive to the next. These temporary faculty have no loyalty to a department or institution, usually do not attend department meetings, and therefore cannot be expected to conform their syllabi and course plans to the outcomes agreed on by the department or to participate in developing rubrics and assessments. When outcomes have been developed and even implemented in colleges with large numbers of adjunct faculty, regular faculty complain that they have no levers to ensure that outcomes are shaping the syllabi in all classes.

A major achievement of the cluster we examined in depth was the extension of the benefits of their collaboration to adjunct faculty. The history departments agreed to require the same outcomes in survey courses, no matter whether the courses were taken at the community college or the university. At one of the colleges, part-time faculty were involved in the decision to align the survey courses because the history faculty had a policy of cultivating a semi-permanent faculty—they called them associate faculty—thus removing a stigma. The permanent faculty also regularly observed teaching by these associates in order to assure uniform quality. At the other community college, most of the history courses were taught by associate faculty, until an administrative decision made it possible to hire a full-time history instructor.

Collegial and mutually beneficial relations among two- and four-year institutions are possible, as this cluster demonstrates. No other cluster was as successful on such a large scale, but faculty in other clusters enjoyed positive experiences. One English faculty member said of her Maryland cluster, "Never for a moment was there any sense of anything other than colleagues working together toward a common goal with mutual respect—unless one adds affection and humor to the mix."

A Georgia university faculty member praised the two-year faculty for their investment of energy:

> In talking to colleagues from our two-year institution who participated in QUE, I know they made a conscious effort to align their survey courses with ours, particularly in terms of skills emphasized. I was impressed in general with the seriousness of the participants from two-year institutions in our discipline group. In many instances it seemed that these faculty made more of an effort to align with the goals of the four-year institution than vice versa.

Determining the causes of and remediating the relations between faculty of two- and four-year institutions are far too challenging a task for one project, but seeing the complex forces at work in a project such as QUE that attempts to bring together a number of very different partnerships can be revealing. As is true in many complex relationships, outside forces play an important role. Two clusters that had good partnerships came from a state whose two- and four-year institutions make an effort to work together. These institutions have discovered that through collaboration they are able to craft educational policy for the state, rather than become the victims. This is not a shotgun marriage but an equal partnership with shared goals.

Cooperation between two- and four-year institutions cannot be left to the luck of having congenial personalities in leadership positions. Projects such as QUE, where cooperation among institutions is crucial for student success, should begin with a careful analysis of factors affecting collaboration: transfer patterns, articulation issues, administrative attitudes, mandates for assessment, responsibility for remediation, the use of adjunct faculty, disparity in faculty teaching loads, and professional contacts among faculty. If some or all of these factors are satisfactorily addressed, social factors—such as the resentment felt by community college faculty—may be controlled, even if the hierarchical structure of the system may prevent their complete elimination.

Conclusion

This chapter, as well as the two preceding it, described how QUE worked (or was intended to work). The following five chapters focus on how QUE was experienced by participants and consultants and convey the energy that was generated by the vital conversations among QUE members. Their differing perspectives demonstrate the richness of the QUE experience in terms of issues facing contemporary postsecondary education.

Endnotes

1) The associate provost was approaching retirement but did not leave his post during QUE's funded period.

2) For example, the California higher education plan designed in 1960 envisioned community college as the entry for almost all students, with the University of California and the California State Universities as primarily upper-level institutions.

References

Forrest Cataldi, E., Fahimi, M., & Bradburn, E. M. (2005). *2004 national study of postsecondary faculty (NSOPF:04) report on faculty and instructional staff in fall 2003* (NCES 2005–172). Washington, DC: National Center for Education Statistics, U.S. Department of Education.

4

Wandering Through the World of Standards: Evolution of a Biologist's Perspective

Barbara Baumstark

In 1998, I accepted an invitation to participate in the Quality in Undergraduate Education (QUE) project and inadvertently stepped into the world of standards-based education. Before then, my instructional perspective as a biology professor at Georgia State University (GSU) was typical of those of my colleagues who know little about educational reform issues but simply enjoy teaching. Despite the fact that our success in academia is measured primarily by our research accomplishments, professors like us put a lot of effort into instruction and feel rewarded when we receive positive student evaluations and the approval of our peers. We tend to be diligent about keeping up with the latest scientific advances and presenting this information in our classes. However, in most cases we are not nearly so eager to test out the latest teaching strategies, particularly if their incorporation into our courses will take a lot of time to implement or risk jeopardizing student perceptions. Our opposition may become intractable if we sense that the instructional style that has been working well for us—whatever that style may be—is under attack. In some ways it is the resistance of professors like us, the ones who take pride in their teaching, that makes it difficult for even the most innovative, well-documented educational reform efforts to make a successful transition from discussion at national conferences to implementation on college campuses. A major strength of the QUE initiative has been its ability to provide a forum where professors in diverse disciplines can learn about new educational initiatives, but where they can also make suggestions and voice concerns in an environment where these matters are respected.

My Introduction to QUE

When I agreed to travel to Reno to attend the first QUE meeting, I had never heard of the standards movement or the controversy surrounding it in the K–12 arena. I knew only that the meeting would focus on two disciplines—history and biology—and that we would spend our time discussing what we expect of students who have completed two years of college (level 14). Attending with me were two other GSU biology faculty members: Therese Poole, a lecturer in our department, and Ahmed Abdelal, who at that time was the dean of arts and sciences. In preparation for the QUE meeting, we were asked to generate a "standards document" in consultation with our department faculty. We were told to bring this draft to the meeting, where we would be working closely with colleagues from other two- and four-year institutions to refine and revise our documents.

In anticipation of the Reno meeting, the three of us from GSU set to work on our biology standards document. At that stage, we didn't actually know what standards were—we had an inkling that they had something to do with what we expected our students to know and be able to do—but we forged ahead anyway. The first thing we did was send memos to all GSU biology faculty members soliciting their input. After receiving a thoroughly underwhelming response, we decided to target a subset of our instructors and pose the following questions:

- *To instructors in our lower-division courses:* What knowledge and skills do you expect students to learn in your classes?

- *To instructors in our entry upper-division (junior level) courses:* What knowledge and skills would you like to see mastered by students before they enter your classes?

Since we knew that our colleagues were unlikely to be any more knowledgeable about educational reform efforts than we were, we decided that our response rate could be improved if we provided them with a piece of prose to modify rather than asking them to come up with a comprehensive set of criteria de novo. We therefore developed our own set of level 14 standards, adorned it with some explanatory verbiage, and submitted it to the faculty for their suggestions. This rough draft included the following items:

1) *Students should be able to pose scientific questions and form testable hypotheses to address these questions.* In conjunction with this, students should be able to design experiments and evaluate their results (and the results of others) in terms of their significance and their limitations. The level of technological sophistication need not be high. For example, a student could meet this standard by a) asking whether drinking coffee causes high blood pressure, b) developing a protocol for surveying populations with high blood pressure about coffee use (and including appropriate controls), and c) interpreting the results in terms of cause and effect (i.e., that correlation does not necessarily indicate causation) and confounding factors (i.e., heavy coffee drinkers may also be heavy smokers).

2) *Students should demonstrate an awareness of the history underlying advances in biological thought.* Learning about important scientific advances in the context of the knowledge that was available at the time of their discovery helps students to gain an understanding of the process by which science is done. Moreover, by recognizing that what is accepted as "scientific fact" is subject to change over time, students are able to continually extend their understanding of biological principles even after they complete their formal education.

3) *Students should be able to use knowledge and skills obtained from other disciplines to approach the study of biology.* Students should be able to address biological problems through the application of quantitative skills and by using concepts mastered through the study of other sciences such as chemistry, physics, and geology. They should be able to communicate their ideas about biology effectively, both verbally and in written form.

4) *Students should demonstrate an understanding of the impact of biology on the lives of individuals and society.* Students should be familiar with social and political movements (e.g., the eugenics movement) that have used the mantel of science to lend credibility to their causes. They should also be able to discuss current controversies (e.g., bioengineering, cloning, or evolution) in terms of their policymaking, ethical, and personal implications, and be aware of the scientific evidence supporting or refuting claims made by both sides in the controversy.

5) *Students should demonstrate an awareness of the information content and an understanding of the fundamental concepts that form the foundation for biological sciences.* While it is understood that the models used to explain biological systems will be modified as additional information becomes available over time, students should be aware that there are certain underlying concepts that define life as we know it, including the mechanism of reproduction as a way to maintain the continuum of life, the need for energy to fuel processes essential for life, and the role played by the environment and other living things in the survival of individual species.

Our faculty colleagues found little to modify in the first four items on our list. Item 5 generated a flurry of activity, however; faculty members were eager to contribute numerous content topics they considered to be essential for a well-rounded education in biology. At this stage in our development of standards, we decided to be inclusive rather than selective and incorporate as many suggestions as possible into our document. It is noteworthy, and indicative of things to come, that the list of content items took up 7 pages of our original 12-page draft.

When we arrived at Reno bearing our standards document, we discovered that the only other biologists at the meeting were Virginia Michelich and Sheryl Shanholzer, two colleagues from our two-year partner institution, Georgia Perimeter College (GPC). Starting with GSU's draft document as a template, our group of five biology professors spent several collegial hours revising and refining our standards. This was not the case with our history colleagues, however. Although none of us biologists were aware of it at the time, we later learned that the standards movement is a highly politicized issue among historians with a long background of controversy. The QUE leadership eventually had to divide the historians into two separate rooms to reduce infighting and keep them on task.

The initial progress of our biology group at the Reno meeting (particularly in contrast to the behavior of the history group) made us feel like the good kids in school who receive the teacher's approval for working well together. Our sense of complacency soon evaporated, however, when it became clear that our understanding of the word *standard* did not conform to the definition favored by our QUE colleagues. We had been thinking of a standard as a goal that we would expect all of our students to achieve in order to receive a degree. In retrospect, I realize that we were interpreting the term as an adjective for classification, much like federal regulators might do (a standard grade of beef, for example, is edible though not as highly prized as choice or prime). In contrast, our QUE facilitators encouraged us to aim high—to think of standards in terms of a set of idealized learning outcomes that all students should strive for, even though few might actually achieve them. Although our inability to arrive at a uniform operating definition for standards was largely semantic, the problem continued to gnaw at us. As professors at state colleges and universities, our concerns with formulating a set of standards that represented our highest expectations focused on public perception: If only 30% of our students were expected to satisfy criteria set forth in a given standard, then would 70% of our graduates be considered substandard?

The lack of agreement on a precise definition of *standard* became an issue that we would revisit again and again in subsequent meetings. It was reflected within the QUE movement itself, where the terminology constantly shifted between *standards* and *learning outcomes*. Once, after participating in yet another discussion where this issue came up, I decided to see if a thesaurus could clear up any of the confusion, at least in my own mind. I found that my initial perception held true for the word *standard,* which included among its definitions terms like *conventional, ordinary,* and *average.* However, adding an "s" to produce the word *standards* generated a completely different set of synonyms. *Standards* were defined as *ideals, principles, ethics, integrity*—all good things to promote among our students, even if they do not always represent the undergraduate norm. Although this did not completely alleviate my sense of befuddlement, it did make me aware that even words in common use can mean different things to different groups of people, and that these differences in perception can be a major roadblock on the way to achieving consensus.

Growing Pains

Over the next several years, our GSU/GPC biology group shrank to three (myself and my two Georgia Perimeter colleagues), but the numbers of biologists attending the QUE meetings steadily increased as more institutions came on board. Because our team was there at the beginning, we achieved the dubious status of "senior members" in the QUE initiative, with the dual obligation of explaining the goals of the movement to new participants and defending the standards put forward in our own document. Given that we were not even sure how to define *standards,* we found our status as experts to be a bit problematic.

As with our experiences in our own department, we encountered very little disagreement about the merit of our first four standards. Newcomers to the biology group uniformly agreed that the ability to pose questions, design experiments, and evaluate data (our Standard 1) is a defining characteristic of the successful biology student. A few raised concerns about the inclusion of standards that deal with the relationship among biology and other disciplines (e.g., history and other social sciences), saying that they did not always have time to address these in an introductory course. (Although we continued to consider these characteristics to be important, we eventually consolidated our description of them into one overarching standard.) However, regardless of their judgment of its importance, nearly every new professor had a strong opinion on the content issue, Standard 5. The controversy over what, and how much, content to include in our introductory courses extended over several meetings and became the focus of our most passionate, and admittedly our most interesting, discussions.

When we originally prepared our department standards document at GSU, we wanted to make certain that all faculty opinions were represented. Since nearly every suggestion involved the inclusion of additional content items, we found that our document soon resembled a laundry list of concepts to be mastered with very little sense of how these concepts were related to one another. At the QUE meetings themselves, we tried several times to come up with different formats for presenting these concepts that would illustrate their interrelatedness. Being biologists, we tended to adopt living metaphors, such as the one represented in Figure 4.1.

Figure 4.1
Information Content in Biology

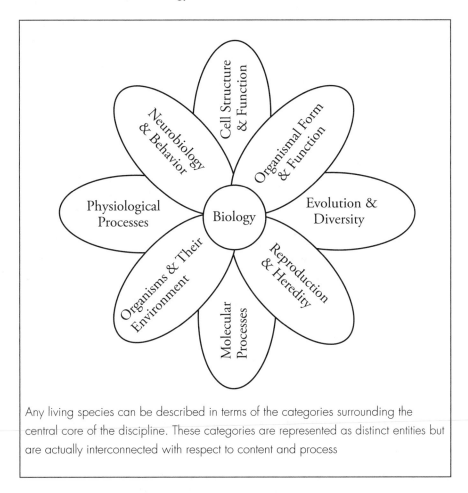

Any living species can be described in terms of the categories surrounding the central core of the discipline. These categories are represented as distinct entities but are actually interconnected with respect to content and process

Still, regardless of the method we used to present content items, the mere mention of content in any form was guaranteed to generate heated debate among our QUE biology group. At one extreme were professors who believed that inclusion of specific content information was immaterial as long as biology majors experienced science as a process and learned to think like scientists. At the other extreme were professors who felt that our particular list of content items was incomplete and needed further detail. Most of us fell somewhere in the middle. We agreed that a grasp of certain fundamental concepts makes the ability to address new questions in any discipline more efficient.[1] In most instances, though, we believed that "process" should take precedence over "facts," since with new discoveries the facts accepted by the discipline will change over time, while the hypothesis-driven nature of scientific research remains constant. Nevertheless, even within this group there were considerable differences of opinion as to where the balance should be struck, and the relative emphasis that should be placed on specific concepts and content items.

The debate over level 14 content kept us occupied for hours over the course of several national QUE meetings. As we considered standards at level 16, concerns about content lessened (although they never disappeared completely). Our biology group agreed that all colleges and universities can provide challenging and rewarding learning opportunities for upper-division students by focusing on their disciplinary strengths. The content information presented in upper-division courses at an institution whose area of expertise is focused in marine biology, for example, might be significantly different from the content information presented by an institution with a focus in molecular genetics, but students at both places could still participate in inquiry-based, research-oriented learning experiences that provide them with the knowledge and skills necessary to succeed in any biology-related field.

How QUE Influenced My Educational Philosophy ———

One of the main points QUE brought home to me personally is how often different disciplines share the same expectations of their students. This became apparent even at our first meeting in Reno, where the history group seemed to have such difficulty reaching consensus. Despite the differences of opinion expressed within the group, in the end many of the history standards developed by different clusters bore a striking similarity to those of the biology groups. This was one of the most important lessons I learned through QUE—that the knowledge and skills valued in academia span disciplinary lines and have little to do with specific content items. As a consequence, my own perception of what should constitute the minimal content requirements for the well-educated biologist decreased dramatically over the course of my association with QUE. I now think of biology content in terms of the following five general concepts:

1) *Life goes on (and on).* Individual living things last only for a limited time, but life itself has been around for billions of years. The characteristics of living things are passed on from one generation to the next through the use of information encoded in DNA, the primary instruction manual for life.

2) *Life doesn't come cheap.* The processes needed to sustain life on earth require a significant input of energy. This energy is derived from the sun and trapped in sugars by plants. Animals use the high-energy compounds they obtain through eating plants and other animals to form ATP, which acts as the energy currency for living things. Enzymes help to overcome the high-energy requirements by lowering the activation energy required for reactions necessary to sustain life.

3) *Life is adaptable.* The most successful species are not necessarily the most complex, but instead the most responsive to change. Through the continual process of mutation and natural selection, living things have become highly diversified, with individual species finding ways to survive under specialized—and in some cases, extremely harsh—circumstances.

4) *Life keeps using what works.* Despite the diversity of life, certain characteristics of successful species have been maintained over evolutionary time. Species that appear to be completely unrelated still share commonalities at the molecular and cellular level. Cells, which constitute the building blocks of life, come together to form tissues, organs, and organisms of high complexity.

5) *Life doesn't stand alone.* The survival of all living things depends on their interaction with other organisms and with their environment. Living things obtain energy from and in turn secrete waste products back into

the environment. They cooperate with and compete with other organisms to obtain the resources needed to survive, grow, and reproduce.

The interrelatedness of diverse disciplines such as biology and history made it increasingly difficult for me to feel comfortable with the representation of standards as stand-alone objectives. Because of this, I eventually found myself taking a cue from the evolutionary biologists and conceptualizing standards more from the standpoint of a branched figure such as a tree rather than as a vertical list (see Figure 4.2).

Figure 4.2
A Standards Tree for Biologists

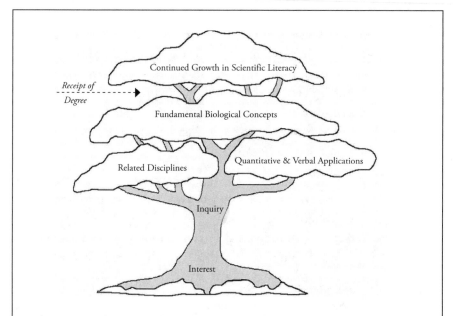

Awakening a student's natural interest in science, followed by the experience of acting on that interest, produces an environment where students can use knowledge and skills obtained from other disciplines to master biological concepts. The inquiry-based nature of their experience provides a framework for understanding future discoveries in biology and the issues these discoveries may generate.

To me, this representation more adequately reflects the process by which students achieve mastery of their subject. For example, by taking advantage of our students' inherent interest in a subject (or generating interest if none is there to begin with), we can pose questions to fuel their curiosity. As they address these questions, they will learn content information that feeds back into their investigations and generates additional questions. The concept of a tree also incorporates a goal that we all share: the production of graduates who continue to grow and learn within the discipline after they have left our sphere of influence.

Bringing the Lessons of QUE Home

Discussions of education reform at national meetings are invigorating, but the ideas tend to lose steam if they are not well received at our home institutions. Some of our biology QUE participants, while agreeing with the standards movement in principle, were highly pessimistic about the likelihood that QUE activities would result in any permanent changes in the way students were taught in their own departments. Our GSU/GPC group ended up feeling optimistic about our ability to introduce QUE-based ideas into our curriculum, in large part because we enjoyed the support of our administrations. Even so, our experiences are probably typical of what our colleagues at other institutions can expect.

- *QUE standards documents provide a conceptual framework for dealing with other educational reform efforts.* Our department, like biology departments all over the country, has felt besieged in recent years by demands for assessment and accountability. Since most of our professors consider time to be among their most precious commodities, any proposal for reform that carries with it a significant time investment is bound to encounter resistance. Critiquing a preexisting document is much less time-consuming than generating a document from scratch. Thus having our QUE standards document already in hand drastically simplified the process of formalizing goals and expectations within our department.

- *The number of items proposed for a list of "essential content" typically expands to reach the number of faculty members taking part in the discussion.* As faculty members work together to formulate their expectations for their students, a tendency to jump on content issues is probably inescapable. We are all aware that the actual information content in biology is simply too large to be covered in its entirety (even superficially) in the time allotted to an undergraduate education. As the amount of knowledge in our discipline continues to mushroom while the amount of class time remains constant, one of the hardest decisions we must make is not which new components to add to our courses, but which old ones to discard. Coupled with this problem is the feeling among individual faculty members that the information represented in their own particular subspecialty is indispensable to the well-trained biologist. This feeling is understandable, since most professors have spent years conducting research on very narrow topics, not only because they need a research component to obtain a position or receive tenure, but also because they presumably find these topics to be exciting and significant.

- *Evolution is better than revolution (incremental changes add up).* As I watch our department struggle to address educational and curricular issues, I am struck by how often the opinions of our faculty members divide along the lines described by Wiggins (1989) more than 15 years ago:

> The traditionalists demand complete cultural literacy; the progressives deify "thinking" and multiple points of view. The former see themselves as the guardians of rigor, standards, and disciplinary knowledge; the latter see such views as elitist, narrowly pedantic, unmindful of nontraditional knowledge and modern epistemology. (p. 45)

Many of our professors are understandably skeptical of the "latest innovations" in education. In some cases, they have watched their own children serve as guinea pigs for politicized and hastily developed educational programs in the K–12 arena. If they are among those faculty members who put a high value on content, they may object to innovations that focus on inquiry, since these typically consume a lot of class time. However, we have found that change does not always need to wait for consensus. Working together or individually, faculty members can try out new teaching approaches in their classes on a small scale. If these approaches are successful, and particularly if they garner a favorable response from students, there is a high likelihood that other faculty members will gradually become interested. Moreover, since the groundwork for each activity will have been laid (meaning that course materials and laboratory procedures will have been developed and tested), the amount of time needed to incorporate the activity into another class becomes considerably less, thus lowering the activation energy required to convince other faculty members to try it.

When I compare our courses today with the courses we offered when I first became involved with the QUE initiative, I can see areas where incremental changes have made a significant difference. This has been particularly true for our introductory courses. Like many other university systems, Georgia requires that all undergraduates in state colleges and universities complete two semesters of a laboratory-based natural science. In the case of GSU, the most popular way to fulfill this requirement is to take our introductory biology series. For at least 20 years, this course was taught using a traditional large-class (70–200 students) lecture format with breakout laboratory sections. Grades were based predominantly on performance on multiple-choice exams that were heavily content oriented. The same series was offered to both majors and non-majors.

In the early days of the QUE movement, our department was in the process of dividing our introductory course series into two, with one series devoted to majors and the other to non-majors. The conventional wisdom at the time was that this would allow us to increase our expectations for our majors. Although a few of us expressed reservations about the split, most faculty members were in favor of it, regardless of their educational perspective. Traditionally oriented instructors saw it as a way to include more content in the majors series, while their progressive counterparts saw it as an avenue for introducing inquiry-based activities into courses for both majors and non-majors.

Our QUE standards documents helped us to formulate our expectations for both majors and non-majors courses. Although the prevailing views of the faculty held that content should still be a driving force in the majors lecture segment, individual faculty members were able to incorporate a significant number of new inquiry-based activities into the laboratory sections.

It is in the non-majors courses that the most striking changes are being implemented, however. For several years, a few faculty members had been interested in offering individualized courses for our non-majors focused on specific themes that would be relevant to the students' chosen areas of study. This option met with considerable resistance from more traditional professors. Their concern was focused on their fear that a theme-based approach, if adopted universally, would run the risk of diluted content and lowered rigor. With the availability of a set of approved learning outcomes, however, instructors who wish to pursue a theme-based approach can specifically highlight those aspects of their course that fulfill each of the standards agreed upon by the faculty as a whole. For example, a course directed at history and other social science majors might deal with the effects of microbes on human history. Initial student interest could be generated by presenting the following scenario:

> A government official receives a letter from his gardener containing a suspicious white powder. As a bioterrorism expert working for the CDC, you must determine whether or not the powder contains *Bacillus anthracis*, the bacterium responsible for anthrax.

Over several weeks, students can pose hypotheses, design experiments aimed at bacterial identification, and interpret their results. (Since we are obviously not going to expose our students to anthrax, their tests would ultimately reveal that the powder contains a closely related but harmless organism such as *Bacillus thuringiensis*, a bacterium used by gardeners to control the spread of insect pests.) The historical significance of microbes becomes clear with a consideration of the political and social upheavals that ensued in the aftermath of major epidemics (such as the "germ warfare" propagated by settlers in the New World, who brought with them measles, smallpox, and other diseases that devastated native American populations). In fact, even if instructors were to limit the number of microbes under consideration to those touted as agents of bioterrorism, they could still describe their effects in a context that incorporates significant biology content information. All bacteria, for example, use DNA as their genetic material, as do the hosts they infect. *B. anthracis* is one of many bacterial species that can survive in oxygen-rich or oxygen-poor conditions, producing energy efficiently in the presence of oxygen by respiration, and less efficiently in its absence by fermentation. In addition, as a spore-forming bacterium, *B. anthracis* can adapt to extremely harsh conditions, surviving for years in a dormant state only to revive when conditions become more favorable. Many of the potential germ warfare organisms in existence today owe their biological success to the "civilizing" forces at work in human society, which resulted in domestication of animals, formation of population-dense urban centers, and increased contact with other societies through war and trade.

By volunteering to offer a theme-based introductory course, Therese Poole, one of our charter QUE members, recently took the first step toward revising our non-majors series. The success of her course has inspired others in the department to develop introductory courses around other themes. Within one year, the number of theme-based introductory sections we will offer has increased from 2 to 10 (out of 26). These courses, even though tailored to a group of non-majors, will still incorporate the types of inquiry-based activities and a level of content that provide a challenging learning environment.

Final Thoughts

The process of developing learning outcomes, and the discussions that this process generates, are taking place at many colleges and universities. Based on my own experiences, however, I believe that there are several unique features of the QUE philosophy that set it apart from other educational initiatives.

From the beginning, the QUE leadership accorded us respect as specialists in our academic disciplines and looked politely away when we betrayed our ignorance of educational reform movements. They made it clear that our work on developing standards was not designed to promote a national "standardized" set of learning outcomes, but instead to identify the knowledge and skills that represent areas of expertise within our institution and are particularly valued by our faculty. By taking this approach, they led us to appreciate, and respect, the enormous diversity within our disciplines and the different perspectives of our fellow biologists. The QUE initiative also performed a great service by opening up the lines of communication between four-year colleges and universities and the two-year community colleges that serve as the source of their transfer students. Although my two GPC colleagues both live within jogging distance of my house, we had to travel 2,500 miles to the first QUE meeting in Reno just to get acquainted! As time has gone by, I have found Virginia and Sheryl to be wonderful sources of new ideas and teaching strategies. Their work on developing performance standards, assessment tools, and, especially, a set of standards for non-majors has had a profound effect on the evolution of my own teaching philosophy.

On their web site (www.gsu.edu/que), the founders of QUE mention that "the process of writing the standards is itself rich and stimulating." This was certainly true for me as a biologist. The path we took to produce our QUE documents had even more influence on my perceptions than the completed documents themselves. Ultimately, the QUE experience made me realize that we college instructors need to strive not only to become good teachers, but to provide our students with the knowledge and skills they need to become good learners. Only then will we be proud of every student we send out into the world.

Endnotes

1) To give an example from mathematics, students confronted with a complex multiplication problem are going to arrive at an answer much more quickly if they automatically know that $5 \times 5 = 25$ and do not have to add $5 + 5 + 5 + 5 + 5$. Of course, students are going to remember that $5 \times 5 = 25$ if they use multiplication regularly to solve problems and don't simply memorize the multiplication tables.

References

Wiggins, G. (1989, November). The futility of trying to teach everything of importance. *Educational Leadership, 47*(3), 44–48, 57–59.

5

Chemical Education Today

Jerry Sarquis

The chemistry disciplinary group within the Quality in Undergraduate Education (QUE) project began its work in 2001. Compared to other QUE disciplinary groups, the numbers involved were fewer. This issue was discussed among the QUE chemists attending the meetings and several reasons were suggested. One was that chemistry as a discipline has a strong organization, the American Chemical Society (ACS), and a very active subgroup, the Division of Chemical Education (CHED), which has more than 5,000 members. Both the parent ACS and CHED are very much involved in curricular matters at the postsecondary level, perhaps mitigating, in many chemists' minds, the need for a set of local standards.

There is a significant difference in the ACS certification guidelines and the specific learning goals and objectives that underlie QUE principles. Content in chemistry tends to be linear, especially in years 13–14. A year of general chemistry and a year of organic chemistry is the overwhelming standard 13–14 curriculum, although a few institutions deviate from this model. General chemistry currently focuses on answers to exercises, and the majority of the content is mathematical. Thus it is easy for students to slip into an algorithmic mode of learning. Organic chemistry is descriptive: Different types of reactions are studied in a systematic way, with a focus on what is happening at the molecular level. The ultimate goal is to be able to predict reactivity based on patterns followed by similar substances. Organic is much more conceptual and is frequently feared by students as an impossible hurdle. Compounding the fear is the fact that organic chemistry is often used as a gatekeeper course for aspirants to medical school.

The ACS Certification Guidelines

To understand the background to the QUE work on chemistry, and the situation in the postsecondary teaching of chemistry in the U.S. today, it will help to take a brief look at the ACS and its influence on chemistry instruction.

One of the most important ACS committees is the Committee on Professional Training (CPT), whose "primary objective . . . is to facilitate the maintenance and improvement of the quality of chemical education at the postsecondary level" (ACS, 2003, p. 1). One way the CPT meets this objective is "by developing and administering the guidelines that define high quality undergraduate programs" (ACS, 2003, p. 1). In order for an undergraduate chemistry program to be ACS certified, the seal of approval for an undergraduate chemistry degree, a chemistry department must meet the guidelines set forth by the CPT. The guidelines specify the number of hours and the content of chemistry courses and supporting courses that must be completed for certification. There are more than 600 colleges and universities with ACS-certified programs. Chemistry courses from a certified institution are more readily transferred to other institutions. Certified graduates are also highly sought by the top chemistry graduate programs and they are eligible for membership in ACS upon graduation.

In addition to satisfying curricular guidelines, institutions must also demonstrate minimum resources in such areas as faculty, library holdings, and equipment and receive assurance that the finances of the institution are adequate to support the necessary resources. Initial certification involves a site visit. Once certified, a department must submit annual reports that indicate they continue to meet or exceed the CPT guidelines, and there is a reevaluation every five years.

In effect, chemistry as a discipline looks to the CPT guidelines as the curricular standard for professional chemists. As a result, there seems to be less need to set forth department standards.

Curricular Reform in Chemistry Education

Nevertheless, the profession is feeling some discomfort about chemical education at the postsecondary level. In 1989, the National Science Foundation (NSF) published a report based on a series of workshops addressing undergraduate science education. The report called for the creation of science education task forces to develop materials for undergraduate education in the sciences for adoption in college and university chemistry curricula. In addition to materials development, science educators were challenged to publicize the new materials and provide workshops for instructors who wished to use them.

In response, the Division of Chemical Education formed the General Chemistry Curriculum Task Force in 1990 (Lloyd & Spencer, 1994). As one of the task force members, Lloyd reviewed curricular reform in chemistry in the 20th century through 1992. This period included two major chemistry curricular reforms which were accepted by the chemistry community, but both involved updating course content to reflect new knowledge. These reforms did not impact the goal of chemical education to develop student ability to explore chemical systems in a rational way, but Lloyd concluded that teaching strategies to reach these goals needed to change. "The courses, as currently structured, are not attracting talented students nor are they providing the experiences needed to produce students who have a firm foundation of basic skills needed to think and act as a scientist" (Lloyd, 1992, p. 636). Lloyd predicted (accurately) that additional reform will not be so easy since it will be necessary to confront " . . . the reluctance of teachers of general chemistry to implement change. . . . [and that] curricular change must be a response to changes in the way students learn chemistry, requiring changes in methods of instruction and evaluation" (p. 636).

Dispelling "Misbeliefs" _____

In the late 1990s, the NSF Division of Undergraduate Education funded four major systemic initiatives focusing on chemistry curricular reform: ChemConnections, Molecular Science, New Traditions, and Peer-Led Team Learning. The goal was to explore how chemistry education could be changed to improve student learning. The National Science Foundation also funded several grants through the Division of Undergraduate Education Adopt and Adapt program to extend the impact of the original four projects. The four systemic initiatives joined forces as the four-year Multi-Initiative Dissemination Project, which presented 45 faculty workshops across the U.S. from 2001–2004. This is the same timeframe as the QUE initiative. The Multi-Initiative Dissemination Project workshops focused on the paradigm shift from teaching to learning and introduced faculty participants to the four curricular reform projects, current education theories, and the ways in which those projects addressed issues of student learning. In spite of these high-profile projects during the last 10 years, most chemistry instruction is still conducted using the traditional lecture. It is teacher-centered instead of learner-centered.

When chemistry faculty are asked why they have not considered reforming the traditional lecture, the response is often that there is no proof that alternative methods are superior to the tried and true methods. But such comments are usually from those who have not explored alternative methods, are not familiar with the literature in chemical education and chemical education research, or do not accept the methods and/or the findings and conclusions of chemical education research. Likewise, the same individuals feel no need to question a system of instruction that was successful to them personally, nor the need to investigate how today's students learn.

Moore (2004, p. 7) noted three prevailing misbeliefs regarding the teaching of chemistry:

- Chemistry is too hard for many students and therefore we ought to find algorithms by which they can obtain correct answers without understanding why the algorithm works.

- Students can learn directly from what we say, without processing information and constructing understanding.

- Students who can answer numeric questions on exams actually understand the principles of chemistry.

Moore makes a compelling case that these beliefs are in fact untrue and supports his assertion with reference to research studies in chemical education. He continues that acceptance of these misbeliefs by chemistry faculty allows them to carry on in chemistry education without reform.

It is ironic that chemists who pride themselves on the integrity of their science can find it all too easy to accept these misbeliefs without requiring any supporting evidence. Doing so is convenient and faster, but it belies the scientific principles that are the foundation of chemistry specifically and science generally. Faculty continue to believe that students listening to lectures and learning to solve algorithmic exercises achieve conceptual understanding.

Students Aren't Molecules

Ignorance of chemistry education research findings among chemistry faculty is prevalent, but such ignorance should not be excused. Many chemistry faculty are skeptical about the methods and protocols of sociological and educational research. It is hard to convince chemists that the methods used, data collected, and the resulting conclusions are valid. They are especially suspicious of qualitative research methods. Credibility of chemical education research is made all the more difficult because chemists are used to manipulating molecules and finding situations in which the conditions of an experiment can be precisely compared to a control that allows unambiguous, definitive results. Research involving molecules is much easier than research with students.

It is impossible to design a "perfect" experiment in chemical education with just one variable controlled. Often the changes observed between experiment and control are small. Even if the same instructor teaches two sections, one traditionally and the other with an innovation, it is rare that dramatic changes are found. The impact of so many variables (background, mathematical ability, language ability, etc.) not possible to control like a chemistry experiment. As a result, one hears comments on chemical education research findings such as "the student populations are not the same," "just because an innovation works in one setting, that is not proof that it will work here," and so on.

Chemical Education Research

Because it is difficult to convince science faculty of the validity of educational and sociological research methods, it is easier for chemistry faculty to hold on to their misbeliefs. However, in the past two decades, the subdiscipline of chemical education research has grown increasingly important. Typically, a chemical education researcher has a content background in chemistry at an advanced level and, in addition, has become an expert in educational research methods. The number of chemical education graduate programs remains small in comparison to traditional areas such as organic, analytical, physical, and biochemistry. According to the Committee on Chemical Education Research (2005), 17 institutions offer a doctoral degree and 7 more offer a master's degree in chemical education. This is in contrast to the more than 600 institutions offering an ACS certified degree and many more that offer chemistry bachelor degrees that are not certified.

In addition, even in departments with a dozen or more faculty, it is not unusual for a chemistry department to have just a single faculty member whose scholarly interest is chemical education research. This presents a major impediment for chemical education researchers. They do not have the same opportunity to discuss and debate their scholarly activities in the same way that traditional chemistry faculty members would have with several colleagues in the same subdiscipline. But intracampus collaboration with colleagues in other departments and colleges and intercampus affiliations—such as that offered in the QUE project—do give the individual chemical education researcher some company.

The Scholarship of Teaching and Learning in Chemistry

In the last two decades, research has become increasingly important in chemistry departments in many institutions, especially in those offering graduate courses in chemistry. Accompanying this trend is the risk that attention to teaching has declined. This, of course, is not unique to chemistry. In 1990, Boyer wrote,

> The most important obligation now confronting the nation's colleges and universities is to break out of the tired old teaching versus research debate and define, in more creative ways, what it means to be a scholar. It's time to recognize the full range of faculty talent and the great diversity of functions higher education must perform. (p. xii)

In 1992, the American Chemical Society's Division of Chemical Education established the Chemical Education Research Task Force to answer the question "What is chemical education research?" and establish criteria by which practitioners of chemical education research can be fairly evaluated (e.g., in tenure and promotion decisions and salary recommendations) by their chemistry colleagues. The results of the task force are reported in the *Journal of Chemical Education* (Bunce, Gabel, Herron, & Jones, 1994). The task force examined research in chemical education and discovered that the purpose of chemical education research is the same as the purpose of research in other branches, despite the fact that the techniques and guiding theories differ from those used in other branches of chemistry. The report concludes with an admonition that chemists recognize that "Without the understanding of how chemistry can be taught and learned that derives from research in chemistry education, the entire field of chemistry is impoverished and its contribution to humanity is reduced" (Bunce, Gabel, Herron, & Jones, 1994, p. 852).

The issue of chemical education research was also addressed by the American Chemical Society. At the fall 2000 meeting of ACS, the board of directors approved the following from its "Statement on Scholarship in the Chemical Sciences and Engineering":

> In addition to discovery research, scholarship in the chemical sciences and engineering includes the integration, application, and teaching of chemical sciences and engineering principles and practices. This expanded definition recognizes that valuable

> scholarship in any of these areas requires originality, creativity, a thorough grounding in the previous accomplishments of other scholars, and effective communication of new contributions in peer-reviewed publications. (as qtd. in Moore, 2000, p. 1383)

Eybe and Schmidt (2001) published an article discussing quality criteria in chemical education research. In spite of such efforts, the evaluation of tenure-track chemical education research faculty is still mostly case by case.

In 1997, the *Journal of Chemical Education* instituted a new feature, Research in Chemical Education. As the premier publication in chemical education, this new initiative is significant. Articles accepted for the feature require that "The research must be theory based; the questions asked should be relevant to chemical educators and able to be tested through the experimental design proposed; the data collected must be verifiable; and the results must be generalizable" (Bunce & Robinson, 1997, p. 1076).

Chemists with a chemical education research specialty contribute their expertise to the chemistry community. They have sound content knowledge, education research credentials, classroom instructional experience in chemistry, a better understanding of the problems facing chemistry students, and the ability to more effectively communicate with chemists due to their knowledge of the language and jargon of chemistry.

Evaluation and Assessment

The increasing focus on program assessment and evaluation at the department and the institutional level is contributing to the need to pay attention to the results of chemical education research. In turn, this focus on assessment and evaluation is being driven by the institutional accreditation agencies. For example, The Higher Learning Commission of the North Central Association of Colleges and Schools lists the following as criterion 2c: "The organization's ongoing evaluation and assessment processes provide reliable evidence of institutional effectiveness that clearly informs strategies for continuous improvement" (The Higher Learning Commission, 2003, p. 6).

As colleges and universities address the issue of demonstrating program effectiveness at the institutional level, based on evaluation and assessment, this will also become a critical component of department program review. Thus chemistry departments will have to devote more resources to collecting and analyzing data to provide evidence of effectiveness and continual improvement in chemistry. These departments will also need to seek guidance from those proficient in evaluation and assessment, meaning the role of the chemical education researcher will become more and more prominent in the future.

Assessment Instruments

How is undergraduate chemistry content evaluated? The ACS Division of Chemical Education Examinations Institute was established in 1930 and its first exam, general chemistry, was published in 1934. Today there are more than 50 exams available ranging from high school level to all subdisciplines in college chemistry. Because these exams are standardized national exams, they are often the instruments used by community colleges, four-year undergraduate, and comprehensive universities to measure the success of their chemistry courses. Each exam is developed by a committee of volunteer chemistry faculty from throughout the U.S. It generally takes two to three years for an exam to be published, and new editions of the exams are developed on a regular schedule. Often when a curricular innovation is tried, the first question asked is "How do the students perform on the ACS exam?" As such, the Examinations Institute has played an important role in curricular assessment.

Zoller, Lubezky, Nakhleh, Tessier, and Dori (1995) examined student abilities toward examinations based on algorithmic low-order cognitive skills, which mirror the traditional university-level lecture mode of content delivery and those based on high-order cognitive skills. They reported that success on algorithmic exams does not mean there is conceptual understanding. The traditional instructional strategies are not compatible with attaining conceptual learning and high-order cognitive skills (Zoller et al., 1995).

As the paradigm shift from teaching to learning became more important in chemistry, the ACS Examinations Institute responded by developing an examination to test conceptual understanding, first released in 1996. Faculty now have an opportunity to test for conceptual understanding with standardized exams.

A multiple-choice instrument of conceptual questions was developed to assess conceptual understanding (Mulford & Robinson, 2002). It consists of one- and two-tiered non-mathematical questions of concepts covered in the first-semester general chemistry course. The instrument was given to 1,400 general chemistry students as a pre-test and a post-test. Out of 22 questions, the average score improved only from 10 to 11 after one semester of general chemistry. This finding indicates that conceptual understanding is improved very little by a typical one-semester general chemistry course. Mulford and Robinson's finding is also consistent with similar analyses based on the Conceptual General Chemistry Examination described earlier. These results confirm that many students come away from chemistry with little understanding of fundamental concepts: " . . . many of our general chemistry students are not fluent with a significant portion of the concepts in general chemistry. They have difficulty with fundamental concepts concerning the properties and behavior of atoms and molecules" (Robinson & Nurrenbern, n.d.).

QUE Chemistry Outcomes

What this all means is that the national picture in chemistry education is conflicted. The ACS standards satisfy the majority of faculty in chemistry, but student achievement does not inspire confidence. The consensus of the QUE chemistry faculty was that the examination of the chemistry curriculum in the context of desired outcomes was useful. The immediate impact of QUE may appear to be modest over the short term. Historically, curricular change in higher education is evolutionary rather than revolutionary.

Two QUE clusters worked on chemistry: the University of Nevada–Reno (UNR) and Truckee Meadows Community College (TMCC), both located in Reno, Nevada, and Salisbury University with its community college partners Chesapeake College and Wor-Wic Community College, all located on the Maryland eastern shore.

The University of Nevada–Reno and Truckee Meadows Community College participated in the first QUE national meeting in August 1998, when the chemistry department at UNR and the Department of Physical Science at TMCC collaborated on a set of outcome-based standards. An important motivation for the two chemistry departments was to facilitate the transfer of chemistry majors from TMCC to UNR. Two of the faculty are also active at the national level in the Division of Chemical Education with issues confronting community college chemistry students and departments. The result of participation in QUE was a set of standards for the levels 14 and 16 in chemistry (see Appendix B).

Not included in Appendix B, but available on the UNR web site (www.chem.unr.edu/undergraduates/standards.html), are detailed assessment rubrics based on those developed by Joseph A. Shaeiwitz from the Department of Chemical Engineering at West Virginia University. The UNR web site makes the standards document available to undergraduate students and also provides a listing of outcomes and assessment tools for each of its three baccalaureate chemistry programs.

At Salisbury University, the chemistry department became actively involved in QUE in fall 2002, when the university was undergoing an intensive period of internal curricular assessment and the goals of QUE meshed with the local charge to develop content and process standards and associated assessment tools. At the same time, Salisbury was establishing a relationship with Wor-Wic and Chesapeake community colleges. The collaboration emphasized a faculty-generated approach to curriculum standards for general chemistry. The Salisbury/Wor-Wic collaboration was especially important since Wor-Wic only offers one semester of general chemistry. Thus their students must take second-semester general chemistry at Salisbury.

Salisbury found the draft chemistry standards published by UNR to be consistent with the operational standards at Salisbury. With the help of the Office of Institutional Research, student outcome data was collected on transfer students. The results confirmed anecdotal data that the Salisbury chemistry standards were comparable with other four-year institutions and provided the basis for discussions with the two-year schools. Thus QUE played an important role in establishing an active, ongoing dialog between Salisbury and Wor-Wic.

While the UNR standards provided a starting point for the Salisbury initiatives, Salisbury is currently working on completing its own version of standards, especially for the advanced-level courses in the major—organic chemistry, analytical chemistry, and physical chemistry. Laboratory practical exams are also being discussed at Salisbury along with the development of scoring rubrics for those exams. Thus it is clear that the process of developing local standards in a discipline is not completely specific to location. QUE has provided a transferable model of curriculum development that others can adapt and adopt.

Barriers

None of the institutions involved in the QUE chemistry initiative had universal buy-in from department colleagues. While it was discussed among the faculty as a whole a few times, the majority of the discussion was within smaller groups or committees. At the University of Nevada–Reno, faculty were skeptical or confused about QUE goals and thought them to be a "moving target." Like all certified ACS degree departments, UNR conducts periodic curricular reviews to maintain certification. In general, the faculty felt that the ACS review process is adequate to maintain program quality. They were not convinced that committing the additional effort and assessment suggested by the QUE initiative would have a major impact on what faculty currently do in the classroom and on improved student learning outcomes.

The major barrier to implementation of QUE standards at Salisbury was a departmental lack of interest or willingness to spend the necessary time and effort. Although QUE was discussed once in a department meeting, it was not considered to be an item of priority. Unless the department chair takes a lead role, it is extremely difficult to get faculty buy-in.

Community College Issues

At the community college level, there are other barriers to implementing QUE principles. First, all the barriers discussed for four-year institutions apply to community colleges as well. In addition, community colleges generally have a relatively high percentage of part-time instructors. Even if the full-time faculty wish to adopt a curricular innovation, it is difficult to get part-time faculty to adopt the same strategies. The reasons for this are many: They often have other work responsibilities; they have less contact with their full-time colleagues, limiting meaningful discussions about curricular reform; there is less time for direct contact with students outside of class; they have limited opportunity to participate in the professional development necessary to institute and support a new teaching style; they fear student backlash as a result of implementing new instructional strategies.

Another barrier is the issue of transferability of courses. The QUE project addressed this issue by forming clusters that included both two- and four-year institutions. Unfortunately, articulation agreements are often written on a course-by-course basis. Nationally, there are more and more students who will take courses to fulfill their degree requirements at multiple institutions. There is some movement in some states for facilitating transferability, but there is much room for improvement.

Likewise, there are significant differences in student populations. Many have the impression that a community college chemistry course is "easier" than its equivalent at a four-year institution. One has to be careful in this analysis and not jump to incorrect conclusions. Community colleges are largely open enrollment institutions and students generally have a weaker academic background and less exposure to higher education culture than their counterparts at four-year institutions.

Community college students transferring to a four-year institution can face social as well as academic disadvantages. They are also used to close personal attention—their instructors seek them out as opposed to the student's having to take the initiative to approach a four-year college instructor. Students find it more difficult to become integrated with chemistry majors in the four-year institution who have already established social and study groups during their first two years.

Another problem is the perception that implementing curricular reform will require more of students. This is a much more important issue at the two-year institution where the average age is 25–30, most students have job and/or family responsibilities in addition to school, and institutional retention rates are closely followed by administration. Once again, full-time faculty are much better equipped to assist students in finding the proper balance between their school and other responsibilities than is the casual instructor.

The Next Step

As more documentation of learning is required by government and accrediting agencies, QUE and similar initiatives may find a friendlier environment. For example, the University of Nevada–Reno has recently introduced a new set of university-wide program assessment requirements. This has resulted in a partial implementation of QUE principles in the chemistry department. The assessment criteria and tools currently used are wholly derived from those identified or developed by QUE. Assessment of student work originally developed for the QUE project is now being reviewed, QUE-derived rubrics are being used in some courses to evaluate student writing and student oral presentations, and more courses are now using standard ACS exams.

Truckee Meadows Community College felt that dialogue was quite useful, but that it was hard to get beyond the initial agreement on outcomes expected for first- and second-year chemistry courses. Two-year college faculty might have fewer attitudinal and institutional barriers to curricular reform because the community college mission is focused on teaching rather than research. But this advantage is mitigated by higher teaching loads, smaller departments (thus fewer opportunities for discussion and debate), and generally fewer possibilities for professional development.

All of the faculty involved reported that their participation in QUE activities and initiatives was, at best, tolerated rather than encouraged at both the department and institutional level.

As consultant for the QUE chemistry discipline group, I thought it a privilege to work with dedicated teachers of undergraduate students of chemistry, as well as our colleagues in other disciplines. It gave me great hope for the future. As higher education is called upon to provide more and more accountability, the QUE project will provide one of the bricks of a foundation upon which others can build.

Resources

We acknowledge the following organizations for material used in writing this chapter:

The Modular CHEM Consortium, University of California–Berkeley
Process and content standards:
http://mc2.cchem.berkeley.edu/
http://mc2.cchem.berkeley.edu/modules/index.html

ChemLinks Coalition, Beloit College
Process and content standards:
http://chemlinks.beloit.edu/summary.html
http://chemistry.beloit.edu/modules.html

American Chemical Society
Committee on Professional Training, topical supplements to *Undergraduate Professional Education in Chemistry: Guidelines and Evaluation Procedures:*
http://www.chemistry.org/portal/a/c/s/1/acsdisplay.html?DOC=education\cpt\guidelines.html

References

American Chemical Society, Committee on Professional Training. (2003). *Undergraduate professional education in chemistry: Guidelines and evaluation procedures.* Retrieved November 1, 2005, from http://www.chemistry.org/portal/resources/ACS/ACSContent/education/cpt/guidelines_spring2003.pdf

Boyer, E. L. (1990). *Scholarship reconsidered: Priorities of the professoriate.* Princeton, NJ: Carnegie Foundation for the Advancement of Teaching.

Bunce, D., Gabel, D., Herron, J. D., & Jones, L. (1994, October). Report of the task force on chemical education research of the American Chemical Society Division of Chemical Education. *Journal of Chemical Education, 71*(10), 850–852.

Bunce, D. M., & Robinson, W. R. (1997, September). Research in chemical education—the third branch of our profession. *Journal of Chemical Education, 74*(9), 1076.

Committee on Chemical Education Research. (2005). *Masters (M.S.) & doctoral (Ph.D./D.A.) programs in chemistry education.* Retrieved November 1, 2005, from http://www.users.muohio.edu/bretzsl/cer/programs.htm

Eybe, H., & Schmidt, H. J. (2001). Quality criteria and exemplary papers in chemical education research. *International Journal of Science Education, 23*(2), 209–225.

The Higher Learning Commission. (2003). *Institutional accreditation: An overview.* Retrieved November 1, 2005, from http://www.ncahlc.org/download/2003Overview.pdf

Lloyd, B. W. (1992, August). A review of curricular changes in the general chemistry course during the twentieth century. *Journal of Chemical Education, 69*(8), 633–636.

Lloyd, B. W., & Spencer, J. N. (1994, March). The forum: New directions for general chemistry: Recommendations of the task force on the general chemistry curriculum. *Journal of Chemical Education, 71*(3), 206–209.

Moore, J. W. (2000, November). Scholarship in the chemical sciences and engineering [Editorial]. *Journal of Chemical Education, 77*(11), 1383.

Moore, J. W. (2004, January). New year's resolution: Expunge misbeliefs [Editorial]. *Journal of Chemical Education, 81*(1), 7.

Mulford, D. R., & Robinson, W. R. (2002, June). An inventory for alternate conceptions among first-semester general chemistry students. *Journal of Chemical Education, 79*(6), 739–744.

National Science Foundation. (1989). *Report on the National Science Foundation disciplinary workshops on undergraduate education* (NSF 89–3). Washington, DC: Author.

Robinson W. R., & Nurrenbern, S. C. (Eds.). (n.d.). Conceptual questions (CQs): Chemical concepts inventory. *Journal of Chemical Education Online.* Retrieved December 1, 2005, from http://jchemed.chem.wisc.edu/JCEDLib/QBank/collection/CQandChP/CQs/ConceptsInventory/CCIntro.html

Zoller, U., Lubezky, A., Nakhleh, M. B., Tessier, B., & Dori, Y. J. (1995, November). Success on algorithmic and LOCS vs. conceptual chemistry exam questions. *Journal of Chemical Education, 72*(11), 987–989.

6

The English Chair's Guide to a Learning-Centered Curriculum

Susan Albertine

Need we say that to the typical Department of English at most colleges and universities assessment of learning is no picnic? English faculty approach the task not so much with energy as with trepidation, even loathing. To those who face an accreditation task, such responses will come as no surprise, and we might as well speak frankly and compassionately about it. Drawing on the work of the Quality in Undergraduate Education (QUE) project and a similar project at my home institution, The College of New Jersey, I offer this chapter as a pragmatic contribution to department chairs and faculty leaders throughout the discipline who find themselves faced with the assessment of learning, wishing that lightning would strike.

Disciplinary Background _____

The discipline of English offers many rewards but virtually nothing for curricular reform. One need only follow the rewards. There are no good jokes about curricular reform. It does not appear in *New Yorker* cartoons or that ubiquitous op-ed piece following the Modern Language Association (MLA) annual meeting. Assessment is likewise a low-status activity. It depends on collaboration, and as such, it has no ready place within the individualistic department or the discipline. Typical among the traditional humanities, scholarship in English (by which I mean research, scholarship, and creative work) prizes the single-author publication. The priority of single authorship enhances the effects of individualism within departments. We tend in any case to defend, and defend strongly, the faculty member's academic freedom, the faculty member's courses, and the faculty member's classroom. The hierarchical status of institutions also affects disciplinary thinking about individuals and individualism. By and large, English departments seek the status of the elite research institutions, with their highly individualized star system. Most of us have thought about or coveted the reputation and salary of the stars—and the teaching load. As they did throughout the 20th century, the elite doctoral institutions prepare students to teach at the elite doctoral institutions. Most of us, of course, go from the elite doctoral institutions to teach and practice elsewhere.

But more specifically concerning assessment of learning, neither the community of the discipline—could one imagine such organization?—nor its principal professional organization, the MLA, has stepped forward to lead. There are no disciplinary handbooks to help departments design programs for learning or construct guidelines for assessment. The MLA has little to say on the subject and has, through its staff, opposed any call to articulate goals or assess outcomes. When QUE invited MLA staff to attend our English meetings in 2000, we learned firsthand of this opposition. We must not, the argument goes, commit ourselves to paper. Any document that introduces anything remotely like standards will be used against us—to standardize—undermining the freedom and flexibility of the discipline. It is dangerous to be clear about what we expect our students to know and do when they complete their programs. These are publicly stated opinions, as can be found in Schramm, Mitchell, Stephens, and Laurence (2003).[1] When I presented the issue at the New England Educational Assessment Network (NEEAN) workshop for English departments at the University of Massachusetts–Amherst in April 2005, I heard from several in the overflow audience that the MLA had sent the same message to them. And while I might here devote myself to a counterargument, I intend to do something different, something less direct but moving toward the same goal. I want to present models for practice and then ask empirical questions about results. Let me be clear from the start: Contrary to what the MLA has stated, there exists a considerable demand for guidance from departments. All regional accreditation associations now ask for evidence of learning; all teacher accreditation programs ask the same.

After five years with QUE, I suspected that many departments were beginning to discover a need for guidance. The NEEAN workshop still surprised me. Nearly 100 faculty attended—more than capacity—from all institutional types in New England. While some departments had reasonably well-developed plans, even the most advanced felt unprepared and uncertain. Nobody wanted to waste time arguing about compliance or dangers. They wanted, it was clear, to take charge of the situation. Not only is it no picnic, but English departments are out on a limb, wondering what to do next. Many, perhaps most, realize that they have to invent some approach, any approach, to assess the curriculum and learning. Otherwise, they are out on a limb, waiting for lightning to strike or somebody to saw it off.

Toward Common Contextual Ground

Individualized as we are and divided among subfields, we ought to begin by seeking common contextual ground. Most departments will assume it is not easy to find; hence the current state of frustration. I have found it helpful to talk with colleagues about the history of the discipline. Given the structure and recent history of English and the shape of the discipline (diversifying, interdisciplinary, spiral, associative, amoeboid, so diffuse, some say, as to lack identity), the typical department will of course resist any call for specific goals for learning. Such activity appears to undermine not only academic freedom but also the emerging and highly contested content of the field. Traditionally, departments have defined pathways to the degree according to content, a set of courses rather than a set of outcomes. They pay more attention to the track than to the learner and the learning. The course and track—curriculum—have a stable foundation in disciplinary culture, though the issues associated with courses and tracks are many and growing. In other words, although fields of scholarship, theory, and creative work compete with increasing urgency—given the culture wars, the growth of interdisciplinary programs, the arrival of the

Internet, and the recent turn to globalization—the status of institutions and faculty activity depends firmly and stably on individual achievement and the course and reading list. Is a highly diversified curriculum—with its leading subfields of literary history, theory, criticism, rhetoric/composition, visual and cultural studies, and creative writing—too contested to be defined or, as many fear, to be reified into a single plan for learning? Many faculty and departments make such an argument. Again and again I hear that too many barriers stand in the way of making a single set of goals achievable by either consensus or fiat (Culler, 2003).

Until recently, it did not matter a great deal. Most departments could meet requirements of review and accreditation by describing the content of the programs, tallying grades and number of degrees completed as evidence. Around the time of a decennial reaccreditation, one might have observed a flurry of activity that barely touched the department. Within the elite institutions, assessment was and may well remain within the purview of the provost's office and institutional research. Until recently, departments of all institutional types have not had to think much about it. Until recently, we could mostly behave as if we were all among the elite.

Not so any longer. Faced with externally imposed demands for accreditation, what is a department to do? Where is the evidence of learning required by regional accreditation associations, the National Council for Accreditation of Teacher Education (NCATE)/specialized professional association, or institutional program review? Without a set of articulated goals, a department has no way to document what students know and are able to do when they finish a degree. The evidence of grades and number of programs or degrees completed and the standby reading lists and syllabi just do not work any more. There are calls for data, but few know what data to collect.

Despite these barriers, can most English departments design a systematic approach to the curriculum and a reflective practice of teaching and learning while maintaining their autonomy and integrity? Certainly, I say, based on the practice of the departments I know. I go further and argue that it is both possible and valuable to find common ground in the work. This chapter emphasizes the traditional English liberal arts degree and is applicable to other majors in English. It calls for leadership and offers specific advice, suggesting possibilities for collaboration and learning from others' experiences.

It provides guidelines for design, starting from scratch or in the middle of a project and working toward an assessment program the department can claim for itself.

The English Story in QUE

The English disciplinary group at QUE struggled and spun their wheels for most of two years before making headway on curricular design and plans for assessment. Every time new people joined us—a regular feature of meetings in the first two years—we had to start over. This highly iterative, not to say instructively exasperating, process taught us lessons that can save time for others. Indeed, QUE enabled me, as dean, to lead the School of Culture and Society at The College of New Jersey as we transformed the entire curriculum of the humanities and social sciences. Work of this kind makes great demands on faculty and succeeds only if people invest collectively and build on earlier experience that they trust. Whatever I have been able to do as facilitator or disciplinary leader has depended on the goodwill and energy of the faculty, and I would encourage any leader to keep this fact in mind from the start.

In the English group at QUE, we made the collective discovery that a project to design a program for learning and then to assess the results was achievable and worthwhile, although it took time to work through the doubts or objections of newcomers. I would like, therefore, to warn those starting such a project to beware the hermeneutics of doubt (and keep a sense of humor). A discipline so steeped in the heritage of interpretation can circle and recycle doubt without end, amen. At the QUE meetings, we became familiar with recurrent issues and learned to answer cogently enough to re-build consensus and thence continue to work. For example, newcomers often objected that program learning goals would undermine academic freedom. Somebody lurking outside—vaguely meaning administrators or legislators—would take such goals and turn them into blunt instruments of standardization. Acknowledging that misuse or abuse of curricular authority is possible, we decided it was wiser to set our own goals than to have them thrust upon us. A well-crafted set of program goals and evidence to show outcomes is an excellent defense, we concluded, against standardized testing or an imposed curriculum—neither of which will find many proponents among English faculty. The great fear the MLA warned us about began to appear more likely to materialize if we did nothing.

As program goals began to emerge among the departments represented at QUE, we saw no threat to academic freedom. A section of the Towson University program goals (reprinted in full in Appendix B) makes the point (see Figure 6.1).

Figure 6.1
Towson University's English Goals: Abilities

Upon graduation, English majors demonstrate instrumental knowledge of reading and writing in the discipline. They can:

- Grasp and interpret metaphor.
- Conduct purposeful analysis of literary discourse, including discussion of the history, forms, and conventions of the different periods and genres.
- Read literary works with understanding of their background, structure, meanings, implications, and relevance.
- Read scholarly works with understanding of their contexts, concerns, and terminology.
- Interpret written materials flexibly, understanding how multiple meanings are possible and, conversely, how individual interpretations sometimes can be wrong.
- Understand and use evidence to support interpretations.

They can use their understanding of the discipline and its contexts to:

- Apply knowledge of the history, theory, and methodologies of the discipline and its contexts in thoughtful discourse.
- Apply to everyday life knowledge gained from literary, rhetorical, and linguistic study.
- Integrate or synthesize knowledge from a range of disciplines as a means to interpret the text.

These are not goals that call for standardized testing. They are reasonable and durable statements of intention that most departments tacitly assume. Certainly, the department may be challenged to locate and present evidence of these abilities. We may argue about the level of ability (after all, secondary English programs also want students to grasp metaphor). But threat to academic freedom in this context is a red herring. Individual faculty members may teach to develop these abilities in a wide variety of courses and in highly individualized ways. The department will not undermine their own freedom by seeking such performance. Once they have a means to present evidence, they can meet requirements for reporting and accreditation as part of their regular business.

By the end of our QUE funding (which meant we could no longer gather twice yearly for meetings), the departments and individuals involved were convinced of the value of the work. Not all departments that sent representatives to the meetings took the next steps to adopt the work programmatically. Some did; some did not. We hope that over time the work will be useful to all. In any case, we had no intention to impose or control it. We shared results generously, imperfect and unfinished as we often thought they were. In fact, we learned that a living curriculum is a work in progress. As long as there is sufficient continuity in the goals, they can be emended. Over time, a department will discover that some goals can be assessed and some cannot—or not easily, as I will discuss. But not all goals need quantitative assessment. Some exist to guide or to be understood holistically or even to be justified anecdotally. Our disciplinary penchant for ambiguity and respect for tension came in handy more than once as we aligned our new sets of goals with plans for assessment.

The Department Chair's Guide

From the lessons of QUE English and my experience with colleagues at The College of New Jersey (TCNJ), I have drawn up some guidelines. The College of New Jersey was not part of the QUE project, but insofar as I learned from QUE, I have urged my colleagues to build on those lessons. If the following materials draw heavily on TCNJ, it is to exemplify what can become of a sustained project like QUE. I am taking the liberty of direct address to department chairs or other faculty leaders in English and the humanities. In case it should not have been apparent in what I have said thus far, my subject is program assessment, a practice of documenting the ways that students learn throughout a program. It may include, but is bigger than and different from, assessment in individual courses. It requires an understanding of the curriculum as something greater than the sum of the courses.

If you want a design for learning that you can document, you need to take the work as seriously as you take your identity as a department, fraught and tension filled though it may be. Your colleagues should care about the work and make it integral to the life of the department, and you ought to be hopeful that it will work. The basic principles are these: Assessment ought to be worth doing; it ought to be valuable to everybody in the department. It should be worth doing well over time, sustained and acceptable as business as usual. It should flow naturally from the curriculum and work sensibly to the benefits of students and faculty. The project needs to be collective and begin with what the department values. If there was ever an occasion for communal activity, this is it. Seize it. Do not, under any circumstances, wait for it to be imposed on you. We may argue long and hard about the root causes and possible nefarious outcomes. Be careful not to get bogged down in such arguments, but deal with them as they come. Focus attention on what you value deeply as a community of literary scholars, critics, and writers. Return to your best hopes for your students whenever consensus dissolves. Revel in your differences and the productive tensions they produce. Find common ground as you express what you value for yourselves and your students. Then figure out how the curriculum gets there and how you can know it is all working.

A Procedure Outlined

1) Set your learning goals or outcomes, aiming to state what you expect students to know and do by the time they graduate. You may want to include attitudes or dispositions also.

2) Align the goals (or draft goals, if the concept of a draft works better politically) with the courses in your major programs.

3) Draft a plan, including a timeline to assess the outcomes both in and across courses. Work backward from your next scheduled self-study or accreditation campus visit to see **what** timeframe you have.

4) Make regular reality checks, reading syllabi and student work against the goals or outcomes and the assessment plan.

5) Understand that this practice is iterative and dynamic. You and your colleagues can improve it as you get to know it better.

More Detailed Procedural Advice

Department Workshop

Arrange to lead a department workshop for four to six hours—a significant commitment. Make sure you communicate in advance to your colleagues the importance of the activity and the objectives of the meeting. If you have a partner college or university or a state system, invite colleagues from the partnership to join. Plan to provide refreshments. If resources are a problem, ask the dean or provost to cover the costs as an endorsement of the work. This is an opportunity for leadership—good humored, hopeful, and realistic. You should commit yourself to the work as essential to the well-being of the department, beyond mere compliance. Consider that it is beneficial for a department periodically to reflect on values and goals. If you take the matter of identity and renewal seriously, your colleagues will also. You might provide models as a point of departure, using material cited here. Most departments are going to devise similar goals. In fact, you might discover that goals for reading or interpretation, writing, and critical thinking across disciplines bear some resemblance.

Working With Drafting Goals or Outcomes

At the end of the workshop, you want to have a viable set of goals or outcomes (we at QUE used the terms interchangeably because we did not want to get hung up on assessment jargon). You need a set in draft that you can work with over time. It is not a good idea to choose too many outcomes. Eight to ten will be much easier to handle than fifteen. If your department has never compiled a list of goals for learning—goals that you expect students to achieve by the time they complete the major—then begin by drafting such a list. If one exists already, then consider it time to revisit it. If you have a mission statement or a description of the major on your web site, you might begin there. Such statements typically address learning, emphasizing goals for students rather than listing courses. The web is full of information that can help you. The Department of English at St. Olaf College, for example, does not describe a learning-centered curriculum on their web site, but their home page presents a statement of goals that could easily be redesigned as a set of outcomes:

> In contrast to majors that cover only British and American Literature, the English Department at St. Olaf places colonial and post-colonial writers from various countries and eras in conversation with influential British and American voices. All majors complete the same three core courses. . . . These courses give majors a common experience, enhance their skills in reading, writing, and interpreting literature, and orient them to this new trans-national conception of literatures in English. (Department of English, 2005)

The work of drafting outcomes is unlikely to be completed in one session. You may want to stay in draft mode for as long as a year or two, if you have the luxury, long enough to build consensus and discover which of the goals are ideal—never to be reached or nearly impossible to document in the performance of majors. We may all wish to promote a lifelong love of literature and engagement with texts. Towson University chose such a goal and remains committed to it. But it is not a goal readily proven through empirical study on the familiar cycles of the accreditation review. Some goals are readily measured or proven by performance. Others never can be. I have taken a liberal approach and encouraged departments to be mindful of the differences between ideal goals and measurable outcomes. We took the time to discuss philosophical idealism and realism in this context. It is worth the investment to discuss the differences, although you may be challenged not to get mired in discussions that stop the group from completing a plan.

If you want students to demonstrate certain abilities, you need to describe the outcome, beginning with a strong active verb: *demonstrate, exhibit, discover, apply.* Everyone in the community is likely to agree, for example, that the English major should be capable of advanced critical thinking, expressed in various forms or acts of textual interpretation, frequently written as essay assignments. The English faculty at TCNJ chose critical reading and writing as their first of nine program outcomes for the English liberal arts program:

> *Critical reading and writing:* Demonstrate an understanding of the power of words by reading critically, interpreting responsibly, writing and speaking with clarity and grace, reasoning intelligently, and arguing thoughtfully and persuasively for a range of audiences and purposes. (Department of English, 2004)

Towson University's list of abilities includes a similar section:

[At graduation, students] can communicate effectively in speech and writing:

- Speak and write academic discourse competently.

- Recognize a range of social, academic, and professional situations and adapt language accordingly.

- Write in a variety of forms (expository, argumentative, imaginative, academic, business/technical, literary, etc.) as appropriate to audience, purpose, and occasion.

- Comprehend the grammatical and syntactical patterns of the English language and use them as a tool in writing and revising.

Valdosta State University, with three broad program goals in the traditional track, embeds critical thinking this way:

> The goals of the traditional track are as follows:
>
> - English majors in the traditional track will develop a comprehensive understanding of English and American language and literature, including a familiarity with key facts, concepts, and values; a sensitivity to the contexts in which that literature was and is written and read; and an ability to interpret that literature in appropriate ways.
>
> - English majors in the traditional track will develop their ability to write and speak with clarity, precision, and sophistication.
>
> - English majors in the traditional track will develop their ability to conduct research carefully and systematically, utilizing appropriate computer technology, and to apply that research to the study of language and literature. (Department of English, n.d.)

Like critical thinking, breadth of knowledge in the field is likely to appear on most department lists of outcomes. Again, it is best expressed in terms of student demonstration or performance. At TCNJ, the faculty put the outcome this way:

> *Breadth of knowledge:* Demonstrate familiarity with a significant body of texts within and on the margins of a variety of literary traditions (e.g., British, American, continental European, Asian, African, and Latin American). (Department of English, 2004)

Towson describes breadth of knowledge as follows:

> At graduation, English majors will have a demonstrably broad and deep knowledge of the principal areas of the discipline and their terminology:

- Criticism: principal schools and history.

- Literature: genres and history.

- Rhetoric and writing: conventions, genres, and history.

- Language and linguistics: awareness of the structure, organic nature, and social implications of language.

- English majors can also demonstrate knowledge of the historical, social, and psychological contexts (as well as the cultural implications) of the discipline, including awareness of race, class, and gender.

Should the department wish to specify knowledge of theory, methodology, and history, I recommend diction sufficiently inclusive to cover the range of departmental commitments. Should disagreement ensue about theory, you might propose to agree on formalism and take a pluralistic approach beyond it. You should set such goals with your own institutional and department culture in mind. If a dispute occurs over the canon, face it. You may be surprised to discover that canonical issues are not as divisive as they used to be. If any point appears intractable, put it on a list and table it. At a subsequent meeting, invite a colleague from a department you admire (which need not be in the humanities), on campus or external, to attend or to comment in writing—someone with a known commitment to the design of the curriculum. Every department I know includes at least one or two colleagues who care energetically about design and who welcome the opportunity to exchange ideas. At QUE, departments borrowed freely from each other and adapted the material as they chose. We trusted each other.

Departments that collaborate across institutions, such as the two-year/ four-year partnership we fostered at QUE, can exchange the program outcomes and associated course materials. If large numbers of students transfer from a college to a university, they will be better prepared if faculty in both institutions know the curricular design.

Aligning Outcomes and Courses

Once you have a working list of program outcomes, you should begin to connect them with your courses, as was outlined in the super matrix described in Chapter 1. This is hard, time-consuming work. The recursive and spiraling structure of learning in the discipline—as opposed to the tree-shaped or branching structures of the sciences (see Figure 4.2 in Chapter 4)—makes a methodical design for learning difficult to achieve. The way students learn metaphor is a case in point. It is a matter of practice and application, learning to recognize and then to do things with metaphor at ever-higher levels. Because of the diversification, fragmentation, bifurcation—call it what you will—of the discipline, departments often find it difficult to imagine sequential learning. How then to associate goals with courses? In two-year colleges, there may be no associate's degree in English and few literature courses offered beyond the composition sequence and general introductory surveys. In regional four-year institutions, large numbers of transfer students enter the major at any number of points. They take courses as they can, without regard to sequence, and may be taking courses at more than one institution at a time. State system rules for transfer credit may conflict with department plans. These are real problems for the majority of public institutions, and they also crop up at private colleges and universities. We discussed them over the years at QUE, and I continue to hear them at every presentation I make.

It is precisely because we face such structural problems that we need to consider design of the curriculum as a solution. It is possible to design a viable structure, communicate it well to students and colleagues, and then devote attention to advising. Such systemic challenges as face most English departments require concrete and systematic thinking about the curriculum. We ought to start with structure, assuming that its strength will arise in its flexibility. If assessment works, it should point out problems and solutions over time—the empirical study that most departments have not had time yet to do.

A number of QUE departments used a matrix to lay out courses and outcomes in a way that presents learning as progression (the super matrix). All the humanities and social science programs at TCNJ also use a matrix, more generalized than the super matrix. The matrix template follows (see Figure 6.2), with some cells filled in to illustrate the pattern. Program learning outcomes are arrayed on the left, vertically, and courses horizontally, grouped as appropriate. The level of learning appears in the cells: basic, intermediate, deep. After experimenting with other designs, TCNJ settled on this model. We expect the design to evolve as we carry out the assessment that is built on this structure, as I will describe below.

Figure 6.2
Outcomes and Courses

Outcomes	Courses			
	101 Foundations	200-Level Language & Linguistics Courses	300-Level Historical Problem Courses	400-Level Seminars or Capstone
1. Critical Reading and Writing	Basic Understanding		Intermediate Understanding	Deep Understanding
2. Scholarship	Basic Understanding	Intermediate Understanding		Deep Understanding

Faculty who teach courses that address the same goals work together on syllabus design, and they do so respecting each other's academic freedom. We also exchange scoring guides or rubrics, which helps to keep the assessment activities aligned across courses that share the same outcomes. The most popular rubric (a six-point design) has made its way through most of our departments, with some modification in each. Our school curriculum committee reviewed the rubric and declared that we should consider it "freeware"—free to adapt and distribute to colleagues. Because we also adopted a template for syllabi, we expect program outcomes to appear clearly in material for each course. Faculty address these goals in any number of ways. Not all program outcomes will be addressed in each course, however. We are learning to discriminate carefully in order to keep the workload within acceptable bounds. You ought to adopt a reasonable number of outcomes and to share assessment within and across courses as reasonably as the economy and culture of your department will permit.

Many departments, and certainly the QUE membership and TCNJ, began by discovering that a "bookend" structure will work, though just for a start. That is, a foundations or methods and approaches course at the beginning of a program addresses basic knowledge and abilities while a capstone course or sequence at the end asks students to demonstrate deep understanding and ability. This structure appears in so many programs that we might by now consider it common knowledge. The QUE departments all considered or adopted such a basic structure and then built on it. As many of us have also discovered, the courses in the middle are notoriously hard to arrange in any predictable sequence. But as the matrix suggests, they may address particular outcomes at progressively higher levels. The College of New Jersey has made a strong commitment to historical understanding, requiring three courses at the 200 or 300 level:

> The 200-level courses in literary history will foster sensitivity to the concrete historicity of texts, introduce basic lexical and historical research, and/or expand the body of texts with which students are familiar. The 300-level courses, on the other hand, will enrich and complicate the students' sense of literary history by focusing students' attention on specific historical problems and issues in the particular time periods, cultures, or texts covered in the course (e.g., by putting discordant voices from the same time period in dialogue).[2]

Midlevel courses allow students to practice and gain breadth of knowledge. A recursive pathway to expertise requires no less. Faculty who teach such courses may find as we did in QUE and at TCNJ that exchanges of syllabi and rubrics, both aligned to the program goals, will foster collaborative think-ing beyond the individual course. In other words, once a program has clear outcomes and a plan to meet those outcomes at appropriate levels within the courses, the next step is to make long-term collaboration on course material and review of student work a regular feature of department life. Outcomes, association of outcomes with courses, redesigned syllabi to reflect both, and regular reality testing through collaborative review of student work all con-verge as a dynamic design. College and university partnerships can do this work together as long as there is functional support and sufficient resources within and across both institutions. Insofar as a department embraces the design, it can describe the results and provide evidence from sampling in a wide variety of ways. Assessment thus becomes regular practice—that is, not something done every 10 years.

Modeling an Assessment Plan

Most departments that practice assessment of their programs have not ad-vanced far into the work. At TCNJ, we designed our new curriculum and assessment plans as we were carrying out the decennial self-study and campus visit of the Middle States Association in 2004. We are now in the second full year of the new curriculum, having successfully completed the reaccredita-tion. At this point, departments are launching at least one program assess-ment activity each year, introducing the work in sequence. Since half of our students in English are in teacher education programs (as double majors) and our next NCATE review is in 2008, we will be able to use the information gathered through assessment for that purpose also. We began by laying out a three-column matrix that aligns program goals with an assessment strategy and a timeframe. Here, for example, is the first learning goal, critical reading and writing (see Figure 6.3).

Figure 6.3
Learning Goals and Assessment Strategies

Learning Goal 1	Assessment Strategy	Timeframe
Critical Reading and Writing Demonstrate an understanding of the power of words by reading critically, interpreting responsibly, writing and speaking with clarity and grace, reasoning intelligently, and arguing thoughtfully and persuasively for a range of audiences and purposes.	*Longitudinal* assessment of a cohort of students using student portfolios containing texts from each semester, student interviews, and an affective instrument. Questions for student interviews would be formulated after faculty reflection on expectation and discussion of course-based measures.	Beginning fall 2005; first phase (assessment of student performance through foundational sequence) complete spring 2007; full assessment complete spring 2009.

Each of the nine learning goals has its own assessment strategy. Several use the longitudinal portfolio project as a source of evidence (Goal 3, critical voice, for example, does so). A number of the strategies also use course-based assessment. As I have mentioned, we have adopted a template for all syllabi at the college, the principal sections of which include program goals to be addressed in the course, learning activities, assessment, and the schedule of assignments. Faculty who teach courses at the same level will, as part of the program assessment, regularly discuss and align their course expectations, including grading and learning activities. They will then be able to sample student work across similar courses and study grading patterns. To understand student engagement, we have asked our office of institutional research to customize a survey developed by that office. The survey collects information about the quantity of work and attitudinal or affective engagement. Any department may use the results for formative purposes, respecting the individuals involved and reporting by cohort according to their own plan. If learning truly comes first, no less is due.

Tips for Design

1) You have resources on campus that you may not have considered, such as the following:

   - Faculty who work in rhetoric and composition or linguistics are likely to be familiar with scoring guides or rubrics and can help modify such documents to address the goals of cohorts of courses.

   - Composition and rhetoric faculty may also have professional resources at hand for scoring essays or portfolios.

   - Faculty in English education are sometimes trained in the social sciences and can help with program and assessment design. They often know how to conduct survey or focus group research. They can also adapt material from state guidelines for teacher certification and translate the language of assessment for colleagues in literature.

   - Colleagues in the social sciences have resources for qualitative and quantitative assessment, including sampling and interview techniques, focus groups, and surveys. Consider a meeting with colleagues in sociology or psychology. They may get a publication out of the work as an added benefit.

   - Consider the value to your faculty of publications on English program assessment. Such publications could be especially helpful to junior faculty in English education or composition and rhetoric. Senior faculty looking toward promotion may also benefit.

   - Your institutional research office may provide the resources noted earlier for surveys, interviews, or scoring. A good partnership with institutional research can help you design an approach to regional accreditation and teacher certification.

2) National resources:

   - The national Council of Writing Program Administrators has developed a set of outcomes for first-year composition that may be adapted usefully for transfer partnerships and for major programs (see www.ilstu.edu/%7Eddhesse/wpa/positions/index.html).

- The National Council of Teachers of English (NCTE) addresses a professional audience who shares an interest in quality of English education. Many English faculty are not inclined to turn to NCTE. It is nevertheless worthwhile to review *Standards for the English Language Arts* (www.ncte.org/about/over/standards) and the new position statement *Good Writing Instruction, Not Testing, Is the Best Preparation for College* (www.ncte.org/about/over/inbox/news/120541 .htm?source=gs). Considerable help is available in the NCTE journal *College Composition and Communication* (e.g., see White, 2005). If you send colleagues to the annual Conference on College Composition and Communication, you will find methods and materials adaptable to the English major.

- If your campus participates in the National Survey of Student Engagement (NSSE), you have additional resources that can be used to assess writing in general education. The NSSE may suggest questions you can use locally to assess engagement in the major (see www.ind ana.edu/~nsse/).

- If you choose to use portfolios, find a copy of Barbara Cambridge's (2001) book *Electronic Portfolios.*

In Closing

A department that takes a pragmatic approach to learning certainly can proceed with respect for the integrity and autonomy of the community and the individuals within it. A period of review and discussion leading to change can only bring health and strength. When we think about the future of English in a global context, we ought to be unsettled—and to use that discomfort productively for curricular reform. If the QUE project taught me one thing, it was that the work of program design and assessment is all about identity— ours as a discipline, ours individually as scholars, our students' as emerging scholars, teachers, and citizens of a deeply fraught world. These lessons came from immersion in the activities of the English faculty at the national QUE meetings—the hours of debate on the best we hoped for our students and then on assessment and draft program goals, alignment of outcomes with courses, design of rubrics and syllabi, and exchange of assignments and student work. It was intrinsically interesting and pleasurable to focus attention on the students' performance and our interaction with them as they learn. It was equally pleasurable to collaborate within and beyond department boundaries.

Over time we expect students' understanding of the curriculum as a whole to be enriched as they work toward expertise through individual courses. Considering also the practical and expedient, we can all save a tremendous amount of time through collective activity. That is a cultural change, and it has particular value: moving departments from individualism that has become isolationist to community action that values individuals. The discipline ought to give it a try.

Endnotes

1) This report claims that there is little demand for outcomes assessment ("few if any departments have yet experienced formal outcomes assessment as a force that affects enrollment, programming in the major, or graduation rates" [p. 80]) and suggests that efforts in that direction lead to standardization, standardized testing, and loss of the traditional freedoms of the English program.

2) From unpublished TCNJ English liberal arts major program material.

References

Cambridge, B. L. (Ed.). (2001). *Electronic portfolios: Emerging practices in student, faculty, and institutional learning.* Sterling, VA: Stylus.

Culler, J. (2003, Winter). Imagining the coherence of the English major. *ADE Bulletin, 133,* 6–10.

Department of English, The College of New Jersey. (2004). *English major goals*. Retrieved November 16, 2005, from The College of New Jersey, Department of English web site: http://www.tcnj.edu/%7Eenglish/academics/englishgoals.html

Department of English, St. Olaf College. (2005). *English major*. Retrieved December 1, 2005, from the St. Olaf College, Department of English web site: http://www.stolaf.edu/depts/english/major/index.html

Department of English, Valdosta State University. (n.d.). *Traditional track program*. Retrieved November 16, 2005, from the Valdosta State University, Department of English web site: http://teach.valdosta.edu/english/Traditional.html

Schramm, M., Mitchell, J. L., Stephens, D., & Laurence, D. (2003, Spring/Fall). The undergraduate English major: Report of the 2001–02 ADE ad hoc committee on the English major. *ADE Bulletin, 134–135,* 68–91.

White, E. M. (2005). The scoring of writing portfolios: Phase 2. *College Composition and Communication, 56*(4), 581–600.

7

The QUE Project and History Learning and Teaching: The Case of Long Beach State

Tim Keirn, Brett Mizelle

This chapter addresses the impact of the Quality in Undergraduate Education (QUE) project within the discipline of history and examines specifically its role in facilitating the reform and development of a standards-based and learning-oriented undergraduate major in the history department at the California State University–Long Beach. With 35,000 students, Long Beach State, as it is usually called, is the largest campus of the 23 universities in the California State University System and the second largest university in the State of California. It is a "minority majority" urban campus where the vast majority of students commute from throughout the region of southern California.

We will discuss challenges to both the design and implementation of a standards-based curriculum, and we will analyze curricular transformations within a broader context of recent trends concerning learning and teaching within the historical profession.

The design and implementation of this type of curricular reform and aligned assessments is a measured and gradual process that requires the generation of faculty consensus at all stages—a grassroots effort, if you like—that in itself also reflects a cultural shift among faculty as they think more about what students learn, not what they teach. What is presented here is a model for the creation and execution of standards-based curricula that emanates from the local context of faculty and individual departments as opposed to the more common (and indeed contentious) top-down model of standards and assessment imposed upon faculty and departments from college, university, and system-wide administrations.

We will argue that locally generated standards and assessment are effective in improving student learning because they specifically and authentically embed the skills, behaviors, and perspective of the discipline. At the same time, taking ownership of the process of outcomes and assessment provides faculty and departments with an intellectual (and political) counterweight to the imposition of standards and evaluation from above. Moreover, through the creation of a senior capstone course and portfolio—and department discussion about student work in both—the model includes an important feedback loop.

Assessment of performance as students exit the major provides the setting for department reflection about their learning up to that point and is the means for transforming what goes on in other courses within the major. The process of designing curriculum and assessment is dynamic and ongoing. Indeed, sustained faculty dialogue and discussion about history learning and teaching have become important outcomes of this project.

National and Disciplinary Contexts: Standards and Learning in History

It has been well over a decade since President George H. W. Bush addressed the National Governors Association in September 1989, declaring that the time had come to "establish clear national performance goals, goals that will make us internationally competitive [and] second to none in the twenty-first century" (as qtd. in Nash, Crabtree, & Dunn, 1997, p. 149).[1] President Bush soon launched America 2000, a comprehensive plan to establish national education goals and performance standards in the core disciplines of the K–12 curriculum. The creation of standards for history was by far the most contentious. The publication in 1996 of voluntary national standards for both U.S.

and world history led to an acrimonious debate among politicians, educators, and historians. These standards were dragged into the nation's culture wars, with most of the controversy around the historical content of the standards, especially U.S. history. In due course, the national standards in history were revised, but public and bipartisan support for national history standards waned. However, energy for creating K–12 content and skills standards in history was maintained at both the state and district levels where, in some cases, the national standards in U.S. and world history served as an important guide (Center on Education Policy, 2005; Hill, 1997; Nash, Crabtree, & Dunn, 1997; National Center for History in the Schools, 1996; Symcox, 2002).

Over the last decade, governors and legislatures have been vigorous promoters of creating grade-level (as opposed to age-level) history standards and performance assessment instruments at the state and local levels. Currently, 25 states have implemented high school exit exams in social science, mostly history (Center on Education Policy, 2005; National Governors Association, 1998). Many states have developed state standards in history, and where state standards are absent they have often been implemented at the district level. In the local Long Beach Unified School District, history teaching is shaped by the California History/Social Science Content Standards, drafted by the state Academic Standards Commission, as well by district standards.[2]

As the standards movement advances throughout most states, the disconnect between K–12 and postsecondary education policies has become more pronounced. Political moves are afoot to rectify this situation by bringing standards-based curriculum into the arena of higher education. Since 1996, the National Governors Association and the National Conference of State Legislatures has sponsored meetings and studies to develop more uniform state educational systems that seamlessly align secondary and postsecondary curriculum and facilitate K–16 reforms. Congress and many private foundations have appropriated money for the creation of K–16 partnerships, and in some states (notably Maryland, Georgia, and Missouri) this process is fairly well advanced. Long Beach State has long been involved in an extensive local K–16 partnership with the Long Beach Unified School District and Long Beach City College entitled the Seamless Education Project (Kirst & Venezia, 2004; National Governors Association, 2004a, 2004b, 2005; Venezia, Kirst,

& Antonio, 2003). Funded by the National Education Association and the Boeing Corporation, an important part of the Seamless agenda is to create standards and curricula at the university level and integrate, articulate, and align them with those of the school district and community college (Schwartz, 1999; Weber, 1997). The chancellor of the California State University System has funded system-wide conferences to promote the formation of standards and assessment within specific disciplines and to articulate them with those of the K–12 and community college systems. The implication of this initiative is that at some point a bachelor's degree earned in history at any campus within the system should indicate similar knowledge and skills to those of the same degree received at any other campus within the system.

However, none of these recent national, state, and local initiatives has fashioned postsecondary standards for the discipline of history, let alone integrated them with those state standards for K–12. But the rapid expansion of standards and grade-level performance assessment in the K–12 history curriculum has significant consequences for the teaching of history at the postsecondary level. A national survey in 2002 showed that 37 states had content and skills standards in K–12 history (Brown & Patrick, 2005). If students are increasingly accustomed to a standards-based learning environment in high school, shouldn't they expect the same in college? If K–12 reforms are raising the achievement levels of students, shouldn't the bar be raised at the postsecondary level as well? History majors preparing for a career in K–12 will eventually teach in a standards-based environment and will be held accountable for the performance of their students. Shouldn't they be taught (and held accountable to) the content and skills that they will eventually teach? Outside the profession of teaching, wouldn't the employer (and the potential employee) benefit from a more specific sense of what someone with a bachelor's degree in history knows and is able to do? History is often a frustrating subject for the student because absolute subject mastery is impossible. The creation of standards and learning outcomes provides the student with a sense of subject mastery, enough to make the discipline attractive.

Of course, the notion that standards and performance outcomes can be created for a bachelor's degree in history across campuses, not just within one department, is perhaps no more than a pipe dream. As we saw in the strident debates relating to the K–12 national standards, historians are not likely to agree on common content standards for a bachelor's degree in history. At the California State University conference on standards and assessment held at Long Beach State in April 1999 (one of the system-wide disciplinary conferences), faculty reported back to the chancellor that

> History as a discipline is less about "facts" than it is about argument and process; this alone makes any effort to develop meaningful "content standards" a very different operation than it might be for other disciplines, particularly for the sciences.

At its core, historians are simply unlikely to agree on "whose history" is to be represented within any content standard.

However, historians have shown some inclination toward consensus and agreement upon a body of historical skills. Indeed, faculty at the conference had little difficulty reaching agreement on sets of standards that related to skills and competencies reflecting the process—as opposed to the content— of history. These conclusions are similar in tone to recent reports from the American Historical Association (AHA) that explicate the skills and competencies to be expected of a history major but make no definitive statements pertaining to a specific content (AHA, 1991; Sievers, 1999).

In this sense, a focus on the skills as opposed to the content of history also parallels new lines of scholarly inquiry within the profession and discipline. Over the past decade a field of scholarship has arisen that concentrates on what it means to learn and understand history and to think historically (Bain, 2000; Lee, 2001; Wineburg, 2001). Much of this early scholarship emanated from Britain and was tied to the cognitive revolution that shifted the focus in learning theory from behavior to issues of meaning and epistemology (Gardner, 1985; Lee & Ashby, 2000; Shemilt, 1987). Moreover, the development of the field was also facilitated by the culture wars of the early 1990s and historians' new interest in issues of historical memory (Le Goff, 1977/1992; Lowenthal, 1985).

History is a human representation of the past—what is represented of the past is a consequence of choice, which in turn is informed by contemporary political and cultural considerations. This recognition involves a shift from a focus on substantive history—the facts and concepts of history—to the procedural ideas of history—historical perspective and skill (Lee, 2005).

The convergence here is in the preoccupation with what is remembered or learned as opposed to what is taught. Given the significance of schools in the construction of collective historical memory, it is not surprising that virtually all of this new scholarship is addressed to historical teaching and learning in the K–12 environment (Seixas, 1993; Wineburg, 2000). Nonetheless, this scholarship is also relevant to postsecondary instruction and has informed and enlightened the discussions surrounding curricular reform and teaching in history at Long Beach State.

Creating the Bookends

Before our participation in the QUE project, the Long Beach State history department had substantial experience with standards-based education at the K–12 level through our commitment to training pre-service teachers. Involvement in QUE, however, served as a vital accelerant of our belief in the efficacy of standards in the postsecondary arena. Our work with other clusters of university and community college history faculty at local and national QUE meetings gave us the opportunity to further think and reflect about what we would like our students to know and be able to do. As a result, our department committed itself to implementing standards-based curricula within the history major (Schwartz, 1999; Weber, 1997).

We decided to start small, attempting to build consensus within the department, avoiding a top-down model of standards and assessment within the department in particular or imposed by California State University in general. Our efforts in standards-based reform focused initially on one specific course: History 301, Historical Methodology. The selection of this course was purposeful. First, the course is entirely dedicated to historical skills and avoids the morass surrounding content standards. Second, a standards-based course dedicated to skills serves as an excellent gateway for entry into upper-division history courses.

Regrettably, history majors often avoided enrolling in History 301 until their last semester. But beginning in the 1998 fall semester, all history majors had to complete the course satisfactorily before (or concurrent with) their entry into upper-division coursework within the major. In conjunction with a standards-based approach, this sequence creates a much better sense of incremental and foundational learning (see Figure 7.1). Henceforth, all students in upper-division courses should have mastered specific skills and competencies that can be applied and expounded upon in their historical concentrations and fields. History 301 also serves as a useful entry point for our community college transfers (who make up approximately half of our majors) as they enter Long Beach State to engage in upper-division coursework. In this sense, History 301 serves as a year 14 benchmark or standard in terms of what a history major has the ability to do before entering upper-division coursework (or, to be precise, a year 14.5 standard, given that most students take the course concurrently with their first upper-division course in chosen fields of study).

Figure 7.1
History Major Curriculum Map

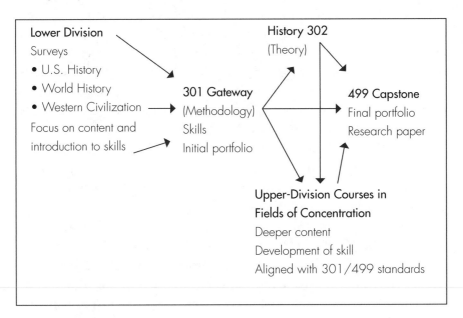

Many of the history faculty who worked on creating the learning outcomes for History 301 were familiar with standards-based curriculum through their collaboration with the Long Beach Unified School District in the creation and implementation of K–12 standards. The development of standards for History 301 was also facilitated by the provision of some external funding for faculty stipends from our Campus Assessment Committee during spring

1998. The development of standards in History 301 was also incorporated with our involvement in QUE.

History faculty from California State University–Long Beach and Long Beach City College met with faculty from universities and community colleges from Georgia, Maryland, Nevada, and California. Not surprisingly, the historians from these institutions agreed that the creation of standards for the discipline of history as a whole was impossible and impractical. Instead, the history faculty involved in the QUE project, drawing on the insights of QUE's critical friends (consultants with special expertise in history education), chose to emphasize the creation of standards on an individual course, degree, and campus basis.

The standards and learning outcomes developed for History 301 were created by a working group of history department members. Membership of the committee was on a volunteer basis, and reward came via small stipends or through the reduction of class size: All sections of 301 were reduced from 25 to 15 students. This committee consulted with student representatives from the History Students' Association for their perspectives and concerns about the types of skills necessary to succeed in upper-division courses. Meetings were also open to all members of the history department to get faculty perspectives on what skills and competencies were deemed necessary for history students. Faculty from other departments—most notably from English—were also consulted for their expertise in creating standards and assessments that related to critical thinking and communication skills. Our work in progress on the skills and learning outcomes for History 301 was also shared and discussed with faculty involved in the QUE project. In fact, feedback from QUE participants (most notably those from Georgia State University) and consultants Jim Roth (Alverno College), Lendol Calder (Augustana College), and Mills Kelly (George Mason University) proved essential to both the creation of History 301 and our subsequent curricular revisions.

Through this process of department, campus, and national consultation, agreement and consensus was reached in the history department about the standards and competencies taught and demonstrated by students in History 301. These standards and learning outcomes are distributed among four distinct sections of the course and include demonstrating a general knowledge of the professional historical literature as well as mechanical, analytical, and presentation skills (see Figure 7.2). These learning outcomes are incorporated into the syllabi of all sections of History 301 (normally eight sections are taught per semester), but instructors are free to teach to these standards by any method, assignment, example, or content area that they see fit.

Figure 7.2
History 301 Competencies

Introduction

1) Students will demonstrate familiarity with major schools of current historical practice.

2) Students will demonstrate the ability to distinguish between various genres of secondary historical literature, including textbooks, monographs, and periodicals, using the resources of the university library.

3) Students will be able to distinguish between a primary and secondary source.

Mechanical Skill

4) Students will be able to demonstrate an organized system of notetaking and the mechanics of research.

5) Students will be able to demonstrate appropriate footnoting and bibliographical entry.

6) Students will be able to locate and retrieve appropriate sources (both primary and secondary) relative to a historical topic.

7) Students will master computer skills appropriate to the discipline.

Analytical Skills

8) Students will demonstrate the ability to formulate focused historical questions.

9) Students will demonstrate the ability to detect bias and point of view in primary and secondary sources.

10) Students will demonstrate the ability to interpret and evaluate certain kinds of evidence: material, media, oral, quantitative and statistical, textual, and visual.

11) Students will be able to make inferences, form generalizations, and draw conclusions based on examined evidence.

Presentation

12) Students will demonstrate the ability to create, organize, and support a thesis in written and oral presentations.

To assess our efforts at helping students to achieve these standards, faculty teaching History 301 arranged to meet several times each semester as a working group to troubleshoot the course and to exchange means of enhancing, refining, and assessing student learning outcomes. All sections require a research paper and oral presentation as a method of demonstrating student competence in meeting some (but not all) of the standards. Students also submit a number of shorter assignments that serve as assessment instruments to ensure that all the standards are examined. All student work in History 301 is then kept in a portfolio that is submitted for final assessment at the end of the semester. The decision to use a portfolio proved critical, as we soon realized that students could continue to develop it in their upper-division courses for submission in a yet-to-be-created capstone course.

Faculty designed and exchanged scoring guides and rubrics for assessing the research paper and oral presentation, developing through consensus a uniform means of assessment that measures not only what is competent but also degrees of competency that correlate with a traditional grading system. Faculty have also developed, refined, and shared shorter exercises and assessment instruments (all kept in an easily accessible binder stored in the department office) to monitor student performance in reaching the standards. The development of uniform means of assessment is, of course, difficult given the restraints of time and resources. In fact, the department has not yet been able to meet its goal of having the entire History 301 faculty assess student performance collectively in the form of a group portfolio reading.

However, it did not take long for the implementation of a standards-based approach to History 301 to bear fruit. Faculty support for the project was strong; all were in favor of raising and applying standards as they relate to student skills and abilities. Once the revised 301 sections had been offered for a year, many faculty reported that they could see the improvement in their students' performance, especially in contrast to the students in their classes from majors other than history which had not implemented a standards-based approach. In fact, the history department had to start limiting the course to majors only, as several other departments began encouraging their students to register for History 301 because of the skills transferable across disciplines that it developed. Most faculty comment was directed toward students' abilities to complete research papers, with many instructors impressed by our students' abilities to create annotated bibliographies with pertinent and diverse sources, accurate citation, and little guidance.

This is not to say that we did not face a few obstacles and challenges. The commitment to a smaller class size made the reform relatively expensive. There were a few logistical glitches tracking students to ensure that they satisfactorily completed the course before enrolling in upper-division courses.

Student responses to 301 were mixed and remain so, but most who complain do so because they find the course difficult—evidence that standards are being raised. While many students describe History 301 as an academic "boot camp," they also find it useful as they proceed through the major. When the department completed its development of a capstone course that required a reflective essay, we found that students frequently refer to 301 as an important, even transformative, course. As one student put it, "although I complained about 301 at the time, it turned out to make a huge difference in my development as a historian."

The creation of expected performance outcomes and competencies for History 301 was a small, labor-intensive but manageable move toward creating a standards-based history curriculum in a postsecondary setting. The department realized, however, that to truly assess student learning in an ongoing manner, we needed to create a new senior capstone course, 499, one in which students would submit an enlarged final portfolio. This collection of students' work from their career in the department would provide an opportunity to enhance and refine their historical skills in more complex ways. These portfolios would serve, in essence, as an exit exam and would measure the development and sophistication of historical skill and the analysis and depth of content knowledge in chosen fields of concentration.

The participation of Long Beach State history faculty in the QUE initiative greatly abetted the development of both form and content guidelines for the portfolio. It proved especially helpful that Alverno College already used electronic portfolios for assessment of all their students. Alverno's Jim Roth provided important feedback on our work in progress; his experience in a small college setting also led us to realize that we were not yet ready to move to an all-electronic format for these portfolios, given our large number of majors. Instead, students would expand the binder that they created in History 301 into their final portfolio. As we began to design this course we also drew upon some of the scholarly literature about portfolio-based assessment, including a helpful essay by Susan Leighhow Meo (2002) about the implementation of such a system at Shippensburg University.

In applying these outside insights to our particular conditions at Long Beach State, we drew first upon our 301 competencies, aligning them to the portfolio's "mastery" category. We realized, however, that students would not necessarily achieve the same levels of mastery at the conclusion of their college career, so we also created a development section where they could establish their own benchmarks and reflect upon their progress as historians. The reflective essay component of the 499 portfolio closed the circle begun in 301, where students wrote reflectively about their participation in the methodology course. These ideas were incorporated into our portfolio guidelines which were given to all students in their 499 and 301 sections (see Figure 7.3).

Figure 7.3
Portfolio Guidelines

Your portfolio should be complete, reflecting your work in history courses from History 301 through the final semester of your work in the major. The portfolio should reflect your progress through the major and include examples of your best work. Your portfolio should be manageable without being too abbreviated and it should include faculty comments on papers.

Portfolio Content
The content of your portfolio should come from upper-division history courses. You may submit any examples of your work so long as the portfolio includes some material from History 301 and the specified minimum number of examples from each of the following sections and categories and demonstrates variety and breadth of material within each category. The weight given to each section and category is specified below.

A. Development (40%), a portfolio section containing the following:
- *A reflective essay* (five to eight pages). This essay explains, reflects, and illustrates your development as a historian. The essay should convey your rationale and justification for the entries submitted in the portfolio. It should also demonstrate the extent of growth in your historical knowledge and skill during your undergraduate career as a history major.

- *The reflective essay* written for History 301 (two to four pages). This essay should reflect and illustrate your development as a historian as a consequence of your participation in the methodology course. In addition to a thoughtful and self-reflective discussion of the process of your development in this course and the progress you made, your essay should discuss and evaluate how the various pieces in the portfolio indicate or represent your level of mastery of the 301 competencies.

- *Examples of work* that illustrate your progress as a history major (a minimum of three and a maximum of five). These should be examples that provide a sense of a benchmark (presumably from early in your career) that demonstrate progress and development relative to the items submitted in Category B below. You may submit lower-division work in this category.

B. Mastery (60%)

This section of the portfolio will demonstrate your level of mastery of the following competencies in four categories. Each of the following four categories should begin with a brief cover (one to two paragraphs) discussing your criteria for selection of the work submitted. Students should recognize and make use of the correlation between the following four categories and the 12 standards and competencies associated with the History 301 course.

- *Understanding* of the discipline of history and its methods (a minimum of two and a maximum of four entries worth 20% in total). Examples of the types of materials you may include: a historiographical essay; research paper that surveys the current state of historical literature on a given topic; paper that pertains to the disciplinary perspectives of history; annotated bibliography; theory paper; other items of your own choosing.

- *Analytical skills* (a minimum of two and a maximum of four entries worth 20% in total). Examples of the types of materials you may include: primary and secondary source analysis; web site evaluation paper; research paper based on primary and secondary sources; book or film review; essay exam (bluebook or take home) that demonstrates historical analysis; paper demonstrating an appreciation of multiple historical perspectives; other items of your own choosing.

- *Mechanical skills* (a minimum of one and a maximum of three entries worth 10% in total). Examples of the types of materials you may include: research proposal; note cards; evidence of computer literacy in history; other items of your own choosing.

- *Presentation skills* (a minimum of one and a maximum of three entries worth 10% in total). Examples of the types of materials you may include: outline or handout for oral presentation; video or audiotape of oral presentation; PowerPoint presentation; teaching unit; other items of your own choosing.

As we moved to implement this final bookend, we realized that we had to educate not just our students but also our colleagues about these changes. Presentations about the 499 course and its concluding portfolio were made in department meetings, while faculty teaching the course were encouraged to attend meetings of the 301/499 working group several times during the semester to reflect on challenges and share best practices. The department designated a faculty member as the portfolio advisor and all undergraduate majors were required to attend portfolio workshops that explained the new system and, importantly, encouraged them to retrieve their coursework from their instructors. These faculty meetings and student-centered workshops played a major role in changing the culture of the history department at Long Beach State.

Learning From the Silences

Effective standards-based and learning-oriented change requires ongoing assessment. As the department began to teach sections of the capstone course in each of our major concentrations, we found ourselves directed toward further areas of improvement based on the gaps and silences in our students' work. Some of the problems were found at the assignment level; for example, we almost immediately discovered that students were not writing effective reflective essays in either History 301 or History 499. We developed detailed guidelines for these essays, asking the students to reflect on their development as they progressed through the major and to advocate for their mastery and competency as historians.

Because students seemed to frequently raise many of the same questions about the portfolio and its contents, several faculty teaching History 499 developed a series of portfolio suggestions that are distributed to students after the review of their preliminary portfolio near the start of the semester. These suggestions, which cover the form and the content of the portfolio (including the vexing question of what work students should include to demonstrate their mastery of skills and content), reflect our interest in assessment for feedback and evaluation of our teaching as well as student learning. A plenary session on assessment and accountability led by Grant Wiggins at the fall 2003

QUE meeting in New Orleans helped confirm our sense of the importance of using History 499 to assess our efforts as well as those of our students.

While many of the changes that resulted from the feedback we received occurred at the level of assignments, others were more substantial. At a meeting of the 301/499 working group after the evaluation of the first set of senior portfolios, we realized that we needed to do a better job of teaching students about historiography. Although we had designated a section of the portfolio guidelines for display of knowledge of the discipline of history and its methods, students were having trouble coming up with work for this category. Although we knew that attention to historical practice and the way historians think was absent in too many of our upper-division courses, it was obvious that History 302, a required course in history and theory, was not sufficiently benefiting students. Up until this point, History 302 had been taught in radically different ways depending on the instructor's interest. Thanks to the 499 portfolio, however, we were increasingly aware that students had a poor understanding of historiography and the relation of theory to history.

To redress this gap, it was decided that 302 would need to undergo substantial revision. Funding from the dean of the College of Liberal Arts (a strong supporter of the department's student-centered, standards-based approach) was given to a group of faculty involved in the QUE project with experience with the theory course to come up with a new standard course outline for History 302 that included learning outcomes and sample assignments. This group met frequently over the course of a year to debate the organization of History 302 and to share sample texts and assignments. Eventually, consensus was reached about the primary components of the course. While an introduction to the profession and an analysis of theory were common elements of prior iterations of 302, we realized that students often began their investigations of theory without ever being introduced to any of the major conceptual categories—such as race, gender, class, and nation—used by historians. Accordingly, an analysis of at least one of these key categories was added to the 302 learning outcomes.

Our work with 499 portfolios also led to the realization that students did not understand historiography; that is, how historians use the tools of the discipline to study themselves. In several of the syllabi examined by the 302 working group, students had been asked to write a historiographic essay, but these projects seldom proved satisfactory. Instead of sending students out to find material upon which to practice historiography, we decided to have students work with sets of material on a topic (or topics) of the instructor's choosing that would be selected in advance. It was hoped that these packets would focus students' analysis of changes in historical trends and interpretations over time, leading to both a clearer and more nuanced understanding of the process of writing history. As the final paper in the course, this historiographic essay, along with the other assignments geared to specific categories in the portfolio guidelines, would better prepare students for the rest of their upper-division coursework by enhancing their ability to see how history works and why it matters.

This new standard course outline was approved by the department and the college curriculum committee. To align the course with 301 and 499 (which are four-unit rather than the standard three-unit classes) and reflect our heightened expectations of our students, an extra unit was granted to History 302. The learning outcomes for this course represent only the most recent result of our ongoing dialogue about history learning and teaching (see Figure 7.4).

Figure 7.4
History 302 Learning Outcomes

Upon successful completion of the course, students will know and be able to do the following in four key areas.

Introduction to the History of the Profession
- Students will be able to define theory, history, and historiography and note the ways in which they are linked.
- Students will be able to trace generally the history of the profession from the ancient period to the current day, with specific emphasis on the professionalization of history in the 19th century.
- Students will recognize major intellectual schools, trends, and debates within the profession and demonstrate how those changes were connected to social developments.
- Students will be able to name significant historians of the modern period and demonstrate their familiarity with a variety of theoretical perspectives historians have used to produce historical knowledge.

Conceptual Categories of Historical Inquiry

- Students will be able to recognize, define, and trace the genealogies of basic categories of historical analysis such as class, race, gender, nation, space, etc.
- Students will identify some of the intellectual tools historians have used to help make sense of these categories.
- Students will demonstrate how these categories of historical inquiry can cross theoretical and disciplinary boundaries.

Theory

- Students will demonstrate knowledge of premodern theories of history within a global cultural and spatial perspective.
- Students will demonstrate how theories are contingent, contested, and reflective of contemporary circumstance.
- Students will recognize the contribution of history to the theories operating within and across other disciplines.
- Students will be able to explain basic components of selected theories, cite major contributors to such theories, and demonstrate the application of those theories to historical practice.

Historiography

- Students will demonstrate that historiography is a mode of analysis in which historians use the tools of historical research to study their discipline.
- Students will recognize that history is an interpretive, subjective process in which individual historians engage in dialogue with larger intellectual communities.
- Students will be able to account for major shifts in a specified body of historical literature, tracing changes in methodology, evidence, and interpretation.

Another consequence of our QUE deliberations and the feedback mechanism engendered by the portfolios in History 499 was an attempt to address and create substantive content standards in addition to those already generated in terms of historical procedure and skill. Many of the QUE clusters in history and other disciplines created level 14 standards that were articulated between community and four-year colleges. Much of our discussion with other institutions then focused on issues about lower-division teaching in history—in particular, survey courses in U.S. and world history. Given the nature of a survey course, much of the dialogue revolved around particular content to be represented in the course standards. From these discussions—and evidenced by the work of other history departments in the QUE project—we recognized that some consensus about content was feasible at a department level.

Moreover, as a consequence of the feedback mechanism generated by the bookend portfolio, there was some department concern about the disparity of content knowledge among students in History 499. Students enter the seminar with a variety of specialized spatial and temporal experiences within, but not across, their fields of concentration. The absence of a common foundational knowledge of content created difficulty in teaching a specialized course where students had no common curriculum in their field of concentration. But the development of a common set of content standards for each upper-division field proved intractable. The creation of upper-division content standards resurrected anxieties about whose history was to be represented. In addition, such an endeavor would have entailed a complete restructuring of upper-division course offerings well beyond the budget of the department.

However, there was some agreement about generating common content standards for the lower-division survey courses, recognizing that establishing basic foundational knowledge for history majors before engaging in upper-division coursework would be beneficial. (History majors at Long Beach State take four courses of lower-division work from a two-course survey in Western civilization and U.S. and world history.) This became our next standards-setting project.

Some members of the department had previous experience in creating content standards as part of their involvement in teacher preparation programs at the university. Approximately one-third of our history majors at California State University–Long Beach go on to obtain Single Subject Teaching Credentials. Many members of the history department work in the credential program, teaching the content of the state curriculum and supervising pre-service teachers in the field.

Long Beach State recently developed an intensive Integrated Teacher Education Program that allows students to earn a bachelor's degree in liberal studies and a Multiple Subject (Elementary) Teaching Credential within four years. All curriculum in the program is standards-based. The campus received

$450,000 from the John S. and James L. Knight Foundation for the development of these courses, including survey classes in early U.S. and world history. Moreover, history faculty have developed standards-based capstone courses for pre-service teachers in the Multiple Subject (elementary) and Single Subject (secondary) Social Science Credential Programs that explicate specific content standards and performance outcomes for U.S. and world history as they relate to the state K–12 history/social science framework (Houck, Cohn, & Cohn, 2004; Martel, 1999; Norton, 1999; Ravitch, 2000). It is striking that historians and historical professional organizations agree about advocating and articulating history content standards for pre-service teachers but not for the history major.

The project to create standards for the lower-division survey courses was based on our experience of the process for History 301 and History 499. However, given that the department offers multiple sections of the surveys, which are mostly taught by part-time faculty, participation in the project was limited to faculty who taught the courses on a regular basis. Small stipends were provided. In addition, faculty from Long Beach City College participated in the process, as a significant percentage of the department's majors transfer from community colleges to Long Beach State. Through these deliberations, standards were created for the survey courses in U.S. history (see Appendix B).

Surprisingly, consensus was rather easily reached concerning the issue of content. More difficult was the acceptance and embedding of an agreed-upon depth and breadth of skills within the survey courses. There was some tension between those concerned that the survey courses were being asked to serve too many mandates in terms of the breadth and depth of content relative to the demonstration of historical skill and thinking and writing competency.

However, the greatest challenges to the lower-division projects were logistical. The standards, once agreed upon, were in fact never implemented. Given the multiple number of sections of the course and the turnover of faculty who teach them at both institutions it proved impossible (especially given budgetary limitations) to monitor the implementation of the standards in all sections beyond a cursory perusal of syllabi. More importantly, efforts to create standards for the survey courses proved futile: Community college transfers to Long Beach State are more or less equally distributed from seven to eight community colleges. Accordingly, to effectively create lower-division standards would require the articulation of consensual standards (and ensure their implementation) across multiple campuses throughout much of southern California. Hence, standards for world history and western civilization courses were never written and those for early and modern U.S. history that remain have never been put into operation.

Conclusion

While we eagerly look forward to seeing how the changes to History 302 (which was taught for the first time in fall 2005 as a four-credit course) manifest themselves in our students' skills and abilities in historiography and theory, we realize that we also still face many challenges. Despite developing a workable, consensus-based model for how to do assessment and foreground student learning at the department level, we have our work cut out for us in getting our upper-division courses to reflect our laboriously crafted standards and prepare students for success in the capstone course. Unfortunately, few faculty, including even some of those involved in the expanded 301/302/499 working group, make it clear how particular assignments in their upper-division courses fulfill portfolio categories and reflect 301 competencies. While some progress has been made, (partly by requiring faculty to include a description of our portfolio-based assessment system on all course syllabi), it will still take time to change the culture of the department from a focus on what we teach to what students learn. We also need to address our lower-division curriculum, perhaps an even greater challenge given the many sections we offer and the number of instructors (most of them part-time) who teach these classes.

Yet despite these concerns, we believe that we have put into place an emphasis on student learning and faculty reflection about teaching that will continue to yield positive results. In fact, while the experience of the history department at Long Beach State may provide a model for the development of standards-based curricula elsewhere in the higher education community, the most important outcome has been our own dialogue about history teaching and student learning.

Endnotes

1) Some of what follows in this section is revised from Keirn (1999).

2) These district standards were developed in collaboration with members of the history faculty at Long Beach State, www.lbusd.k12.ca.us/curriculum/Curriculum%20Services/Hist.Social/history.htm. The California History/Social Science Content Standards Grades K–12 can be found at www.cde.ca.gov/be/st/ss/hstmain.asp.

References

American Historical Association. (1991). *Liberal learning and the history major.* Retrieved November 16, 2005, from www.historians.org/pubs/Free/LiberalLearning.htm

Bain, R. B. (2000). Into the breach: Using research and theory to shape history instruction. In P. N. Stearns, P. Seixas, & S. Wineburg (Eds.), *Knowing, teaching, and learning history: National and international perspectives* (pp. 331–352). New York, NY: New York University Press.

Brown, S. D., & Patrick, J. (2005). *History education in the United States: A survey of teacher certification and state-based standards and assessments for teachers and students.* Retrieved November 16, 2005, from http://www.oah.org/reports/surveys/50state/index.html

Center on Education Policy. (2005). *State high school exit exams: States try harder, but gaps exist.* Washington, DC: Author.

Gardner, H. (1985). *The mind's new science: A history of the cognitive revolution.* New York, NY: Basic Books.

Hill, J. (1997). Whatever their merits, the national standards will not be widely implemented. *The History Teacher, 30*(3).

Houck, J. W., Cohn, K. C., & Cohn, C. A. (Eds.). (2004). *Partnering to lead educational renewal: High-quality teachers, high quality schools.* New York, NY: Teachers College Press.

Keirn, T. (1999). Starting small: The creation of a year fourteen history standard. *Organization of American Historians Newsletter, 27*(4), 9–10.

Kirst, M. W., & Venezia, A. (Eds.). (2004). *From high school to college: Improving opportunities for success in postsecondary education.* San Francisco, CA: Jossey-Bass.

Lee, P. (2001, June). History in an information culture. *International Journal of Historical Learning, Teaching, and Research, 1*(2).

Lee, P. J. (2005). Putting principles into practice: Understanding history. In M. S. Donovan & J. D. Bransford (Eds.), *How students learn: History, mathematics, and science in the classroom* (pp. 31–78). Washington, DC: National Academies Press.

Lee, P., & Ashby, R. (2000). Progression in historical understanding among students ages 7–14. In P. N. Stearns, P. Seixas, & S. Wineburg (Eds.), *Knowing, teaching, and learning history: National and international perspectives* (pp. 199–222). New York, NY: New York University Press.

Le Goff, J. (1992). *History and memory* (S. Rendall & E. Claman, Trans.). New York, NY: Columbia University Press. (Original work published 1977)

Lowenthal, D. (1985). *The past is a foreign country.* New York, NY: Cambridge University Press.

Martel, E. (1999, October). Can "social studies" standards prepare history teachers? *Perspectives, 37*(7), 33.

Meo, S. L. (2002, February). Portfolio assessment for history majors: One department's journey. *Perspectives, 40*(2), 26–31.

Nash, G. B., Crabtree, C., & Dunn, R. E. (1997). *History on trial: Culture wars and the teaching of the past.* New York, NY: Alfred A. Knopf.

National Center for History in the Schools. (1996). *National standards for history.* Los Angeles, CA: Author.

National Governors Association. (1998, September 1). *High school exit exams: Setting high expectations* (Issue brief). Washington, DC: Author.

National Governors Association. (2004a, July 22). *ECW-05. Great expectations: The importance of rigorous education standards and K–12/postsecondary alignment.* Washington, DC: Author.

National Governors Association. (2004b, February 27). *ECW-13. High school reform: Aligning secondary and postsecondary education policy.* Washington, DC: Author.

National Governors Association. (2005, March 3). *ECW-15. Principles of federal preschool–college (P–16) alignment.* Washington, DC: Author.

Norton, M. B. (1999, September). Standards for history teacher preparation: Another view. *Perspectives, 37*(6), 53.

Ravitch, D. (2000). The educational backgrounds of history teachers. In P. N. Stearns, P. Seixas, & S. Wineburg (Eds.), *Knowing, teaching, and learning history: National and international perspectives* (pp. 143–155). New York, NY: New York University Press.

Schwartz, D. (1999, August). Can history professors learn from K–12 teachers? *Organization of American Historians Newsletter, 27*(3), 8.

Seixas, P. (1993). Popular film and young people's understanding of the history of native-white relations. *The History Teacher, 26*(3), 351–370.

Shemilt, D. (1987). Adolescent ideas about evidence and methodology in history. In C. Portal (Ed.), *The history curriculum for teachers* (pp. 39–61). Philadelphia, PA: The Falmer Press.

Venezia, A., Kirst, M. W., & Antonio, A. L. (2003, March). *Betraying the college dream: How disconnected K–12 and postsecondary education systems undermine student aspirations.* Retrieved November 17, 2005, from the Stanford University, Bridge Project web site: http://www.stanford.edu/group/bridgeproject/betrayingthecollegedream.pdf

Sievers, S. (1999). *Retrospective comments on the conference.* Unpublished manuscript.

Symcox, L. (2002). *Whose history? The struggle for national standards in American classrooms.* New York, NY: Teachers College Press.

Weber, W. (1997, September). Seamless education in Long Beach: University/college/school collaboration. *Perspectives, 35*(6), 21–25.

Wineburg, S. (2000). Making historical sense. In P. N. Stearns, P. Seixas, & S. Wineburg (Eds.), *Knowing, teaching, and learning history: National and international perspectives* (pp. 306–325). New York, NY: New York University Press.

Wineburg, S. (2001). *Historical thinking and other unnatural acts: Charting the future of teaching the past.* Philadelphia, PA: Temple University Press.

8

Mathematics and QUE: Oil and Water?

Bernard L. Madison, Susan L. Ganter

The traditional and still dominant culture of collegiate mathematics and the culture sought by the Quality in Undergraduate Education (QUE) project differ greatly, with little basis for even a conversation about agreement. However, the evolving reform in U.S. collegiate mathematics has opened doors for the ideas of QUE, and the QUE mathematics faculty participants are well ahead of many other mathematicians in thinking through the very difficult issues involved in making collegiate mathematics education more relevant and effective. The issues include curricular learning goals, pedagogical methods, and assessment of learning in programs—issues neither well understood by nor familiar in the practice of many U.S. collegiate mathematics faculty.

Four of the QUE clusters had mathematics components.[1] The faculty in these components joined the QUE project with different motivations, but with shared beliefs, problems, and practices derived largely from the traditional culture of collegiate mathematics.[2] At first, these faculty struggled with the language of educational reform and with interpreting that language in the context of collegiate mathematics. They struggled to get past their dependence on lists of mathematics content as the primary method for defining curricula, while also trying to accommodate their professional roles and the role of mathematics in the larger arena of general education. Overcoming these and other obstacles took time and, as a consequence, the QUE mathematics faculty lagged in their participation in the broader QUE discussions with colleagues from other disciplines. However, national initiatives in mathematics reform and faculty development provided encouragement and direction. The philosophy of these initiatives meshed very well with the philosophy being promoted by QUE. The synergism pushed the QUE mathematics faculty forward.

In this chapter, we describe the context of collegiate mathematics that created the culture in which the QUE mathematics faculty worked. We investigate details of how this culture interacted with QUE, as well as the support found in other national reform initiatives in mathematics. Developments within QUE are traced against the backdrop of these national initiatives.

Profile of the QUE Mathematics Faculty ⸺

The mathematics faculty who participated in QUE shared common beliefs and practices but came from individual institutions with varying experiences and priorities. Participants started with different levels of awareness about reform efforts (both within U.S. mathematics and in broader educational arenas) and different attitudes toward reform (from very negative to positive but cautious). Very few—possibly because of lack of information—expressed support for the need for reform to the extent articulated by those promoting paradigm change in undergraduate education (e.g., Barr & Tagg, 1995).

There were contrasting perspectives on QUE activities among the mathematics faculty. For example, one institution's effort was led by a person who, as a university administrator, had been very involved in a top-down institutional assessment program. On the other hand, some faculty from two-year institutions viewed instruction and assessment from the perspective of one or two lower-level courses. Between these two extremes, meaningful two-way communication required adjustments in thinking.

Mathematics faculty in QUE had varying roles within their institutions. Some were instructional managers, some were focused on remedial mathematics, some on mathematics majors, and a couple on institutional assessment. Some came from a research environment, but most were primarily devoted to instructional activities. Initially, many of the faculty were concerned with local issues, and it took time for the group to detach from the details and begin to think in broader educational terms.

The beliefs of all QUE mathematics faculty were influenced by the culture of researcher-driven collegiate mathematics. Although the cultures of mathematics departments at two-year colleges, four-year colleges, and research universities are very different, they all share a common influence from mathematics research. The values of mathematics graduate programs, dominated by research, are imprinted on faculty throughout college mathematics. Consequently, the culture of research mathematics has considerable influence on college and university mathematics, even at the introductory level. The values inherent in that culture conflicted with the values promoted by QUE and with the more progressive values from other reform movements within mathematics.

The Research Mathematics Culture

Mathematics research is the principal activity of the "mathematics fraternity," described by distinguished U.S. mathematician Paul Halmos (1968) as a "self-perpetuating priesthood" (p. 381). "Mistakes are forgiven and so is obscure exposition—the indispensable requisite is mathematical insight" (Halmos, p. 381). Prestige in mathematics is gained through manifestations of mathematical insight—developing new mathematics—and those who have prestige wield power over academic mathematics.

Mathematics research is a demanding taskmaster requiring dedication, concentration, even obsession. Although most mathematics research does not aim at immediate applications, the history of unanticipated uses of mathematics provides strong support for its value to society. Consequently, in the research mathematics world, educating mathematicians and creating new mathematics often takes precedence over educating people to use mathematics, whether in the workplace or in undergraduate coursework.

Mathematicians see great value and power in abstract mathematical structures and seek students who can master advanced mathematics. This strongly influences mathematicians' views of the goals of mathematics courses and curricula, and those views are reflected in school and college mathematics.

This culture of collegiate mathematics was reflected in the learning goals developed by the QUE mathematics faculty. Indeed, early lists of these goals read like the list of topics to be covered in a course or the table of contents of a mathematics textbook. The same phenomenon was even more pronounced in the group's approach to assessment, with standard mathematics tests (over the lists of topics to be covered)—perhaps even multiple choice in format—chosen as the appropriate assessment instrument. Learning goals were to master mathematical procedures, using assessments that demonstrated mastery of these procedures.

Circumstances such as enrollment patterns complicated responses to QUE goals, while national collegiate mathematics reform initiatives reinforced and promoted progress toward QUE goals. This environment in which the QUE mathematics faculty worked on a daily basis greatly influenced their efforts within QUE.

Collegiate Mathematics

Much of the mathematics offered in college, especially the first two years, is organized as courses that have always been a part of U.S. higher education. Basic courses in algebra, trigonometry, and geometry were a part of the classical collegiate curriculum prior to the shift to majors (plus general education) about a century ago (Hawkes, 1910). Even after the introduction of majors, the same mathematics courses were offered for both general education and preparation for further study in mathematics, science, or engineering—making mathematics unique among mainline academic disciplines in not developing introductory college-level courses for general education.

Now, in the early 21st century, the mathematics curriculum from grade nine through general education courses in college continues to be dominated by a long-established sequence of geometry, algebra, trigonometry, and calculus, referred to as GATC. Until the recent growth of calculus courses in high school, the widely acknowledged first college mathematics course was calculus. That was the position taken in the 1950s when the College Board's

Advanced Placement (AP) program began and calculus was selected as the AP course in mathematics. However, over the past 30 years, survey results from the Conference Board for the Mathematical Sciences have shown that approximately two-thirds of college enrollments are in the GAT of GATC (Lutzer, Maxwell, & Rodi, 2002). Consequently, any discussion of collegiate mathematics must focus on GATC.

The content of the GATC courses has remained essentially the same for 150 years, and is heavily—if not totally—influenced by algebraic methods needed for success in the methods of calculus. The dominance of the content and the long history of the GATC sequence in secondary and postsecondary education have cemented attitudes and practices among many academic mathematicians. Questions about relevance, purpose, and learning goals often are not considered.

The GATC sequence is long, narrow, and hurried as it runs through the high school and early college years. The number of students who have trouble with this sequence has grown enormously as larger fractions of Americans participate in postsecondary education (Madison, 2003). Consequently, in efforts to increase student success, multiple courses have been introduced that break the GATC sequence into a multitude of courses (still sequential) such as pre-algebra, algebra 1A, algebra 1B, algebra 2, algebra 3, beginning algebra, intermediate algebra, college algebra, geometry, trigonometry, precalculus, and calculus. It is not unusual for colleges—especially two-year colleges—to offer three or more sequenced courses in algebra alone (Lutzer, Maxwell, & Rodi, 2002). This creates a spectrum of competency levels in mathematics among entering college students and disperses the students across a variety of courses designed to reach the ultimate goal of calculus. Many—in fact, most—do not enroll in calculus, thus never realizing much of the proposed value of their learning in the initial part of the uncompleted GATC sequence.[3]

College mathematics faculty have become accustomed to guiding students through algebra and trigonometry toward calculus, and some into calculus. Learning goals are considered clear, specified by the well-known sequential content of these courses and determined largely by the point where the student is in this GATC sequence. More general learning goals such as critical thinking or quantitative literacy are assumed to be corollaries of the more specific and traditional goals of learning in the GATC sequence.

As a result of this dispersion of students along the GATC sequence, collegiate mathematics has no clear beginning. There is no introductory college mathematics course analogous to that of other disciplines. Collegiate mathematics is a continuation of high school mathematics and has multiple entry points. In fact, the situation is much cloudier than the nonexistence of a clear line between school and college mathematics. Most enrollments in college mathematics are in courses whose content is taught in high school, and the fastest growing component of high school mathematics is in courses that carry college credit (Madison, 2003).

More specifically, the Conference Board for the Mathematical Sciences 2000 survey showed that approximately 60% of the mathematics enrollments in four-year colleges and 80% of those in two-year colleges were in courses whose content is taught in high school. (Although calculus is taught in high schools, it is not included in these totals. If the first calculus course is included, the 60% rises to 77% and the 80% rises to 87% [Lutzer, Maxwell, & Rodi, 2002]). The number of high school mathematics courses being offered with dual college credit is increasing rapidly. The murky division between school and college mathematics clouds learning goals and assessments for collegiate faculty, especially at the general education level. This clouding was evident in the work of the QUE mathematics faculty.

College mathematics courses with content covered in school courses are of two distinct types. One type consists of courses with content that is required study in almost all schools, namely arithmetic and a first course in algebra, usually designated as algebra 1. Courses of this type—accounting for one of three college mathematics enrollments overall and over half in two-year colleges—are usually designated as remedial or developmental in college and do not carry college degree credit. However, definitions and uses of remedial or developmental courses vary from college to college and within a college from major to major. Nonetheless, except for returning students who have been away from school for some time, students in remedial courses are repeating material they failed to learn in recent and possibly multiple efforts. Having to repeat work, not making progress toward a degree, and studying uninspiring—and to students, illogical—subject matter makes remedial mathematics courses unusually dreary. The subject matter of these courses is the kind of content—much of it algebraic methods—that appears to be best learned with attentive practice the first time. Misunderstanding and bad habits are hard to undo. Consequently, the proportion of students who are unsuccessful in remedial college mathematics courses is often high, sometimes 50% or more (Madison, 2003).

The second type of college courses with high school content consists mostly of algebra courses beyond algebra 1, analytic geometry, and trigonometry. Increasingly, the first course in calculus also is moving toward this category since many high schools now offer a course in calculus. These courses often carry degree credit, especially for students majoring in areas outside of science and engineering. Many students in these courses are repeating study of high school content, but this time for college credit. The maladies of remedial courses are also present in these courses, which tend to be unpopular and have comparatively low success rates.

Dual Credit Courses

The enormous overlap between college and high school mathematics has fueled the recent growth of dual credit courses in high schools. The expansion is typified by this common scenario: A two-year college enters into an agreement with a high school to give college credit to high school students for specific courses taken in the high school that also count for high school credit (hence the term *dual credit*). Agreements of this type have been made for college credit in most core disciplines. In mathematics, dual credit is being awarded in courses from beginning algebra through calculus. These agreements are generating considerable college credit in courses taught in high schools by high school teachers as well as courses taught in colleges for both high school and college credit. The Conference Board for the Mathematical Sciences 2000 survey reported that 15% of all sections of college algebra (including algebra and trigonometry) taught in two-year colleges in fall 2000 were for dual credit (Lutzer, Maxwell, & Rodi, 2002).

A 2001 national survey estimated that one-half of all juniors and seniors in U.S. high schools (approximately 3.5 million) are enrolled in courses (in all disciplines) that carry credit for both high school graduation and college degrees (Clark, 2001). Some of these courses are in examination-based programs such as International Baccalaureate (IB) and College Board's AP in which college credit depends on scores on national or international examinations and not merely on high school course grades. However, most dual credit enrollees (57%) are in courses that, unlike AP and IB, have no uniform examination (Clark, 2001). Because the significant growth of dual credit has been so recent, reliable data on how students with this credit fare in college does not yet exist. But if the primary change in these courses has been simply the awarding of college credit, the knowledge gained by many of these students may be insufficient for success in subsequent college courses.

The largest examination-based dual credit program is AP, a 50-year-old program of the College Board aimed at providing opportunities for advanced study in high school, with the possibility of receiving credit or advanced placement in college. Enrollment in AP courses has been growing by about 10% per year for the past 20 years, and AP now offers 34 courses and examinations (soon to be 38 with the addition of four new world language courses). Approximately two million AP examinations will be given in 2005 to about 1.2 million high school students, mostly juniors and seniors—or one in three high school graduates. About 250,000 of these will be in AP calculus and about 75,000 in AP statistics (projected from 2004 College Board reports).

The huge overlap between school and college mathematics both complicates the school-to-college transition and confuses establishment of learning goals for college mathematics. Very often, when learning goals are established in this context, they strongly resemble the analogous goals for high school mathematics. This phenomenon is reflected in some of the learning goals articulated by the QUE mathematics faculty.

Calculus Reform

Curriculum reform in collegiate mathematics has been an occasional issue at various times over the past century, but changes have been relatively minor. One of the most extensive efforts focused on calculus and took place during 1985–2000.

The national calculus reform movement began with two small conferences, one at Williamstown College in 1983 and another at Tulane University in 1986. The Williamstown conference focused on the possibility of discrete mathematics replacing the traditional calculus as a basic course, especially for computer science majors. Partly as a response to the Williamstown conference, the Tulane conference produced a vision of a "lean and lively" calculus. Mathematical Sciences in the Year 2000, a major national assessment project, included a large national colloquium titled Calculus for a New Century in October 1987 at the National Academy of Sciences under the sponsorship of the Mathematical Sciences Education Board and the Board on the Mathematical Sciences of the National Research Council (Steen, 1987). At the same time, the National Science Foundation (NSF) announced a program of support for calculus reform projects.

Handheld graphing calculators were appearing in the late 1980s and soon became generally available at affordable prices. Use of these calculators was one of the major reform issues, and nearly 20 years later it remains a controversial topic among college and university mathematics faculty. However, in 1989 and 2000, the National Council of Teachers of Mathematics (NCTM) promoted using calculators in teaching and learning mathematics, as did a 1995 publication of the American Mathematical Association of Two-Year Colleges. In 1989, the AP Calculus Development Committee (responsible for test construction, course descriptions, and policy recommendations) began discussions about the use of calculators on the AP calculus examination. Subsequently, scientific calculators were required on AP calculus examinations in 1993 and 1994, and graphing calculators were required beginning in 1995. In 1998, a new course description for AP calculus reflected many of the reform ideas, and by 1999 calculators with computer algebra systems were permitted. These movements at the national level were the primary motivators for the current, almost universal use of graphing calculators in high school calculus courses. Several reform textbooks that emerged from the NSF-funded projects—as well as many traditional textbooks that adopted parts of the reform ideas—have changed the landscape in many college calculus courses as well.

Just how much calculus has changed as a result of these recent efforts is unclear (see Ganter, 2001; Solow, 1994; Tucker & Leitzel, 1995). Some say not much, while others say quite a bit. Nonetheless, the calculus reform movement was very high profile within the U.S. mathematics community and it prompted widespread discussions about educational reform questions. It also helped to pave the way for the more substantial philosophical changes in the college mathematics curriculum that have been recommended in recent years. These changes opened doors that enabled the QUE mathematics faculty to embrace more completely the reform philosophy of QUE.

Recommendations of the Committee on the Undergraduate Program in Mathematics

Beginning in 1953, the Committee on the Undergraduate Program in Mathematics (CUPM) of the Mathematical Association of America (MAA) began issuing recommendations for the major in mathematics. These recommendations have been revised approximately every 10 years, with the most recent version issued in 2004. Until 1990, these recommendations focused on a list of recommended courses for the major in mathematics, with the 1990 report (CUPM, 1991/1992) moving beyond this list to include some broader recommendations about student learning and how that learning might be prompted. The list of courses is still very much as it has been for 50 years, with a core of three courses in calculus and one or two each in differential equations, linear algebra, advanced calculus, and abstract algebra. However, the 2004 Committee on the Undergraduate Program in Mathematics report moved far beyond the modest changes of the 1990 report by addressing all of undergraduate mathematics, including general education and service courses. The report is built around six recommendations, all of which include an element of reform and movement toward a more learning-centered and interdisciplinary environment. The topics of the recommendations read like an agenda for QUE:

1) Aligning courses and programs with the needs of students

2) Using courses to promote general competencies

3) Increasing variety of perspectives and connections into courses

4) Promoting interdisciplinary cooperation and collaboration

5) Promoting appropriate use of technology

6) Encouraging faculty innovations in teaching and learning

Other National Initiatives

The Curriculum Foundations Project

Much of collegiate mathematics consists of what have been called service courses or courses in support of client disciplines. Traditionally, the disciplines being served by mathematics courses have been sciences and engineering, with majors that typically include three courses in calculus plus courses in differential equations and sometimes linear algebra. More recently, students from business and the social sciences typically study a semester of calculus and one of finite mathematics or probability and statistics. As a consequence of this service function, collegiate mathematics has a long history of loose cooperation with many disciplines. However, this cooperation has usually been restricted to including certain mathematics content in these courses, without discussions of common learning goals. For example, the mathematical methods necessary for analytical chemistry or engineering mechanics might be targeted for inclusion in the calculus-level courses without further comment. This approach is consistent with practices reflecting the belief that general learning goals such as problem solving, critical thinking, and quantitative literacy are natural outcomes of the skills attained in traditional mathematics courses. That is, mathematics faculty generally assume that the goal is to learn mathematics and that then the general competencies will follow, rather than using mathematics as a vehicle for achieving the sought-after competencies. As a consequence of these long-accepted practices—and in spite of the extensive service role to other disciplines—mathematics faculty are surprisingly insular in many colleges and universities.

In part to address this issue, the Mathematical Association of America (through a subcommittee, Curriculum Renewal Across the First Two Years) developed an initiative to promote more substantive educational cooperation between mathematics faculty and colleagues in other disciplines. The initiative, called the Curriculum Foundations Project, was more than a formalization of what had gone on in many universities for decades; that is, ask the science and engineering faculty what mathematics they wanted their students to learn. In 1999–2001, the project sponsored 11 workshops consisting of 20–35 participants, the majority chosen from the discipline under consideration, the remainder chosen from mathematics. The workshops were not intended to be discussions between mathematicians and colleagues in the partner disciplines, although this certainly happened informally. Instead, each workshop was a dialogue among the representatives from the partner discipline, with mathematicians present only to listen and serve as a resource when questions about the mathematics curriculum arose (Ganter & Barker, 2004).

Distilled from these workshops was a collective vision of collegiate mathematics in the first two years. This vision includes an emphasis on conceptual understanding, problem-solving skills, mathematical modeling, communication skills, and a balance between perspectives such as continuous and discrete or pure and applied. This is a clear departure from the what-topics-should-be-covered-in-calculus mode.

The 11 workshops focused on the "mathematically intensive" disciplines that are served by collegiate mathematics, but now the process is being expanded to the social sciences, arts, and humanities. The first new discipline is journalism, with a workshop now in the planning stages.

Crossroads in Mathematics

The American Mathematical Association of Two-Year Colleges (AMATYC) is revising its 1995 report, *Crossroads in Mathematics.* Now in a near-final draft form, this revision—*Beyond Crossroads*—is based on eight principles under the very brief headings of assessment, balance, broadening, equity, inquiry, literacy, relevance, and research into practice. As these headings indicate, this document also is reform-minded and generally consistent with the Committee on the Undergraduate Program in Mathematics 2004 report (AMATYC, 2004).

The Quantitative Literacy Movement

The need for a mathematics course that actually addresses general education has prompted the development of courses in quantitative literacy or quantitative reasoning. The quantitative literacy movement has gained considerable momentum in the past decade. Led largely by mathematicians but with contributors from many collegiate disciplines (especially statistics), a major national conversation on strengthening quantitative literacy education has taken place.

In 1996, the Committee on the Undergraduate Program in Mathematics Subcommittee on Quantitative Literacy issued a report emphasizing the role and responsibility of collegiate mathematics in quantitative literacy education (Sons, 1996). This report did not have much effect until the advent of another quantitative literary movement, originating with the College Board as a result of looking at the quantitative literacy content of AP science and mathematics course descriptions and examinations (Steen, 1997). Subsequently, the National Council on Education and the Disciplines published *Mathematics and Democracy* (Steen, 2001) and sponsored a national forum on quantitative literary at the National Academy of Sciences in December 2001. The Mathematical Association of America and the Mathematical Sciences Education Board at the National Research Council partnered with the National Council on Education and the Disciplines to present this forum, and the National Council published the commissioned papers and the forum proceedings in 2003 (Madison & Steen, 2003). In 2004, the Mathematical Association of America published a slimmer version of the forum proceedings that summarized the findings and recommendations (Steen, 2004). Finally, an interdisciplinary membership organization, the National Numeracy Network, grew out of the National Council on Education and the Disciplines' work. As the National Numeracy Network was incorporated in 2004, the Mathematical Association of America approved a new special interest group on quantitative literacy called SIGMAA-QL (Madison, 2005).

Initiatives in the Research Mathematics Community

The American Mathematical Society, traditionally focused on research and graduate study, has been increasingly active in educational issues. Their 1999 report had a simple message: To ensure their institution's commitment to excellence in mathematics research, doctoral departments must pursue excellence in their instructional programs (Ewing, 1999). Furthermore, the American Mathematical Society has partnered with the Mathematicians and Education Reform network (see www.math.uic.edu/MER/pages/) on numerous activities and forums centered on reforming mathematics education in colleges and universities.

Another initiative in the research mathematics community is worth noting. The Mathematical Sciences Research Institute, located at the University of California–Berkeley and one of the premier centers for mathematical sciences research in the world, recently created a committee on education. In 2004, one of the first activities of this committee was to sponsor a conference on assessment of student learning.

The Influence of Statistics, Computer Science, and Mathematics Education

The work of QUE, as well as the normal operation of many U.S. college mathematics departments, is complicated by the relationships among mathematics, statistics, computer science, and mathematics education. The extent and variety of these relationships is indicated by the enrollments in various courses in all four areas, as documented by the Conference Board on the Mathematical Sciences surveys (Lutzer, Maxwell, & Rodi, 2002). In all the QUE clusters that included mathematics, some aspects of these related disciplines were in the mathematics department, while other aspects were housed outside mathematics.

Teacher education is an important concern for most mathematics departments and, in recent years, there has been a renewed emphasis on the mathematical education of teachers. This renewed emphasis was evident in discussions within QUE, both about mathematics courses for future elementary teachers and the major program for future secondary teachers.

College and university mathematics faculty have played significant roles in supporting school mathematics. During the 1960s, research mathematicians were involved in developing new school curricula and in conducting workshops for in-service teachers. Shortly after, in the wake of problems with the "new math," mathematicians largely withdrew from school mathematics and the preparation of teachers. Discussions following the introduction of standards for school mathematics in 1989 by the National Council of Teachers of Mathematics caused some mathematicians to reengage with school mathematics. Throughout the 1990s, this reengagement took various forms, including some rather contentious debates about fundamental approaches to mathematics education. The 2001 Conference Board on the Mathematical Sciences report, *The Mathematical Education of Teachers*, made that reengagement real and constructive. In 2003, the Mathematical Association of America launched a major four-year faculty development program supported by the National Science Foundation, titled Preparing Mathematicians to Educate Teachers, to help implement the recommendations of *The Mathematical Education of Teachers*.

These and parallel efforts by National Science Foundation centers, as well as by organizations such as the American Mathematical Association of Two-Year Colleges and the American Statistical Association, has made mathematics faculty more aware of the progressive thinking about stronger teacher preparation. For example, the work of the American Statistical Association and the National Council of Teachers of Mathematics in the 1980s and 1990s formed the basis of the Data Analysis and Probability strand in the national mathematics standards (NCTM, 2000). This has prompted changes in teacher education and the learning goals for college students in data analysis, probability, and statistics, and has increased the need for professional development of both in-service K–12 teachers and college faculty who teach courses for future teachers. One major recent activity in professional development for teacher education has been a project implemented by the American Mathematical Association of Two-Year Colleges entitled "Teacher Education, Mathematics, and Technology: A National Dialogue."

Stages of QUE and Mathematics

As these national initiatives demonstrate, the most progressive thinking in collegiate mathematics education was moving essentially in parallel with the development of QUE. The Curriculum Foundation's collective vision and the Committee on the Undergraduate Program in Mathematics recommendations mesh very well with QUE and made the work of QUE faculty at level 16, level 14, and general education much more palatable. The other national initiatives discussed also served as a stimulus for QUE work. The mathematics faculty in QUE would no doubt have been more immediately receptive and understanding of the reform philosophy of QUE if they previously had been more aware of and influenced by the thinking represented by these activities. Nonetheless, the QUE mathematics faculty were participating in a faculty development project that was essentially paralleling reform developments in the discipline itself.

The work of QUE was divided into four stages.

- Stage 1: Developing student learning outcomes at level 14, level 16, and general education (cross-disciplinary competencies)

- Stage 2: Ensuring course-level alignment and assessment

- Stage 3: Ensuring curriculum-level alignment and assessment

- Stage 4: Matching pedagogy and content with cognition

While addressing Stage 1, the four clusters with mathematics components responded differently. The development of student learning outcomes for level 16 will be discussed first.

Level 16 Learning Outcomes

Student learning outcomes for level 16 were more apparent for several reasons. Although there are a few non-mathematics major curricula in colleges that require mathematics beyond the second year of college, level 16 was uniformly interpreted by QUE mathematics faculty as the mathematics needed to major in mathematics (including mathematics education and occasionally statistics). The program for mathematics majors was most familiar to the QUE mathematics faculty, as it is to most U.S. mathematics faculty. Part of the reason for this familiarity is, of course, due to faculty attention to major courses, but part of it is due to a fairly uniform major offering across the U.S. The uniformity stems from national attention given to recommendations for the undergraduate major in mathematics, as explained in the earlier discussion of the recommendations of the Committee on the Undergraduate Program in Mathematics.

The level 16 standards for future secondary teachers in QUE mathematics institutions reflect many of the changes suggested by the Mathematical Education of Teachers report as well as the Data Analysis and Probability strand from the National Council of Teachers of Mathematics and the American Statistical Association. Some of these ideas, particularly those related to statistical issues and the education of future elementary teachers, were reflected in the level 14 standards.

Computer science and statistics remain connected administratively to mathematics in many two- and four-year institutions. For example, one QUE institution had a department of mathematics and computer science. Aside from computer use (peripherally related to computer science), influences of computer science on learning in mathematics has elevated the importance of discrete mathematics where enrollments have been increasing (Lutzer, Maxwell, & Rodi, 2002). In addition to teacher education courses, statistics has become more prevalent in general education because of the increasing quantification of public discourse and the ubiquitous nature of data generated and analyzed by computers. All these changes have affected mathematical education standards at both levels 14 and 16 as confronted by the QUE mathematics faculty.

Level 14 Learning Outcomes

Developing learning outcomes for level 14 in mathematics presents more difficulties and options than is the case for level 16. The question for college mathematics faculty is—Which students at level 14? Different degree programs require different mathematics courses. These program requirements break roughly into four groups: science and engineering, business, social science, and liberal arts.

- *Science and engineering* programs often require two or three courses in calculus and a course in differential equations, essentially the same courses required in the first two years of a mathematics major.[4] One exception is that some mathematics major programs require an introductory course in mathematical proofs. For example, one of the four-year QUE institutions required such a course in proofs and others did not.

- *Business* programs usually require two mathematics courses, and these are often a course in finite mathematics (logic, probability, and linear programming) and a course in calculus (differential and integral calculus of polynomials).[5] In recent years, some different mathematics courses for business majors have been developed. These are mostly courses organized around business case studies that use some of the concepts from finite mathematics and calculus.

- *Social science* programs usually require a course or courses in statistics, sometimes calculus-based but most often algebra-based. The statistics courses are sometimes taught in a social science department and sometimes in a mathematics or statistics department. The aim is to prepare the students for empirical research requiring data analysis (e.g., McKinney, Howery, Strand, Kain, & Berheide, 2004).

- *Liberal arts* programs typically require a single course, sometimes with college algebra as a prerequisite and sometimes not. Sometimes the course is college algebra or a mathematical modeling version of college algebra. Whatever the name, it is the course at the individual institution that most closely resembles a college mathematics course aimed at general education. Over the past half-century, several versions of "mathematics for liberal arts students" have been described and developed (Lutzer, Maxwell, & Rodi, 2002). One of the first was essentially the original version of the contemporary finite mathematics course (Allendorfer, 1947).

With this array of degree options and reform efforts as a backdrop, QUE mathematics faculty formulated level 14 standards. Each of the four mathematics clusters responded differently.

- The Metro Atlanta cluster (Georgia State University and Georgia Perimeter College) concentrated on level 14 standards for mathematics majors and on common learning goals for three non-major courses: college algebra, precalculus, and mathematical modeling. In the process, they described their interpretation of quantitative reasoning and made it a goal for all students.

- The Middle Georgia cluster (Fort Valley State University and Middle Georgia College) developed an extensive description of learning goals and methods of assessment for the college algebra course taken by liberal arts students.

- The SWItCH cluster (Salisbury University, Wor-Wic Community College, and Chesapeake College) developed level 14 standards for non-majors by partitioning them into content areas, including number sense and estimation, algebra, geometry, continuous mathematics, probability and statistics, and discrete mathematics.

- The Northern Nevada cluster (University of Nevada–Reno and Truckee Meadows Community College) developed two sets of level 14 standards, one for science and engineering majors and one for other majors. Quantitative reasoning is described and included as a level 14 goal. Faculty in this cluster also have been actively involved in the national quantitative literacy movement and a national MAA project on faculty development in assessment.

General Education Learning Outcomes

A big part of QUE was addressing crosscutting competencies (e.g., critical thinking, quantitative literacy, communication, and metacognition) and shared responsibilities among the QUE disciplines. Disciplines contribute toward achieving these competencies through their courses for general education, service courses, and courses for majors.

The traditional view of general education mathematics courses is that they do not differ greatly from the standard courses in the GATC sequence. In fact, various versions of the traditional college algebra course continue to be the primary general education mathematics course (Lutzer, Maxwell, & Rodi, 2002). In recent years, algebra courses that emphasize mathematical modeling and problem solving have become more common but still have small enrollments nationally. However, following the momentum of the calculus reform movement and the recommendations of the Committee on the Undergraduate Program in Mathematics and others, several innovative courses at the level of college algebra are being developed and piloted.[6]

Beyond its own general education courses, the collegiate mathematics community has been rather inactive with initiatives addressing crosscutting competencies. Consequently, QUE mathematics faculty had little experience of their own in this area. Nationally, writing across the curriculum (or writing in the disciplines) is the sole example of mathematics faculty being involved in coaching a broad competency. Mostly, mathematicians see a very limited role for their discipline in competencies such as communication or meta-cognition. They do accept that competencies such as problem solving, critical thinking, and quantitative literacy are related to mathematics, but many believe they are consequences of mathematical literacy, which means learning the material in the GATC sequence. The QUE mathematics faculty were typical in this regard.

However, the discussions within QUE challenged this traditional view of the role of mathematics in crosscutting competencies, and reform developments within mathematics reinforced this challenge. For example, some of the experimental efforts in quantitative literacy have drawn tight connections between number and word. In fact, one definition of quantitative literacy (due to Robert Orrill) is that it is a cultural field where language and quantitative constructs merge and are no longer one or the other. Consequently, education for the 21st century seems to require coordinated cross-disciplinary teaching, and most QUE mathematics faculty are working toward this end.

Course-Level Alignment and Assessment

The second stage of QUE consisted of course-level alignment and assessment. More specifically, faculty looked at the learning goals they had established in the first stage and investigated whether or not course content and pedagogy were likely to lead to these goals. Further, assessment of learning in the courses was analyzed and adjusted so that it would measure progress toward achieving the learning goals. In short, they asked if courses are aligned with learning goals and if assessments align with the course content and the learning goals.

Mostly because the learning goals were derived largely from the content of required courses, this alignment was relatively easy for QUE faculty. Learning goals (at level 14 or 16) mapped nicely to courses. For this reason, QUE mathematics faculty failed to see the substance of this component. Assessment of student learning was only slightly more difficult because it was viewed as assessment of learning within courses and that was standard practice anyway. Essentially, the only new twist was considering whether or not the learning goals were covered by the assessment.

Curriculum-Level Alignment and Assessment

The third conceptual stage of QUE, curriculum-level alignment and assessment, moved beyond the experience of most QUE mathematics faculty. Mathematics faculty are trained to think in terms of courses when they think of learning goals or assessment. Consequently, this conceptual leap to curriculum was troublesome. Fortunately, QUE's efforts to push faculty to think in terms of programs rather than courses was reinforced by existing faculty development activities within the mathematics community that support the assessment of student learning.

The QUE mathematics faculty could find examples and resources in those Mathematical Association of America programs that assess student learning, some developed more than a dozen years ago. Beginning in 1990, the Committee on the Undergraduate Program in Mathematics Subcommittee on Assessment explored the assessment movement in higher education that was rooted in accountability and continuous improvement efforts (Banta & Associates, 2002) and related it to mathematics programs. As a result, the Committee on the Undergraduate Program in Mathematics (1995) issued guidelines for the assessment of learning aimed at program improvements. The Mathematical Association of America then published a volume of 72 case studies on assessment programs in colleges and universities (Gold, Keith, & Marion, 1999). In 2001, the MAA received support from the National Science Foundation for an extensive three-year faculty development program titled Supporting Assessment in Undergraduate Mathematics. A major component of this program was a series of workshops for teams of faculty who were working on assessment of student learning. The program promoted assessment of learning in coherent curricular blocks of collegiate mathematics rather than individual courses and advocated an assessment cycle that largely mirrors the activities of QUE. The cycle included three questions:

What should the students learn? How well are they learning? What program changes can improve the learning?

Most of the QUE mathematics faculty were at least partly aware of the Mathematical Association of America's work on assessment, since assessment was being pushed by accrediting agencies and governing boards. One of the QUE institutions sent a team of participants to a Supporting Assessment in Undergraduate Mathematics workshop.

Matching Pedagogy and Content With Cognition

The final conceptual stage of QUE is described as matching pedagogy and content with cognition; that is, considering alignment between results on learning research and educational practices. This was by far the most complicated and conceptually difficult stage of QUE. Reconciling the reform ideas of QUE (essentially those proposed by Barr and Tagg [1995]) with the results from research on learning (e.g., Bransford, Brown, & Cocking, 2000; Halpern & Hakel, 2003; Pellegrino, Chudowsky, & Glaser, 2001) offered significant challenges on top of the issues related to learning goals, alignments, and assessments.

Educational research is largely empirical and results are often tentative and conditional. Research in mathematics is quite different, mostly founded in precise results derived logically from axiom systems based on centuries of thought. Partly because of this difference in ways of knowing, mathematicians are skeptical of research results on learning. Instead, they trust the power of the intellectual developments of mathematics to inspire and prompt learning. Few mathematics faculty have ever questioned how they teach or what they teach in light of research on learning.

The mathematics faculty in QUE were typical in their lack of knowledge about and attention to research results on learning. Some of them had limited experience utilizing learning research results in designing and implementing assessment programs. But this limited awareness was not enough, and this stage of QUE was largely ignored by the mathematics faculty.

Conclusion

The culture sought by QUE is at the forefront of progressive thought in educational reform. The challenge of QUE in mathematics was enormous—getting faculty who are mired in the mechanics of traditional collegiate mathematics instruction to break away and think deeply about seemingly radical ideas. Aside from the merit of these ideas, arguments abound that push the faculty away. Nonetheless, the leaders of QUE persisted with convincing rhetoric. However, had it not been for the synergism of QUE ideas with the most progressive thought in collegiate mathematics reform, the QUE mathematics faculty would have faltered, alone on an educational island. Consequently, QUE mathematics faculty found bridges and encouragement that connected the possible island of QUE to the mainland of their discipline. The bridges can be described as follows:

- QUE asked mathematics faculty to *think programmatically* rather than in terms of courses and components of mathematics content. The Committee on the Undergraduate Program in Mathematics' (2004) *Curriculum Guide,* the American Mathematical Association of Two-Year Colleges' (2004) *Beyond Crossroads,* and even the American Mathematical Society's *Towards Excellence* (Ewing, 1999) encouraged similar thinking.

- QUE asked mathematics faculty to *articulate program-level learning goals, align them with courses and pedagogy, and assess for progress toward these goals.* This was precisely where the Mathematical Association of America's assessment guidelines and faculty development workshops were pointing.

- QUE asked mathematics faculty to *cooperate more substantially with other disciplines.* The Mathematical Association of America's Curriculum Foundations Project reinforced this.

- QUE asked mathematics faculty to *consider a broader role in general education.* The quantitative literacy movement provided a model, an analysis of the issues and challenges, and resources for the task.

- QUE asked mathematics faculty to *be better role models for future teachers.* The Conference Board of the Mathematical Sciences (2001) *Mathematical Education of Teachers* report outlined how this could be accomplished, and the Mathematical Association of America's "Preparing Mathematicians to Educate Teachers" project is currently supporting faculty's efforts to make it happen.

- QUE asked mathematics faculty to *broaden their view of learning beyond content* into process and long-term retention. Results from learning research and the ideas from both the Committee on the Undergraduate Program in Mathematics' (2004) *Curriculum Guide* and the American Mathematical Association of Two-Year Colleges' (1995) *Crossroads* affirmed the possibilities.

The oil and water image may fit with QUE and traditional collegiate mathematics, but such is not the case with QUE and the most progressive forms of collegiate mathematics.

Endnotes

1) The four clusters with mathematics components were Metro Atlanta (Georgia State University and Georgia Perimeter College), Middle Georgia (Fort Valley State University and Middle Georgia College), SWItCH (Salisbury University, Wor-Wic Community College, and Chesapeake College), and Northern Nevada (University of Nevada–Reno and Truckee Meadows Community College).

2) Ten to twenty mathematics faculty participated in each national QUE meeting, with each cluster having three or more mathematics faculty providing leadership within the cluster.

3) Data gathered every five years since 1965 by the Conference Board for the Mathematical Sciences show that about three of four students in algebra courses in college never enroll in a calculus course.

4) The uniform nature of these requirements is driven by the mathematical needs in the sciences and engineering and reinforced by accrediting and certification criteria. See www.abet.org/forms.shtml and www.chemistry .org/portal/a/c/s/1/acsdisplay.html?DOC=education\cpt\guidelines .html for examples.

5) The uniform nature of these requirements is driven largely by accrediting criteria. See www.aacsb.edu/accreditation/standards.asp for an example.

6) At recent national meetings, contributed paper sessions and panel discussions have highlighted innovative approaches to courses similar to college algebra. The Mathematical Association of America's Committee on the Undergraduate Program in Mathematics has instituted a project that will promote and report on such efforts at selected institutions.

References

Allendorfer, C. B. (1947, December). Mathematics for liberal arts students. *American Mathematical Monthly, 17,* 573–578.

American Mathematical Association of Two-Year Colleges. (1995, September). *Crossroads in mathematics: Standards for introductory college mathematics before calculus.* Memphis, TN: Author.

American Mathematical Association of Two-Year Colleges. (2004, October). *Beyond crossroads: Implementing mathematics standards in the first two years of college* (Draft version 6.0). Memphis, TN: Author.

Banta, T. W., & Associates. (2002). *Building a scholarship of assessment.* San Francisco, CA: Jossey-Bass.

Barr, R. B., & Tagg, J. (1995, November/December). From teaching to learning—a new paradigm for undergraduate education. *Change, 27*(6), 12–25.

Bransford, J. D., Brown, A. L., & Cocking, R. R. (Eds.). (2000). *How people learn: Brain, mind, experience, and school* (Expanded ed.). Washington, DC: National Academies Press.

Clark, R. W. (2001, June). *Dual credit: A report of programs and policies that offer high school students college credits.* Philadelphia, PA: The Pew Charitable Trusts.

Committee on the Undergraduate Program in Mathematics. (1992). The undergraduate major in the mathematical sciences. In L. A. Steen (Ed.), *Heeding the call for change: Suggestions for curricular action* (pp. 225–247). Washington, DC: Mathematical Association of America. (Original work published 1991)

Committee on the Undergraduate Program in Mathematics. (1995). Assessment of student learning for improving the undergraduate major in mathematics. *FOCUS: The Newsletter of the Mathematical Association of America, 15*(3), 24–28.

Committee on the Undergraduate Program in Mathematics. (2004). *Undergraduate programs and courses in the mathematical sciences: CUPM curriculum guide 2004.* Washington, DC: Mathematical Association of America.

Conference Board of the Mathematical Sciences. (2001). *Mathematical education of teachers.* Providence, RI, and Washington, DC: American Mathematical Society and Mathematical Association of America.

Ewing, J. (Ed.). (1999). *Towards excellence: Leading a doctoral mathematics department in the 21st century.* Providence, RI: American Mathematical Society.

Ganter, S., & Barker, W. (Eds.). (2004). *Curriculum foundations project: Voices of the partner disciplines.* Washington, DC: Mathematical Association of America.

Ganter, S. L. (2001). *Changing calculus: A report on evaluation efforts and national impact from 1988–1998.* Washington, DC: Mathematical Association of America.

Gold, B., Keith, S. Z., & Marion, W. A. (Eds.). (1999). *Assessment practices in undergraduate mathematics.* Washington, DC: Mathematical Association of America.

Halmos, P. (1968, Winter). Mathematics as a creative art. *American Scientist, 56*(4), 375–389.

Halpern, D. F., & Hakel, M. D. (2003, July/August). Applying the science of learning to the university and beyond: Teaching for long-term retention and transfer. *Change, 35*(4), 36–41.

Hawkes, H. E. (1910, September). Mathematics in the college course. *Educational Review, 20,* 145–156.

Lutzer, D. J., Maxwell, J. W., & Rodi, S. B. (2002). *Statistical abstract of undergraduate programs in the mathematical sciences in the United States: Fall 2000 CBMS survey.* Providence, RI: American Mathematical Society.

Madison, B. L. (2003). Articulation and quantitative literacy: A view from inside mathematics. In B. L. Madison & L. A. Steen (Eds.), *Quantitative literacy: Why numeracy matters for schools and colleges* (pp. 153–164). Princeton, NJ: National Council for Education and the Disciplines.

Madison, B. L. (2005). Building bridges for quantitative literacy education: National numeracy network and SIGMAA QL. *FOCUS: The Newsletter of the Mathematical Association of America, 25*(5), 12–13.

Madison, B. L., & Steen, L. A. (Eds.). (2003). *Quantitative literacy: Why numeracy matters for schools and colleges.* Princeton, NJ: National Council for Education and the Disciplines.

McKinney, K., Howery, C. B., Strand, K. J., Kain, E. L., & Berheide, C. B. (2004). *Liberal learning and the sociology major updated: Meeting the challenge of teaching sociology in the twenty-first century.* Washington, DC: American Sociological Association.

National Council of Teachers of Mathematics. (1989). *Curriculum and evaluation standards for school mathematics.* Reston, VA: Author.

National Council of Teachers of Mathematics. (2000). *Principles and standards for school mathematics.* Reston, VA: Author.

Pellegrino, J. W., Chudowsky, N., & Glaser, R. (Eds.). (2001). *Knowing what students know: The science and design of educational assessment.* Washington, DC: National Academies Press.

Solow, A. (Ed.). (1994). *Preparing for a new calculus* (MAA Notes No. 36). Washington, DC: Mathematical Association of America.

Sons, L. (Ed.). (1996). *Quantitative reasoning for college graduates: A complement to the standards.* Washington, DC: Mathematical Association of America.

Steen, L. A. (Ed.). (1987). *Calculus for a new century: A pump, not a filter* (MAA Notes No. 8). Washington, DC: Mathematical Association of America.

Steen, L. A. (Ed.). (1997). *Why numbers count: Quantitative literacy for tomorrow's America.* New York, NY: The College Board.

Steen, L. A. (Ed.). (2001). *Mathematics and democracy: The case for quantitative literacy.* Princeton, NJ: National Council for Education and the Disciplines.

Steen, L. A. (2004). *Achieving quantitative literacy: An urgent challenge for higher education* (MAA Notes No. 62). Washington, DC: Mathematical Association of America.

Tucker, A. C., & Leitzel, J. R. C. (Eds.). (1995). *Assessing calculus reform efforts: A report to the community* (MAA Notes No. 6). Washington, DC: Mathematical Association of America.

9

Reflections on Success and Recommendations to Ensure It

Ruth Mitchell, Ronald J. Henry

The QUE project provided participants with opportunities to discuss most of the major issues facing faculty in U.S. postsecondary education today. In some cases, solutions were found to local problems, but solutions and products were less important than the process of faculty development, especially its productive conversations.

In the eyes of its participants—the faculty, who were its focus and its beneficiaries—QUE was a success. They found it valuable for the conversations with colleagues, for connections with their two- and four-year partners, and for the resources it offered them. These are their reflections in their own words.

Conversation With Colleagues

- "What did QUE do best? [It] provided a forum for people from different parts of the country to share ideas."

- "The most important thing . . . was the interaction with the other schools in our cluster and across the nation. It was also quite obvious that we all shared many of the same concerns, but often approached them differently."

- "I am glad that I had the opportunity to participate in the program. I found it useful and stimulating. . . . For me it represented a good opportunity for faculty development, to grow more aware of my own teaching practices, to get to know other practitioners in my field that otherwise I would not have met. It was a positive experience indeed."

- "QUE began as a somewhat fuzzy Utopian project that evolved over time, after many trials and tribulations, into a fine faculty development project. We rarely have time to pause and talk about instruction with colleagues from other institutions. . . . Thanks for the ride."

- "Time is always an element of limitation for participation. One thing that QUE allowed us to do is to legitimize the time and effort for the process, which we are incorporating into our educational process. Change is hard—something that I saw as a result of this process. And a process it is."

Two- and Four-Year Connections

- "I think QUE was a real success for my department, in large part because we were already discussing matters that the QUE initiative then gave us an incentive to focus and collaborate with community college colleagues on."

- "I think building the bridge across the two-year/four-year school divide was valuable. . . . I observed several institutions realizing the work is the same work and the need to collaborate is a good step forward."

Resources

- "One unforeseen benefit to QUE was the terrific aid it was for self-assessment for the SACS [Southern Association of Colleges and Schools] accreditation process, which occurred while we were involved with QUE."

- "I appreciated my experiences and value what it helped me bring into the classroom."

- "I feel fortunate to have had this experience—thank you! I benefited not only personally (from making the acquaintance of some pretty terrific people) but also professionally from the conferences and materials that were developed and shared."

- "[QUE] 1) provided some excellent consultants and experts in the disciplines to facilitate discussion groups and give presentations. 2) . . . plenty of time to interact with others in the same discipline. . . . I appreciate the opportunity to have grown professionally through the QUE experience."

- "[QUE] defined a pedagogy for learning outcomes and the necessity for their use."

- "QUE provided the resources I needed to attain my goal of contacting other instructors across the U.S. to exchange information on student content and performance objectives."

Nevertheless, despite success and wishes that QUE would continue ("I would like to be part of QUE II, which seems to me to be a very good idea," wrote one faculty member), reflection reveals flaws in design and execution that emulators can learn from. In the hope of encouraging other institutions to embark on the QUE process, and of giving them the advantages of our hindsight, we discuss next the trials and tribulations we encountered and offer recommendations for success.

1) Involve high-level administrators throughout the project.

Projects such as QUE that seek to change fundamental attitudes and actions must involve administrators at a level high enough to command some degree of compliance. Coburn (2003) suggests including four interrelated dimensions: depth, sustainability, spread, and shift in ownership.

For depth, are underlying pedagogical principles embodied in such a way that faculty engage students in using the materials and tasks? For sustainability, do changes persist over time? Is assessment of learning outcomes becoming the norm for the involved faculty in all their courses? For spread, do the underlying beliefs and practices extend to other faculty in the department, and is there an impact on reward, recognition, and incentive policies in the department? For shift in reform ownership, are changes in practices in QUE departments adopted more widely in other departments?

Although we would like the answers to Coburn's questions to be a resounding yes, QUE's success—varied largely according to the involvement of high-level administrators. We know now and would like to stress for emulators that they must be involved from the beginning—this means right from the selection of institutions, especially when outside funding is involved. Administrators at the provost, dean, and department chair levels should be invited personally to meetings with the project director and asked to commit not only their faculty but also their own time to the project. An astute project director will know what pressures are facing the institutions that want to be involved so that he or she can show administrators how the project will assist with accreditation reviews, legislative mandates for assessment, and curriculum revision. Most clusters saw QUE as an opportunity to continue or enhance work they were already engaged in. We should not lose sight of the ultimate objective of providing a supportive learning environment for student success.

These administrators should be responsible for selecting faculty so that they are committed from the beginning—faculty should not attend meetings because they're the only ones available that weekend. Selection of course depends on a clear understanding of the project's aims and purposes, which reinforces the need for thorough initial explanation by the project director.

Administrators should be kept abreast of developments throughout the project. Dates should be scheduled for their attendance at national or regional meetings, and a special session should be arranged to explain progress, especially at the final meeting, so that they know what is necessary to continue the project's work. The evaluators of QUE, Policy Studies Associates, repeatedly urged the participation of administrators, but it was sporadic, except for department chairs who were team members.

Involving administrators continuously would help with disseminating the benefits of QUE. One faculty member highlighted the issue:

In addition, involving more than one institution-level administrator at each institution will assuage if not prevent the anxiety felt by faculty when a president, provost, or dean leaves. If it is clear that the administration at a high level knows about the probable effect of a leadership change on the project, then steps can be taken to maintain continuity. At least two QUE clusters were deeply affected by abrupt changes not cushioned by thoughtful intervention.

2) Select and match two- and four-year partners carefully.

Administrator involvement throughout the project applies especially to the selection of community colleges to match with four-year institutions. Of the nine QUE clusters, only the two Maryland clusters and the University of Nevada–Reno were natural partners, in the sense that they had established feeding patterns for transfer students. All the Georgia clusters had different problems—plural campuses at Georgia Perimeter College, mismatches and lack of communication in the others—that might have been resolved with either the formation of different partnerships or with extensive preparation before the project began. The California State Universities at Long Beach and Fullerton are situated in the midst of numerous postsecondary institutions so that they deal with a web of transfer relationships instead of a straight line. This problem might have been resolved with involvement of administrators and commitment to work with only one partner that shared the largest number of transfer students.

Community college faculty need special support so that they do not feel disrespected by their four-year colleagues. As a faculty member commented, "the work is the same work." Helping them to take an active role is the job of the project director and the facilitators of meeting groups. More involvement from these leaders might have allowed community college faculty to realize that level 16 standards are important to them because they need to show their students the expectations they will be facing in the upper division.

3) Work with administrators for reward, recognition, and incentive policies for teaching.

Community college faculty need encouragement and support to participate in projects like QUE, but university faculty also need support. Many of the faculty who rejected involvement in QUE—and, it must be admitted, some participants—feared that paying attention to their teaching to the extent required by learning-centered pedagogy would jeopardize their chances for tenure and promotion. Four-year faculty are tenured and promoted based on three aspects of their work: research, teaching, and community service. The perception is widespread that research is all that really matters.

According to Coburn (2003), for the successful spread of an initiative such as QUE that involves a cultural transformation, there has to be a positive impact on the reward, recognition, and incentive policies in the department and the institution. Sustainable cultural change only occurs incrementally and on a small scale, but it does happen, particularly when people engage collectively in the process at all phases. Once the change becomes theirs, the faculty become the change agents. But to be successful, administrators have to recognize contributions to student learning as an important part of the reward system.

State institutions are often the source of teachers for K–12 schools. Conversations at QUE national meetings frequently focused on the quality of teaching, with the realization that letters and science faculty are responsible for future teachers' content knowledge. Some of the standards written by QUE clusters were specifically for courses where future teachers predominate. Good teaching in these courses reverberates through the educational system, for K–12 teachers teach the way they were taught. Needless to say, improved teaching at the postsecondary level would produce better-prepared students coming into colleges and universities.

This is only one argument for enlarging the role of teaching in tenure and promotion reviews. The literature on the scholarship of teaching abounds in arguments supporting teaching as equally important as research in modern universities. What projects like QUE can do is involve administrators in discussions with faculty to design systems where teaching is acknowledged, fostered, and rewarded. For example, deans or provosts could provide discretionary funds to support faculty involved in initiatives like QUE.

4) Explain the structure and financial arrangements to all participants.

All participants in a large-scale project like QUE should know the structure of the project, including details such as the amount of money available to each unit (or cluster, in QUE's case). Institutional administrators have the responsibility of working with their financial departments, which are notorious for delaying projects with bureaucratic procedures, but cluster coordinators have a similar responsibility to ensure that all cluster participants know where the money is and who gets it. Several clusters were creative in their use of QUE funds, but some were almost immobilized by inability to access them.

Deans and provosts can provide discretionary funds to support faculty involved in initiatives such as QUE. In particular, administrators for a local cluster of two- and four-year institutions could mount an initiative such as QUE at relatively modest cost (as Susan Albertine demonstrated in Chapter 6). Recommended expenses include one-day retreats where faculty can participate in a workshop format facilitated by disciplinary experts.

5) Set goals and schedules for expected work.

The QUE leadership had a utopian view of participants' capacity to fulfill their obligations, especially between national meetings. The leadership thought that it was enough to explain at national meetings what was expected and that cluster coordinators would see that expectations were met. Increased communication with cluster leaders (including special meetings for them) was needed, but even more, the leadership should have specified a timetable for expected work.

Clusters should be given a schedule for expected meetings between national meetings; a structure for those meetings, including general cluster meetings and meetings of discipline subgroups; a deadline for expected products; and directions about sharing standards and the like with non-QUE colleagues.

6) Make explicit the value of outcomes (standards) for all institutions.

This is a corollary to fostering the participation of community colleges and using the cluster work productively. A major emphasis should be on the importance of standards (outcomes) to the two- and four-year institutions, both individually and to ensure a smooth transfer process. Clusters should be encouraged to use curriculum maps (the super matrix) jointly, so that community colleges can see where their courses overlap with those at the four-year institution, or where there are gaps at both institutions.

The significance of learning outcomes for students and faculty depends a great deal on how seriously they are viewed as requirements in courses and programs. The QUE project attempted to forge substantive links among the three curricular levels that operate in the academy: individual courses, programs of study at the department level, and general education programs at the institutional level. The links are the learning outcomes.

7) Appoint a communications facilitator from the beginning.

The QUE project struggled for three years until our program officer at ExxonMobil Foundation suggested we hire a communications facilitator and apply to the foundation for the necessary additional funds. Administrators and faculty have quite enough to do in a large-scale project without being responsible for communicating with more than 100 participants (albeit through cluster coordinators for the most part) and another 10–15 consultants. A communications facilitator not only sends out notices about meetings and collects ideas for meeting agendas, but also distributes pertinent references to journal and newspaper articles. He or she acts as a clearinghouse for information within the project and brings information into its network.

Since an initiative such as QUE is multi-departmental, if a local cluster of two- and four-year institutions wanted to start a similar project, a director of assessment or of a teaching and learning center could be an appropriate communicator and facilitator.

Although exchanges of information and materials were a highlight of the national meetings for many participants, listservs were not effectively utilized, possibly because faculty do not think of their computers as an access route to their colleagues in general, as opposed to email messages to individuals. Listservs are an economical means to exchange assignments, assessments, and curriculum revisions, and some way of encouraging their use should be found.

8) Train participants as proselytizers.

Participants in QUE had mixed success in introducing standards and learning-centered pedagogy to their colleagues. This is partially the responsibility of institutional administrators, who should work with cluster coordinators to arrange congenial settings where QUE participants can explain how explicit outcomes and the conversation they entail contribute to intentional teaching and learning. However, QUE leaders could have scheduled a workshop discussion at each national meeting about strategies and tactics for proselytizing. The success of some clusters in prompting emulation (especially of assignments and assessments) among their peers could be analyzed and communicated. As it is, in some clusters standards-based education will not get the department and institutional support it needs to be sustained.

9) Employ discipline-specific consultants from the beginning— and use them.

When QUE introduced discipline consultants in 2002, faculty began to feel the benefits of QUE as professional development. They saw the standards as tools of their discipline, rather than ends in themselves, connecting them to rubrics, assignments, and assessments in their own disciplines.

The time to this realization might have been shortened by introducing consultants from the beginning, thus making performance levels and alignment of standards and assignments more accessible than they were. At one level, the process of drafting standards is essentially the same in all disciplines, especially to those familiar with the process; but to a historian or a biologist, the differences loom much larger than the similarities.

The QUE consultants might have played a larger role if they had been part of the project initially. The process of developing standards would clearly have been easier and consultants could have visited clusters where progress was stalled or nonexistent in a specific discipline as well as encouraged the use of the listservs by posting weekly teaching ideas. They could also have paid particular attention to community college faculty in their disciplines and helped to bolster their participation, especially in the development of level 16 standards.

There is an advantage in connecting with national projects at the disciplinary level such as the Carnegie Academy for the Scholarship of Teaching and Learning. Administrators who would like to emulate QUE at their institutions should ask their faculty to inquire with disciplinary associations about similar national initiatives.

10) Provide discipline-specific, practical help for participants.

Faculty may consider themselves abstract thinkers, but when they are thinking about teaching and students, they reach as eagerly as any K–12 teacher for Monday morning help. Such help must be discipline specific, although crosscutting competencies may be included. Among QUE's successes were the contributions of a discipline to general education and the consciousness faculty developed about writing across the curriculum. The QUE leadership should have designed the national meetings so that participants went home with at least one practical idea that could be adapted for their circumstances.

If the discipline consultants had been present from the beginning to provide these ideas, we might have dealt with some issues that were forced out by time. Chief among these is the poor state of students' reading skills. Repeatedly, faculty complained about how poorly their students read and how little experience they bring to postsecondary institutions. One history faculty member expressed his dismay when a student told him he was reading a complete book for the first time. Faculty were crying out for specialists who could teach students to read in each specific discipline.

Conclusion

Although these reflections may draw attention to the less successful aspects of QUE, they should not discourage future projects of this kind. Postsecondary education in the U.S. is quickly shifting to the direction QUE is pointing; similar projects will profit from the mistakes we made by not repeating them.

The major lesson we learned is to support faculty in every way possible so that they can develop professionally within their institutions and within their disciplines for the benefit of their students.

References

Coburn, C. E. (2003, August/September). Rethinking scale: Moving beyond numbers to deep and lasting change. *Educational Researcher, 32*(6), 3–12.

Appendix A

The Quality in Undergraduate Education (QUE) project began in early 1997 as an extension of K–12 standards development into postsecondary education by the Education Trust, Inc., which has been involved in standards development since 1995, and the National Association of System Heads (NASH). It seemed logical to extend the notion of developing standards—written public statements of expectations and outcomes—to postsecondary institutions, where they would have similar effects on educational quality as at the K–12 level: focus the curriculum on student learning, provide a yardstick for the quality and content of courses, and serve as a basis for assessment.

Feasibility Meeting, March 27, 1997

After intensive study of available writing on the subject of standards, or outcomes, we decided to put our ideas before a task group. On March 27, 1997, we convened a group consisting of the following individuals:

- Barbara Cambridge, then assessment coordinator at the American Association for Higher Education

- Helen Giles-Gee, then associate vice chancellor for academic affairs in the University of Maryland System

- Ronald J. Henry, provost at Georgia State University

- Joyce Justus, then special assistant to the president at the University of California–Santa Cruz

- James L. Ratcliff, director of the National Center on Postsecondary Teaching, Learning, and Assessment

- Six staff members from the Education Trust and NASH

At that meeting we asked the group to consider standards for writing in two major areas—science and history. We hoped to use writing as an indicator of cognitive and intellectual knowledge and skills. We chose science and history as two poles—writing is the essence of history, but in science it is often considered antithetical to the precision desired in mathematical models. We believed, however, that being able to write in science would be a fair test of deep understanding. Although our thinking changed about writing, our focus on the relationship of two- and four-year institutions did not.

The task group encouraged our project to varying degrees. James Ratcliff believed that standards would be institution specific because American postsecondary education provides opportunities for students of all levels—a B.A. from one institution does not mean the same as a B.A. from another. Others thought the campuses of a large state university should aim for equal quality in their degrees.

We emerged from the meeting determined to proceed. We would focus our recruitment efforts on state systems, not single campuses, and would ask participating institutions to join in pairs—a four-year campus and its feeder community college.

State Systems K–16 Councils Summer Meeting, 1997

State Systems K–16 councils were organized by NASH and the Education Trust to focus the major state education policy forces on the academic achievement of poor and minority students at all levels K–16. The K–16 councils consisted of leaders and staff from the state department of education, state universities, state boards of regents, state boards of education, statewide business committees on education, legislative and governors' advisors on education, and committees or boards that coordinate educational institutions at the state level. The State System K–16s held meetings twice a year, in the summer and in conjunction with the Education Trust's annual national conference in November.

To test interest in the idea of standards-setting at the two- and four-year postsecondary level, we proposed the Quality in Undergraduate Education project to a group of representatives from California, Vermont, Nevada, Texas, Maryland, Oregon, Missouri, and Georgia. Although skepticism about standards at the postsecondary level was expressed, the group saw enough merit in approaching the issue through graduation standards for writing in the sciences and history to offer encouragement. They agreed that it would be advisable to select an institution from those composing the state four-year system and identify a major feeder community college to that institution, then write to the presidents of both institutions. The first meeting of a volunteer group of institutions would take place at the Education Trust's annual national conference in Washington, DC, in November 1997.

Recruitment, Summer and Fall 1997

The Education Trust staff led by Ronald Henry and Janis Somerville (staff to NASH) prepared a prospectus and call for participation in two forms: a 12-page fully argued and documented paper, and a 2-page summary. This was then sent to all the state systems who attended the summer meeting. We were looking for six clusters of institutions to volunteer.

In these documents we were still talking about standards for writing in history and science because we believed that standards for writing would prove to be a lever to improve the quality of undergraduate education across the board. (Writing as a separate area did not survive the next meeting of QUE.) A major obstacle to participation for some institutions was the lack of financial support. We had to ask institutions to pay travel costs for team members to attend QUE meetings and to contribute faculty and administrator time to work on campus.

The Education Trust Annual National Conference, November 1997

A large number of institutions sent representatives to the inaugural QUE meeting, held the morning of the initial day of the Education Trust's annual conference. The program included an introduction to QUE, a short history of standards at the K–12 level to provide context, and (after discussion) the development of a single standards statement so participants could experience the kind of thinking needed to describe outcomes.

We decided to drop writing as the focus of the standards. We found that the presidents, provosts, and deans had asked directors of writing institutes, programs, or centers to attend the meeting—mostly in addition to, but in some cases instead of, disciplinary faculty. Because we were aiming at standards in disciplines, we thought it better to focus attention solidly on them and introduce writing as a standard within the disciplines.

The meeting was encouraging about the future of QUE, and as a result, the Education Trust and NASH wrote a preliminary proposal to the Fund for the Improvement of Postsecondary Education (FIPSE) for three years of funding. In the proposal there were seven partners—the state universities of Georgia, Maryland, Missouri, and Nevada; Portland State University; California State University–Long Beach; and the University of Vermont—each with at least one partner community college. Unfortunately the proposal did not get past the preliminary stage and QUE remained unfunded.

K–16 Council Leaders' Meeting, March 1998

By March 1998, it was clear that a core group was determined to see QUE thrive, despite lack of funding. This core group consisted of Georgia State University, with Georgia Perimeter College, led by Provost Ronald Henry; California State University–Long Beach, with Long Beach City College, led by Dean Dorothy Abrahamse; and the University of Nevada–Reno, with Truckee Meadows Community College, led by Vice President William Cathey. The other partners in the FIPSE proposal were reluctant to proceed without external funding.

The group felt strongly that we should begin with standards at a working meeting during a summer weekend. Bill Cathey offered the use of facilities at the University of Nevada–Reno's School of Education without charge and suggested that inexpensive accommodations could be arranged at Reno hotels.

The First Standards-Writing Meeting, University of Nevada–Reno, August 1998

Thus the first QUE standards were written by participants from these three clusters only. The 23 faculty produced standards at the two-year level in biology; two- and four-year standards in chemistry; and preliminary sketches of standards in history and physics. To our surprise, faculty from the three pairs of campuses wanted to work together to produce a single document in their disciplines. We had carefully avoided the question of interinstitutional standards because we did not want to raise the suspicion that we were trying to develop national standards for postsecondary education. But with colleagues from the six institutions (3 two-year and 3 four-year) present, the groups decided to cooperate on their documents.

The Education Trust Annual National Conference, November 1998

The active participation of representatives of professional associations was urged on the Education Trust, NASH, and the senior advisor, Ronald Henry, during the Reno meeting, so we invited representatives to the November meeting. Noralee Frankel from the American Historical Association (AHA) and Jay Labov of the National Research Council brought the perspectives of professional historians and biologists, respectively. Labov continued as consultant in biology for the life of QUE. A number of faculty participated in presenting QUE and its work to an extended session at the Education Trust conference.

K–16 Council Leaders' Meeting, March 1999

This meeting marked the low point in QUE's history. Progress had stalled. Standards were not being developed beyond the point arrived at in Reno in August 1998, discussions on campuses with faculty did not seem productive (possibly because no one was responsible for conducting them and recording the conclusions), and there seemed no hope of funding QUE. Despite these setbacks, the core group did agree to meet again at the University of Nevada–Reno under the same conditions.

Spring and Early Summer, 1999

In fact, conditions did not remain the same, for funding became available for the summer 1999 meeting. Ronald Henry and Ruth Mitchell met with program officers at the Pew Charitable Trusts in Philadelphia in late March and submitted a three-page preproposal to Russell Edgerton, then director of the education department at Pew, on April 9. The response was encouraging and a full proposal was submitted in September.

By June, Patte Barth of the Education Trust had reestablished contact with Edward Ahnert of the then Exxon Education Fund, who had funded projects when both Barth and Mitchell were working at the Council for Basic Education. Barth was able to tell Ahnert that because of interest from the Pew Charitable Trusts, the number of QUE partnerships in Georgia was increasing—Fort Valley State University and Valdosta State University were interested in joining QUE with their feeder community colleges, the University of Nevada was thinking of launching QUE statewide so its two campuses and their feeder community colleges would be involved, and Towson University was also interested in joining QUE to produce standards in English. The Education Trust letter requested a small grant of $45,000 to assist with the summer meeting to be held in Reno in August 1999.

The ExxonMobil Foundation provided the funds. It was QUE's big break. By the end of 1999, we had funding for three years from the Pew Charitable Trusts and had submitted a long and definitive proposal to the fledgling ExxonMobil Foundation.

The Second Annual Summer Meeting, University of Nevada–Reno, 1999

The grant of $45,000 from the ExxonMobil Foundation enlarged QUE. Where 23 faculty from three clusters had met in Reno the year before, we now had almost twice that number from three clusters in Georgia, two in Nevada, and one each in California and Maryland. We added English to the list of disciplines, making five. In addition to the Education Trust staff, several participant observers and consultants were present at the Reno meeting, including Susan Albertine, then vice provost of undergraduate studies at Temple University, who later acted as consultant in English to QUE and then project director.

Although only four of the original attendees of the 1998 national meeting were also at the final meeting in Denver in April 2004, many more faculty were constant attendees from 1999–2000 onward.

Progress at the second Reno conference varied according to the length of time the participants had been involved and therefore how developed the standards were and how many new participants there were. The biologists had brought student work and began trying to describe it, although they also had new colleagues in their group who needed orientation. They revised their level 14 standards and extended them to level 16. They even wrote tentative performance descriptors for papers, examinations, and lab reports at levels 14 and 16. The historians also brought student work and engaged in strenuous discussions about quality, while the all new English group was able to work together to produce preliminary standards.

The ExxonMobil Foundation Proposal, November 1999

A definitive "federal" organization for QUE was detailed in the proposal to Exxon-Mobil. The structure followed these policies:

- QUE would expand to a total of 10 partnerships in four states: four in Georgia, and two each in Maryland, Nevada, and California.

- We would confine our standards work to six academic disciplines: biology, chemistry, physics, English, history, and mathematics.

- In each discipline, we would write two- and four-year standards, both for the major and for general education.

- Policy Studies Associates would conduct an ongoing formative evaluation and a summative evaluation at the end of each of four years, funded by a combination of the Pew Charitable Trusts and the ExxonMobil Foundation.

- Georgia State University Foundation would be the fiscal agent for QUE.

- The Education Trust would subcontract for services to QUE.

- The leadership would consist of Ronald Henry and Tim Crimmins at Georgia State University (Crimmins was succeeded by Susan Albertine in 2002) with a cluster coordinator in each partnership to ensure that standards-setting activities continued on the campuses.

- Representatives of professional associations would be actively recruited to advise on the standards.

The Education Trust Annual National Conference, November 1999

This meeting continued the work begun in Reno in 1998. New participants needed orientation, but each disciplinary group made progress from its starting point. This was the first meeting evaluated by Policy Studies Associates.

As a result of this meeting, the English group sent draft standards for level 16 (the baccalaureate level) by email to QUE participants. In January 2000, Towson University published "Learning Outcomes of the Towson University Bachelor of English" on its web site and noted that the document "is largely the result of a QUE workshop, a collaborative project to establish learning outcomes for American universities."

Historians circulated some examples of standards through Noralee Frankel of the AHA, but in general they remained focused on writing standards for individual courses, such as History 301 at California State University–Long Beach and a capstone course at Georgia State University.

K–16 Council Leaders' Meeting, March 2000

By coincidence, QUE was back in Reno, although at a different hotel and under different auspices. From this point on, QUE meetings were held separately from either K–16 council leaders' meetings or the annual Education Trust conference. This decision was made so that faculty and administrators did not have to be absent from their campuses more than three days.

The March 2000 meeting included eight of the ten proposed clusters (the second California and Maryland campuses had not been selected). The meeting focused on QUE's purpose through invited speaker Peter Ewell of the National Center for Higher Education Management Systems, who described statewide assessment in higher education and made clear that standards, or outcomes, are essential for assessment.

The Funded QUE Project

The QUE project received $994,000 from The Pew Charitable Trusts and $1,014,000 from the ExxonMobil Foundation. To reorganize QUE, a special meeting was held in June 2000. It included QUE leadership, Policy Studies Associates, representatives of the funders, and the coordinators of the 10 clusters. Dates and locations of future meetings were fixed, and a mechanism was established for maintaining the QUE archives.

In September 2000, at the first national meeting of the funded and reorganized QUE, the leadership declared as a policy that participants new to QUE would receive a separate orientation because veteran participants wanted to proceed from their point of development rather than return to the beginning and fight the same battles repeatedly. Participants developed a FAQ (Frequently Asked Questions) document to explain QUE to new participants and to the increasing numbers of faculty who wanted to know what QUE was about.

During this year, the need for a communications specialist or facilitator became obvious, as the leadership struggled to maintain communication with and among 10 clusters. The ExxonMobil Foundation approved a request for a small additional grant, and a communications specialist was appointed. Gloria John took over the post in 2002.

The Tipping Point: Discipline Consultants

Until 2002, the meetings followed a single agenda for all participants, usually a plenary speaker with breakout sessions for reporting on progress toward the standards and further plenary sessions on topics such as performance standards and crosscutting competencies. In March 2002, this pattern changed. The meeting was organized with separate agendas for the academic disciplines—biology, chemistry, English, history, and mathematics—with national consultants assisting each group. Only two plenary sessions, including the Friday night welcoming dinner, were included.

Not only did this become the pattern for the four succeeding meetings of QUE (September 2002, February and September 2003, April 2004), it also produced positive responses from the participants. "This is the best meeting I have attended" was a common response not only to the March 2002 meeting but to the subsequent ones as well.

Clearly 2002 was a tipping point for QUE. Earlier meetings with their repeated attempts to explain standards or outcomes, their cajoling and persuading faculty that standards help student learning and do not threaten academic freedom, their attempts to provide models and arguments—all these were like an engine grinding slowly and erratically up the hill until 2002, when the summit was reached and a clear road lay ahead. At that point, faculty participants seized QUE and owned it through the discipline groups.

As a consequence of following that road, QUE participants have changed their teaching and experienced the encouraging results documented in this book. It took a long time to establish the pattern of working with discipline consultants in pursuit of outcomes, rubrics, and assessments, but change at the postsecondary level is notoriously slow. QUE's experiences may help others move faster.

Appendix B

The following standards (outcomes) exemplify what the QUE participants produced. More examples in each discipline can be found on the QUE web site: www.gsu .edu/que.

Biology

The following is a complete set of standards for level 14, biology majors; level 14, non-majors; and level 16, biology majors. These standards were widely copied and/or adapted by other QUE clusters. The details of knowledge and skills expected at the three levels will demonstrate how standards (outcomes) shape a rigorous postsecondary course of study.

I. Level 14, Biology Majors

Standards for the Major in Biology at Level 14

A draft version developed in 2002 by Barbara Baumstark (Georgia State University), Therese M. Poole (Georgia State University), Virginia Michelich (Georgia Perimeter College), and Sheryl Shanholtzer (Georgia Perimeter College).

In recent years, the field of biology has entered a state of unprecedented growth and opportunity. The development of new technology has enabled biologists to ask fundamental questions that appeared insoluble a few years ago. Because of the rapid accumulation of new information, the knowledge base available to the student of biology is constantly changing. Those seeking to develop standards for the biological sciences must build a set of criteria that encompass the theoretical framework and scientific information essential to the modern biologist, while at the same time maintaining the flexibility to accommodate and evaluate new hypotheses as they arise.

The successful identification of learning outcomes that apply to all students in the biological sciences will ensure that these students possess the knowledge and skills necessary to maintain a high level of scientific literacy throughout their lives. The following three steps are each essential for this to occur.

1) Definition of Standards

   - *Scientific process.* At what level should students be familiar with the hypotheses, experimental techniques, and data analysis that have formed the foundation supporting currently accepted scientific principles?

   - *Content.* What information are students expected to accumulate during the course of their education?

   - *Application.* What skills do students need to develop in order to use and extend their accumulated information base throughout their lives?

2) Implementation Strategies

   - How are the standards being addressed through the current curriculum?

   - What new courses or initiatives are needed to meet the standards?

3) Assessment Procedures

   - What tools are used to evaluate the success of implementation strategies?

   - How will the results of the evaluation process be interpreted?

Definition of Standards

The goal of any set of standards should be to ensure that students possess a defined core of information coupled with the skills to use that information as well as the expertise to evaluate its validity. Students will be equipped with the ability to use and extend their scientific knowledge base throughout their lives if that knowledge base is presented in a context that stresses:

- Scientific inquiry, reasoning, and communication

- History of biology and its past and present impact on society

- Information content in biology

Like the organisms that are the subjects of biological study, disciplines in biology can be viewed as continuously evolving entities that rely on the mutual interaction of many different components. At the root of every scientific discipline, including biology, is an acknowledgement of the importance of *scientific inquiry.* Scientific inquiry forms the support structure responsible for the development of each discipline. The information obtained from scientific inquiry, the generation of new principles to explain this information, and the communication of the results to others strengthens the entire scientific process, thereby fueling further inquiry.

The ability to convey the true nature of scientific inquiry is greatly enhanced by an understanding of the historical and social contexts that provide the settings for scientific discovery. A thorough background in the *history and nature of science* and in the ways that *science and technology* impact human society provides students with the necessary perspective to critically evaluate the scientific basis for debates involving developments in the biological sciences. In order to appreciate the quantitative aspects of biology, it is essential that the curriculum apply the principles of mathematics, chemistry, and physics to the theoretical foundations of biological processes. This integration of biology with other related disciplines is a crucial element for the mastery of biology.

Students should be informed of the *personal and societal impact of developments in biology.* The developments interface with many aspects of human life, such as cloning and the potential for genetic testing and gene therapy, human health and emerging infectious diseases, and environmental concerns.

Mastery of scientific concepts requires a minimal facility with basic scientific vocabulary. Students who cannot define a *ribosome,* for instance, will be unable to comprehend the process of protein synthesis. Therefore, it is essential that students exhibit a familiarity with currently accepted hypotheses, observations, and other material that make up the *information content in biology.* However, just as the commitment of vocabulary lists to memory does not provide one with mastery of a foreign language, so memorization of terminology outside an appropriate scientific context will not endow students with a lasting proficiency in the biological sciences. To obtain fluency in biology, students must continuously reinforce their skills by applying their newly achieved knowledge to the understanding of hypotheses and the interpretation of experimental observations. They must also be given the opportunity for hands-on participation in the research process. This will give them an appreciation for the events that lead to the accumulation of scientific knowledge. Furthermore, it will provide them with the ability to evaluate the strengths and limitations of scientific evidence that is used to support new hypotheses that may be proposed in the future.

Implementation Strategies

Two elements are vital to the successful implementation of undergraduate standards:

- Expectations for levels 13–16 must build on the foundations established in K–12.

- Facility in biology must be accompanied by an understanding of processes traditionally assigned to other disciplines, including mathematics, chemistry, and physics.

Assessment

In its simplest form, assessment involves an evaluation of instructional outcomes; that is, it determines the degree to which the standards have been met. Deficiencies in reaching the goals set by the standards committee promote a reevaluation of many aspects of the standards process, raising the following questions:

- Are the strategies used for implementing the standards providing students with adequate opportunities to gain a thorough understanding of biology?

- Are the standards themselves realistic?

- Are the assessment tools providing an accurate measurement of the students' knowledge?

Academic Standards

The information content in the biological sciences has traditionally covered such a broad range of topics that it has been difficult to identify with precision the "facts" that every biology student should know. As a consequence, two students who have obtained a comprehensive education in the biological sciences might exhibit distinctly different levels of familiarity with specific details about a given organism. However, information recently obtained through the application of new technological innovations (including molecular and cellular cloning techniques, high resolution microscopy, and automated DNA sequence analysis) is making it clear that biological systems are better defined by their similarities than by their differences. The scientific study of virtually any living organism can be addressed from one or more of the following perspectives. The information gained from one perspective does not stand alone, but overlaps with and modulates the knowledge base of each perspective.

- Evolution and diversity

- Reproduction and heredity

- Cell structure and function

- Molecular processes
- Organismal form and function
- Interdependence of organisms and their environment

In Standard 3, a short description of each perspective is given along with the knowledge base expected of all students who major in biology. Typically, an undergraduate biology student would be expected to accumulate this information in the first or second year of study (by year 14). With this knowledge as a foundation, the student would then be able to focus on specific areas of interest, applying the basic concepts learned in his or her general studies to address questions in more specialized biological subdisciplines (e.g., microbial pathogenesis, toxicology, immunology, benthic ecology). The material outlined in Standard 3 is not static. Its content would be expected to evolve in response to new scientific discoveries, so that certain topics may diminish in importance or vanish altogether while others take on a new significance for those wishing to become literate in modern biology.

Standard 1: Scientific Inquiry, Reasoning, and Communication

Students will be able to:

- Read scientific literature for content
- Critique and analyze claims of others in a scientific context
- Ask scientific questions of their world
- Construct reasonable hypotheses
- Design and conduct investigations about a variety of biological problems
- Perform laboratory skills and procedures
- Formulate and defend alternative explanations and models on the basis of evidence
- Communicate effectively in oral and written forms demonstrating an awareness of different learning styles
- Use basic equipment in laboratory courses and demonstrate awareness of specific technology that is used to carry out biological investigations
- Understand basic principles behind major biotechnology
- Use computers for data analysis, literature searches, and retrieval of data from reliable databases

Standard 2: History of Biology and Its Past and Present Impact on Society

Students will be able to:

- Analyze how progress in biology depends heavily on the political, social, economic, and cultural influences occurring within a society at any given time

- Discuss historical changes in biological theories over time

- Recognize the integration of mathematics, physics, chemistry, and geology into the study of biology

- Understand the impact of science and technology on the global society

- Discuss and identify ethical issues that new technology raises

- Demonstrate the application of biological concepts to personal issues, society, economics, technology, and ethical issues

Standard 3: Information Content in Biology

Students will be able to:

- Demonstrate knowledge of general principles and applications of biology

- Exhibit a functional understanding of biological forms, processes, and relationships

Evolution and Diversity: Underlying Principles

Evolution describes a process in which selection acts upon random changes to allow certain individuals to leave more offspring. When more of one progeny type is produced, this type will tend to dominate in future generations. Evolution results in *diversity* because different environments will have different selection pressures and thus individuals with different traits will be allowed to leave offspring in different environments. Evolution and diversity can apply to organisms, cells, viruses, or molecules.

Specific topics:

- Darwinian concepts
  - Modern theory: macroevolution, microevolution, prebiotic
  - Natural selection
  - Evidence
- Speciation and diversity
  - Systems of classification
  - Organism classification (plant, animal, prokaryotes, monera)
  - Endosymbiosis

- Evolutionary tree(s) and timeline
  - The Age of Microbes
  - Geological gradualism
  - Structural and reproductive adaptations
- Population genetics as a tool to study all of the above

Reproduction and Heredity: Underlying Principles

Reproduction involves replication, recombination, and partitioning of genetic material in all organisms. In higher organisms, mitosis and meiosis are essential for cellular and sexual reproduction, respectively, and have predictable genetic consequences.

Heredity involves the passage of traits from parents to progeny. The processes of inheritance and replication occur at the organismal, cellular, and molecular levels.

Specific topics:

- Classical genetics
  - Mendelian genetics
  - Other patterns of inheritance: epistasis, linkage, polygenics
  - Pedigree analysis
- Chromosome partitioning
  - Cell cycle: stages and regulation
  - Mitosis: apparatus and process
  - Meiosis: apparatus and process
  - Synapsis, crossing over
  - Prokaryotic binary fission
  - Sexual life cycle
  - Chromosome structure
  - Genome structure
- Information flow
  - Molecular basis of inheritance
  - DNA: structure, function, replication, types, and effects of mutation
  - RNA: structure and transcription and modifications from DNA
  - Translation of RNA message into protein: genetic code
- Genetics of viruses

Molecular Processes: Underlying Principles

Molecular processes, including molecular interactions and the synthesis of macromolecules, are governed by basic chemical and physical laws. Chemical and physical interactions, particularly covalent and non-covalent bonding patterns, have a significant effect on macromolecular structure and function. The application of thermodynamic principles to biochemical reactions can be used to characterize the processes that drive these reactions and predict the likelihood that they will be energetically feasible under cellular conditions. Enzyme kinetics can help to understand rates of reactions in cells.

Specific topics:

- Atomic structure: properties, structures, carbon compounds
- Chemical interactions
  - Covalent (polar/nonpolar) ionic
  - Hydrogen
  - Hydrophobic
- Energy
  - Potential/kinetic
  - Storage in ATP
  - Thermodynamics
  - Enzymes and activation energy
- Relationships between chemical reactions and energy
  - Glycolysis, fermentation
  - TCA cycle and respiration
  - Electron transport
  - Photosynthesis
- Regulation of cellular reactions: feedback

Cell Structure and Function: Underlying Principles

In both prokaryotes and eukaryotes, there is a clear relationship between *cell structure and function.* Single-celled organisms are capable of independent self-replication. Multicellular organisms are generally composed of collections of cells with specialized functions. The organelles present in eukaryotic cells play well-defined structural, metabolic, and protective roles.

Specific topics:

- Organelle structure and function from the nucleus on out
  - Nucleus
  - Membrane components: nucleus, ER, golgi, lysosomes, peroxisomes
  - Mitochondria
  - Chloroplasts
  - Vesicles
  - Cytoplasm
  - Vacuoles
  - Cytoskeleton
  - Movement of substances in cells
- Prokaryotes versus eukaryotes
  - Structure
  - Cell division
  - Metabolic pathways
  - Regulation of gene expression
- Exterior of cell
  - Cell membrane
  - Cell wall
  - Extracellular matrix
  - Transport into/out of cells
  - Signal transduction
- Differentiation
  - Sperm and egg structure
  - Fertilization
  - Cleavage, gastrulation, and formation of germ layers
  - Organogenesis

Organismal Form and Function: Underlying Principles

Basic anatomical structures and physiological processes play distinct roles in determining overall *organismal form and function*. Molecules and cells combine to form different tissues and organ systems, which interact with each other to enhance the efficiency and adaptability of the whole organism.

Specific topics:

- Unifying concepts
  - Energy source
  - Oxygen source/CO_2 removal
  - Water balance
  - N_2 waste removal
- Concerns of multicellular organisms
  - Circulation
  - Information transfer
  - Support
  - Movement
- Animals
  - Animal organ systems: form and function
  - Homeostasis
  - Interactions with environment
  - Reproduction and development
- Plants
  - Plant tissues (roots, shoots, leaves): form and function
  - Plant regulation
  - Adaptations to environment
  - Reproduction and development: cloning and alternation of generations

Interdependence of Organisms and Their Environment: Underlying Principles

Organisms interact with each other and the environment in complex ways. The *interdependence of organisms and their environment* can strongly influence the evolution and development of organisms and the composition of the populations to which they belong.

Specific topics:

- Organismal ecology
    - ⁓ Adaptations to ecosystem dynamics
    - ⁓ Abiotic factors, Law of Tolerance
    - ⁓ Organism responses to environmental variation
    - ⁓ Ecological niche
    - ⁓ Environmental cues and mating
- Population ecology
    - ⁓ Biotic potential and exponential growth
    - ⁓ Environmental resistance
    - ⁓ Density independent limits and boom-bust cycles
    - ⁓ Density dependent limits, logistics, population curves, and carrying capacity
    - ⁓ Population demographics
    - ⁓ Survivor strategies
    - ⁓ Human population growth
    - ⁓ Competitive mating and social behaviors
    - ⁓ Inclusive fitness and altruistic behavior
- Community ecology
    - ⁓ Geographical distribution of terrestrial and aquatic biomes
    - ⁓ Selection processes
    - ⁓ Intraspecific and interspecific community interactions
    - ⁓ Symbiotic relationships
- Ecosystem ecology
    - ⁓ Ecological succession
    - ⁓ Ecological pyramids and trophic levels
    - ⁓ Biogeochemical cycles (matter recycling)
    - ⁓ Alterations of biodiversity secondary to human activities

II. Level 14, Non-Majors

Proposed Standards for a Non-Majors Biology Course

Submitted to the QUE initiative by Barbara Baumstark (Georgia State University), Sheryl Shanholtzer (Georgia Perimeter College), and Virginia Michelich (Georgia Perimeter College) in September 2001.

Goals and Objectives

The primary objectives of a non-majors science course are:

- To introduce students to the process of scientific thinking

- To help students gain an appreciation for how science is conducted

- To provide a knowledge base in a particular scientific field that students can use as a foundation for lifelong learning in the sciences

Standards 1 and 2 are envisioned as having application to the biological sciences, as well as other scientific disciplines. Standard 3 is specific for biology and provides an overview of the informational content that can serve as the foundation for the implementation of Standards 1 and 2. Informational content provides the background knowledge required for a general understanding of scientific concepts, the tools which students must use to hone their skills in inquiry-based investigations, and the perspective for understanding the impact of science on society.

At most colleges and universities, non-science majors are given a great deal of flexibility in their choice of courses to fulfill their science requirements. The non-major at a typical undergraduate institution is allowed to choose among several disciplines, including (though not necessarily limited to) biology, chemistry, geology, and physics. Thus, unless there is a required multidisciplinary core science course in place, the informational content presented to non-majors will extend across the scientific spectrum.

With the recent explosion of knowledge in the biological sciences, the information base for biology has become so broad that it is nearly impossible to produce a set of standards with a precisely defined content requirement. However, certain fundamental concepts (listed in Standard 3) are expected to appear in any college level biology course. Programs requiring a general survey course in biology may seek to give uniform coverage to all of these concepts. Alternatively, other programs may opt to focus on a limited number of concepts as a way to give students in-depth exposure to the process of scientific inquiry. Such programs should still present the underlying principles behind these concepts in enough detail to ensure that students have the background knowledge necessary to achieve Standards 1 and 2.

Standard 1: Scientific Inquiry, Reasoning, and Communication

Students will be able to:

- Ask scientific questions of their world

- Demonstrate the ability to read and understand scientific literature written for the educated lay reader

- Critique and analyze claims of others in a scientific context

- Construct reasonable hypotheses

- Formulate and defend alternative explanations and models on the basis of evidence

- Communicate effectively in oral and written forms

- Use basic equipment in laboratory courses and demonstrate awareness of specific technology that is used to carry out biological investigations

- Use computers for data analysis, literature searches, and retrieval of data from reliable databases

Standard 2: History of Biology and Its Past and Present Impact on Society

Students will be able to:

- Analyze how progress in biology depends heavily on the political, social, economic, and cultural influences occurring within a society at any given time

- Discuss historical changes in biological theories over time

- Recognize the integration of mathematics, physics, chemistry, and geology into the study of biology

- Understand the impact of science and technology on the global society

- Discuss and identify ethical issues that new technology raises

- Demonstrate the application of biological concepts to personal issues, society, economics, technology, and ethical issues

Standard 3: Information Content in Biology

Explanatory statement: The following information is designed to serve as a guide to general biological concepts that can form the foundation for lifelong scientific literacy. It is anticipated that all biology courses will address the underlying principles in some form. However, the specific topics used to illustrate these principles may vary, depending on the area of biology that forms the focus for the course.

Concept 1: Life's Common Plan

Underlying principles: At first glance life seems to have so many forms, sizes, and activities that there appears to be little commonality among living organisms. However, all living things are made of fundamental units called cells. Cells are organized structures in which the activities necessary for the maintenance of life are carried out. Within their membranes they maintain their chemical integrity in the face of a changing environment. They obtain energy to power their activities and the materials that are required for growth, and they are able to rid themselves of the wastes generated by these activities.

Specific topics:

- Structural organization of cells
  - Prokaryotic/eukaryotic cells
- Basic cellular processes essential for sustaining life
  - Energy and nutrient requirements
  - Reproduction
  - Adaptation
- Response to environmental cues
  - Cell-cell interactions
  - Homeostasis
  - Response to external stimuli

Students will be able to:

- Compare and contrast prokaryotic and eukaryotic cell structure
- Explain strategies for acquiring energy and nutrients needed to sustain life
- Understand that reproduction ultimately occurs at the cellular level
- Describe how organisms respond to environmental stimuli

Concept 2: Continuation of Life (Genes, Chromosomes, and DNA)

Underlying principles: Although no single biological entity lasts forever, life in one form or another has existed on earth for approximately 3.5 billion years. For most organisms, the components of life are passed from one individual to another through the process of reproduction, with all of the information necessary to carry out life's processes being transmitted to the next generation. Reproduction includes heredity, the passage of traits from parent(s) to progeny.

Specific topics:

- Basic laws of inheritance
- Chromosomal basis of inheritance
  - Cell duplication
  - Formation of reproductive cells
- Molecular basis of inheritance
  - Chemical composition of DNA
  - DNA structure
  - DNA replication
  - Translation from DNA to protein
  - Mutation
- Human manipulation of genetic material

Students will be able to:

- Explain the basic processes of inheritance and expression of genes
- Describe the processes involved in duplication of cells and in formation of reproductive cells
- Understand that DNA is duplicated and determines the structure and function of proteins
- Explain how scientists use biotechnology for practical purposes

Concept 3: Physiological Processes

Underlying principles: Cells and all organisms, since they are made of cells, carry out their basic activities in similar ways. All rely on enzymes to catalyze chemical reactions. All must obtain concentrated energy and nutrients to power their activities, and they all have similar mechanisms for transporting materials into and out of the cell.

Specific topics:

- Energy and enzymes
  - Potential/kinetic
  - Storage in ATP
  - Enzymes as catalysts

- Energy transformation in living systems
  - Photosynthesis
  - Nutrition
  - Digestion
  - Respiration
- Transport
  - Transport into/out of cells: diffusion, osmosis, active transport
- Waste removal

Students will be able to:

- Define enzymes and relate their activity to their structure
- Explain why cells require energy and give examples of energy uses by cells
- Identify the sources of energy for plant and animal cells and discuss its release and storage within an organism
- Describe how materials enter and leave cells, distinguishing between active and passive processes
- Identify waste products, how they are produced, and mechanisms for removal

Concept 4: Adaptations of Life's Common Plan

Underlying principles: While all life exhibits similar modes of organization, shares information with succeeding generations through similar processes, and makes use of similar molecular and physiological mechanisms, the differences in life forms are often more evident to the observer than the similarities. This leads to scientific inquiry concerning both the extent of the variations and how they could have arisen from a common stock.

Specific topics:

- Evolution as an ongoing process
  - Mutation
  - Selection
- Results of evolution
- Biologists' scheme for organizing life

Students will be able to:

- Explain how mutation and selection are instruments of evolutionary processes and give examples that demonstrate evolution as an ongoing process

- Recognize that diversity is a result of the evolutionary process as organisms adapt to different environmental pressures

- Understand that scientists have a framework in place for grouping organisms according to ancestral relatedness and that this framework is constantly being refined and extended as new information becomes available

Concept 5: Connections Among Organisms and Between Organisms and Their Environment

Underlying principles: Organisms are discrete entities; however, they cannot and do not exist without interacting with their environment. They must obtain energy and supplies from the environment, some of which may come from or be passed to other organisms. They must also rid themselves of wastes, which then become additional components of the environment. Finally, they must deal with other organisms as they compete with and help each other.

Specific topics:

- Energy movement through organisms and the environment
- Material cycling through organisms and the environment
- Mutual support and dependence of organisms

Students will be able to:

- Describe the pathway of energy transfer from sunlight through primary producers and consumers to waste heat returned to the environment
- Explain how atoms pass back and forth between organisms and their environment
- Give examples of and describe interdependence among organisms

III. Level 16, Biology Major

Addendum to the Level 14 Standards That Extended Them Through Level 16

Barbara Baumstark (Georgia State University), March 2000

During the last half of the 20th century, scientific advances have caused the information base in biology to increase at an unprecedented rate. As a consequence, no student can be expected to become an expert in all areas of the biological sciences during four years of undergraduate education. An academic program that attempts to give equal priority indiscriminately to all biology subject matter will be forced to limit itself to a surface-level treatment of the field. On the other hand, a program that balances general content knowledge with an in-depth investigation of specialized topics gives students the opportunity to ask questions, evaluate alternative scientific theories, and take an active role in deciding the direction their education will take. This approach teaches students fundamental biological concepts and enables them to acquire the skills necessary to continue their exploration into the field of biology long after they complete their undergraduate education.

Ideally, biology instruction at the introductory level (level 14) provides students with a general body of scientific knowledge that serves as a foundation for further study in the field, along with the basic skills to use this knowledge in experimental situations. Then, as students progress to more advanced levels of study, they use this broad knowledge base to develop a deeper understanding of selected biological concepts. As their understanding of these concepts matures, students usually discover that their interests become focused in areas of increasing specialization. Thus, for most undergraduate majors, education in biology proceeds in three stages:

1) An introductory stage, where they learn general biological concepts

2) An intermediate stage, where they are exposed to several broad-based subdisciplines that serve as a foundation for subsequent specialization

3) An advanced stage, where they use the information they have accumulated to delve more deeply into a few limited areas that excite their curiosity

Immediately following the completion of level 14 coursework, undergraduate majors begin to receive more intensive instruction in several broad-based biology subdisciplines. The material learned at this intermediate stage of their programs can then serve as the foundation for subsequent specialization. Subdisciplines may include (but need not be limited to) animal/plant biology, biochemistry cell/molecular biology, genetics, and microbiology.

Students can gain content knowledge related to these subdisciplines in a variety of ways. For example, a single gateway series may cover all or a subset of topics in an integrated fashion. Alternatively, individual courses may be designed around a single subdiscipline. It is important to note that at any given undergraduate institution, variations in faculty research and instructional interests (which will influence the types of advanced courses available for undergraduates) may cause some subdisciplines to receive more emphasis than others.

As students progress to increasingly advanced levels, they find that their studies become focused into more specialized areas of concentration, especially as they identify specific topics that are of particular interest to them. Undergraduate biology majors can usually tailor their curriculum to fit their chosen area(s) of concentration by selecting from a variety of advanced elective courses. Depending on the courses they choose, two students may acquire distinctly different specialized content knowledge by the time they complete their level 16 coursework. However, as long as they have mastered fundamental biological concepts, developed critical thinking skills, and acquired proficiency in a research setting, each will graduate with the expertise necessary to become successful biologists, regardless of the area of specialization they ultimately choose.

Standards for Level 16 Performance

A top priority of any curriculum designed to meet level 16 standards, regardless of content material, is to ensure that students are provided with experiences that hone their skills in using, generating, and evaluating scientific information. Students should demonstrate the ability to:

- Form hypotheses, design experiments, collect data, and evaluate results

- Read and comprehend the current scientific literature

- Place reports of new discoveries into the context of previous scientific progress

- Develop an understanding of the impact of these discoveries on society

The following is an example of a standards-based undergraduate experience at Georgia State University. In this example, it is assumed that the student gradually develops an interest in molecular genetics, which ultimately becomes the preferred area of focus.

A Standards-Based Experience in Molecular Genetics

This example assumes that the student either entered the program with an interest in molecular genetics or became interested in exploring this field after the experiences of his or her level 14 coursework. As the student progresses through intermediate and ultimately advanced-level biology coursework, increasing numbers of elective courses can be selected that expand and extend his or her expertise in this field.

Introductory Stage (Level 14)

The student will meet Standards 1–5 as outlined in the Standards Document (8/98; revised 8/99). A course or set of courses will provide the basic content knowledge outlined in Standard 5. In addition, the student will be given experience in conducting laboratory experiments and using appropriate technology. He or she will be made aware of the historical context in which scientific advances are made, as well as the impact of these advances on society. The student will also be receiving instruction in the fundamental concepts of chemistry, mathematics, and other fields related to biology.

Intermediate Stage (Level 16)

The student will acquire a firm foundation of content knowledge in:

- *Genetics:* Mendelian genetics, genetic linkage, chromosome mapping, chromosome structure, population genetics, quantitative genetics, regulation of gene expression, recombinant DNA technology

- *Microbiology:* structural characteristics of microbes, microbial metabolism, classification (bacteria, fungi, viruses), mechanisms of pathogenesis; epidemiology, host defense mechanisms

- *Cell/molecular biology:* structure and function of organelles, the flow of genetic information (nuclear structure and communication with the cytoplasm), cell structure and function (cytoskeleton and cell movement), the ER system and protein transport (mitochondria and bioenergetics), cell-cell communication, cell regulation (signaling molecules and their receptors, the cell cycle, cancer)

- *Biochemistry:* macromolecular structure and function, bioenergetics, biosynthetic and degradative processes, enzyme kinetics, acid/base chemistry, redox reactions, regulation of enzyme activity, regulation of gene expression

The student will gain experience in designing experiments, collecting data, making appropriate calculations, and discussing results. Laboratory experiences will focus on:

- *Genetics:* genetic crosses, complementation analysis, mutagenesis (model systems could include *Drosophila melanogaster, C. elegans, E. coli,* etc.)

- *Microbiology:* sterile technique, methods of microbe identification, measurement of growth patterns under varying environmental conditions, selection procedures for isolation of mutants

- *Cell/molecular biology:* cell fractionation techniques, macromolecular isolation techniques (particularly DNA and protein), basic recombinant DNA technology (transformation, gel electrophoresis, PCR amplification)

Advanced Stage (Level 16)

The student will acquire a subset of specialized information that complements and extends the fundamental principles of genetics and related fields that were learned at the intermediate level. Examples might include:

- *Advanced genetics:* mechanisms of genetic exchange, control of gene expression in prokaryotes and eukaryotes, developmental genetics, epistatic mechanisms, non-Mendelian genetic patterns, DNA topology and its effects on gene expression, chromosome structure, genome organization

- *Eukaryotic molecular genetics:* non-Mendelian inheritance patterns, chromosome structure (nucleosomes, centromeres, telomeres, repetitive sequences), gene structure (introns, pseudogenes), control of gene expression (transcription factors, enhancer elements, post-transcriptional processing, translational regulation), genetics of development, molecular cloning techniques

- *Human genetics:* pedigree analysis, simple and complex genetic disorders, molecular techniques for diagnosis of genetic variation, non-Mendelian patterns of inheritance, genetics of behavior, genetics of aging, genetics and cancer, gene therapy

- *Molecular microbiology:* genetic exchange in prokaryotes, bacteriophage (mechanisms of infection and gene regulation), molecular mechanisms of pathogenesis, transcriptional and translational regulatory mechanisms, membrane topology, stress response patterns, defense mechanisms (restriction/modification, colicin production)

- *Immunology:* the nature of antibodies, mechanisms of action by B and T cells, lymphokines and cytokines, genetics of antigen recognition, the complement system, transplantation and tolerance, regulation of the immune response

- *Virology:* virion structure, viral genetics, RNA viruses and DNA viruses, retroviruses and HIV, viral immunology, viral pathogenesis, viral epidemiology, new and emerging viruses, viral diagnosis, immunization and antiviral chemotherapy

The student will gain experience in laboratory techniques and will demonstrate the ability to:

1) Pose scientific questions

2) Generate hypotheses

3) Design experiments to test these hypotheses

4) Evaluate the results of these experiments

5) Identify sources of error and assess the limitations of the data

6) Revise or extend the original hypotheses

7) Suggest additional experiments

Sample Laboratory Experiences for the Molecular Genetics Student

Intermediate Experience

The student is presented with a hypothetical scenario involving a problem that can be solved by DNA technology. DNA samples from a crime scene are provided, along with a group of suspects. The student is then asked to use restriction enzyme analysis coupled with gel electrophoresis to characterize the DNA samples and determine whose DNA corresponds to the DNA at the crime scene.

Advanced Experiences

- *Problem-based laboratory.* The student is asked to conduct an experiment that provides initially unexpected results. The student must then revise his or her initial hypothesis to conform to the observations and test the revised hypothesis.

- *Reversion analysis.* The student is given a mutant strain of *E. coli* that is lacZ- and trpE- (both are amber mutations) and told to isolate Lac+ and/or Trp+ revertants.

  A) Initial Experimental Design

  The student devises growth media that will select for Trp+ (omitting tryptophan from the media; providing glucose as a carbon source), Lac+ (providing tryptophan but including lactose as the sole carbon source), or Lac+Trp+ double mutants (omitting tryptophan and providing only lactose as a carbon source).

  B) Initial Hypothesis

  The student predicts the frequency of reversion (Lac+Trp- or Lac-Trp+: about 10^{-7}; Lac+Trp+ double reversion: $10^{-7} \times 10^{-7}) = 10^{-14}$.

  C) Results

  The student discovers the frequency of double revertants (10^{-7}-10^{-8}) is nearly as high as the frequency of single revertants.

  D) Revised Hypothesis

  The student generates a hypothesis to explain his or her observations. (Hypothesis: The fact that both original mutations are amber mutations raises the possibility that a single mutation in a tRNA gene can produce a translational suppressor that restores the Lac+ and Trp+ phenotypes simultaneously.)

  E) Predictions of Revised Hypothesis

  1) Phenotypic double revertants should be able to support the growth of bacteriophage containing amber mutations in essential genes. Spot-test amber mutant phage on lawns of revertant bacteria. The student devises appropriate controls.

  2) Phenotypic double revertants retain the original Lac- and Trp- mutations. Conduct a bacterial mating with a strain that is defective at proA (a gene closely linked to lacZ). Select for Pro+ recombinants and test for the co-transfer of the lacZ- mutation.

  F) Analysis of Results, Suggestions for Further Experiments

- *Open-ended laboratory.* In an open-ended laboratory, the student designs and carries out a set of experiments in which the final answer is unknown. Gene cloning experiments and "mutant hunts" are two types of laboratory exercises that, if designed appropriately, can lead to the isolation of previously uncharacterized genes (and, in the best of circumstances, to a publishable piece of work). An example of each type of experiment follows. In these cases, the bacteriophage P1 is used as a model system (just about any organism can be used as long as it is easy to grow, makes lots of easily extractable DNA, and, in the case of the mutant hunt, exhibits an easily selectable mutant phenotype). P1 is well known as a generalized transducing phage; however, it also exhibits a complex but relatively unstudied mechanism for differentiating between lytic and lysogenic growth. The gene cloning experiment has the advantage of providing more in-depth experience with cutting-edge technology; however, it generally is more expensive than a mutant hunt.

Because so little is known about the P1 genome, both the cloning experiment and the mutant hunt have a relatively high probability of turning up a promoter or regulatory gene that has never been reported before. Thus, each student can experience the excitement of searching for something that is yet to be discovered.

Gene Cloning

Search for transcription initiation sites on the genome of bacteriophage P1.

A) The student digests P1 DNA with restriction enzymes that produce multiple small fragments. The resulting fragments are then ligated into a promoter probe vector (a plasmid that contains a promoter-less copy of lacZ [the gene for b-galactosidase]).

B) The student transform the ligated samples into an *E. coli* lacZ strain, then plates the mixture on media containing X-gal, a lactose indicator dye that turns blue when broken down by b-galactosidase, the lacZ gene product. Normally, lacZ colonies are white, since the bacteria contain no enzyme to break down the indicator dye. Bacteria that have picked up a recombinant plasmid coding for a P1 promoter will be able to express the lacZ gene, resulting in the cleavage of X-gal by b-galactosidase and the appearance of a colony that is blue in color.

C) The student picks blue colonies, purifies the recombinant plasmid DNA, and identifies the size of the cloned fragment by restriction enzyme digestion and gel electrophoresis.

D) Depending on his or her findings, the student will:

1) Test the strength of the promoters by conducting enzyme assays to measure b-galactosidase activity

2) Conduct Southern hybridization experiments to localize the promoter on a previously derived restriction map of P1

3) PCR amplify the cloned fragment and determine the DNA sequence

4) Subject the promoter to site-directed mutagenesis and assay for alterations in b-galactosidase production

Mutant Hunt

Isolation and characterization of regulatory mutants of bacteriophage P1.

As a lysogenic phage, P1 is able to undergo two alternative modes of growth. If it enters the lytic mode of growth, it kills the infected cell, which then lyses and releases about 100 progeny phage. If it enters the lysogenic mode of growth, it does not kill the cell, but instead allows its genome to be maintained as a plasmid by the host for many generations in a quiescent state. The decision to let the cell live is mediated by several regulatory molecules, which repress the expression of proteins that would normally cause the cell to die. The strain of P1 used in this experiment is wild-type for lysogeny and, as a consequence forms turbid plaques (composed of about 90% lysed bacteria and 10% surviving lysogens). The purpose of this exercise is to isolate regulatory mutants that are no longer able to enter lysogeny. These mutants are easy to detect because they produce clear plaques in which all infected cells are lysed. Using a purified lysate of P1 phage as their stock, the student will:

A) Perform serial dilutions to determine the titer and to look for clear plaque mutants

B) Calculate the numbers of clear mutants and divide by the total number of phage to determine the mutation frequency

C) Purify their clear mutant phage and grow up high-titer stocks

D) Test the mutant phage for virulence

E) Conduct complementation analysis against known clear plaque mutants to determine whether their phage contains a defect in a previously characterized regulatory gene; subsequent experimental design will depend on the results of this test

1) If the complementation test localizes the mutation to a previously characterized gene, mutant phage DNA will be isolated, the gene will be amplified by PCR, and the mutation will be identified by DNA sequence analysis. The amplified DNA fragment containing the

mutant gene will be cloned into a high-level expression plasmid and the mutant gene product will be isolated and characterized.

2) If the complementation tests are all negative (i.e., the mutation is not located in any previously characterized gene) or if the mutant is virulent (i.e., the mutation affects a regulatory site rather than a gene product) the mutation will be localized by genetic mapping studies. A restriction fragment corresponding to that region of the P1 genome will be cloned into a multicopy vector and subjected to DNA sequence analysis.

Chemistry _____

University of Nevada–Reno (UNR)
Truckee Meadows Community College
Western Nevada Community College

See www.chem.unr.edu/undergrad/standards.html for latest version.

1.1 Overview of the Chemistry Curriculum

The predictive capability and therefore the utility of chemistry are based on a huge body of observation and deduction that has produced a model for the physical world that appears internally consistent. Though fundamental chemical ideas are mostly formulated in pure mathematics, these ideas must survive tests of quantitative measurement. Chemistry is an experimental science. This document is a catalog of the skills and knowledge base a baccalaureate graduate should possess.

The periphery of chemical knowledge is frequently a province of extreme specialization, high technological sophistication, and healthy scientific contention regarding new interpretations and observations. However, chemists doing both routine work and those involved in research and development in all areas share an extensive core set of skills, standardized terminology, and a body of experimentally measured factual knowledge. The baccalaureate degree aims to impart these core skills through formal coursework and laboratory exercises and—through involvement in undergraduate research—to give the upper-division student the opportunity to savor the frontiers of chemical knowledge in some area of mutual interest to the student and a faculty member.

Section 3 partitions the outcomes of a baccalaureate degree in chemistry into two components: operational skills (Section 3.1) and knowledge base (Section 3.2). This categorization parallels how chemistry is taught at UNR. Chemical ideas and demonstrated facts are commonly presented and discussed in faculty lectures or in problem solving discussion sections guided by instructors. Training in operational skills—how to do chemistry—is provided in the laboratory. Without these essential hands-on laboratory components, the classroom components of the curriculum would become increasingly abstract and dry as students advance. The chemistry curriculum therefore includes associated laboratories at all levels of instruction.

1.2 Ultimate Objectives

- Graduates will be successful in their professional careers as demonstrated by their abilities to solve important chemistry problems, to solve problems in areas different from their training, and to develop new and valuable ideas.

- They will be able to work in a variety of professional environments as demonstrated by their abilities to work in teams and alone, to provide project leadership, to mentor junior coworkers, and to communicate scientific results effectively to the chemistry community and the public.

- They will possess professional character as demonstrated by their ethical behavior, their pursuit of professional registration, and their commitment to safety and the environment.

2.1 General Education Outcomes

- Graduates will be proficient in the oral and written communication of their work and ideas.

- They will be able to learn independently and to participate effectively in groups.

- They will be proficient in the scientific method (formulating hypotheses and logically supported answers and conclusions).

- They will be prepared for a lifetime of continuing education.

- They will understand their professional and ethical responsibilities.

- They will have broad education in areas outside science that is necessary to understand the impact of science in a global and societal context.

- They will be proficient in the use of computers, recent computer software, and computer-based information systems.

2.2 Chemistry Knowledge Training Outcomes

- Graduates will possess a broad set of factual chemical knowledge concerning naming and chemical and physical properties of substances, molecules, and atoms.

- They will possess a thorough knowledge of the basic principles of chemistry, including atomic and molecular structure, chemical dynamics, and the chemical and physical properties of substances.

- They will possess a thorough knowledge of the subfields of chemistry, including analytical, inorganic, organic, and physical chemistry.

- They will possess cognitive skills in areas such as mathematics and physics to facilitate the understanding and manipulation of fundamental chemical theories.

2.3 Quantitative Reasoning Skills Outcomes

- Graduates will have a practical understanding of applied mathematics, including algebra, geometry, calculus, and topics in differential equations and matrix theory.

- They will be able to solve problems competently involving extrapolation, approximation, precision, accuracy, rational estimation, and statistical validity.

- They will be able to read, evaluate and interpret numerical, chemical, and general scientific information.

2.4 General Laboratory Skills Training Outcomes

- Graduates will be able to perform accurate quantitative measurements, interpret experimental results, perform calculations on these results, and draw reasonable, and accurate conclusions.

- They will be able to synthesize, separate, and characterize compounds using published reactions, protocols, standard laboratory equipment, and modern instrumentation.

- They will understand the theory and use of modern chemical instrumentation.

- They will be able to design effective laboratory experiments, perform laboratory experiments, gather data, analyze data, and test theories.

- They will understand the safety and environmental consequences of their work as chemists and be able to design safe processes.

2.5 Information Skills Training Outcomes

- Graduates will be able to make effective use of information resources, including:
  - Finding chemical information utilizing the primary literature, whether in a traditional library or electronic indexes and journals
  - Critically evaluating chemical information
  - Finding and evaluating chemical information utilizing secondary sources such as electronic databases
- They will be able to make effective use of computers in chemistry applications, including:
  - Using a computer as a tool in technical writing, drawing chemical structures, and presenting data in order to communicate scientific information

- Having a familiarity with the applications of computers in the modeling and simulation of chemical phenomena

- Appreciating the applications of computers in data acquisition and processing

3.1 Process Standards

3.1.1 Level 14

1) Critical Thinking and Problem Solving
Skills inventory:

- Organize and categorize information and data

- Recognize trends and patterns in data

- Deduce hypotheses from patterns and groupings

- Deduce hypotheses using analogical reasoning

- Formulate questions to test a hypothesis

- Order of magnitude estimation

- Use extrapolation and interpolation to infer unobserved properties

Performance expectations:

- Group a diverse collection of phenomena or substances according to specific chemical or physical properties or reaction mechanisms.

- Given information about trends in chemical or physical properties of related substances, identify the underlying features responsible for those properties and predict those properties for substances for which data is unavailable.

- Evaluate whether a calculated result or reported measurement is physically plausible by crude estimation of the quantity.

- Given multiple hypotheses consistent with a set of observations, propose a question of utility in discriminating among the hypotheses.

2) Laboratory Procedures
Skills inventory:
- Synthetic methods

- Analytical methods

- Operation of simple chemical instruments

- Basic laboratory safety

Performance expectations:

- Perform basic chemical manipulations (e.g., distillation, crystallization, filtration, refluxing) in the synthesis and purification of inorganic and organic compounds.

- Assemble synthetic apparatus using standard laboratory glassware.

- Make accurate quantitative assays and measurements (e.g., titration, thermometry, preparation of standard solutions).

- Use pH meters, absorbance spectrometers, and so on to make quantitative determinations.

- Anticipate, recognize, and respond properly to laboratory hazards.

- Understand procedures for proper storage and disposal of chemicals.

3) Data Analysis
Skills inventory:

- Evaluate reliability of data

- Statistical analysis of data

- Analyze impact of results on society (economic, moral, political)

Performance expectations:

- Propagate the uncertainty on a datum through a series of calculations in order to assess the uncertainty of a derived result.

- Graphically represent data and indicate error bars appropriate to the uncertainty in the data.

- Distinguish between and estimate random and statistical sources of error in a measurement.

- Quantitatively calculate random error in a collection of replicate measurements by calculation of the standard deviation.

- Given a set of objective observations and a proposed hypothesis, critically evaluate the hypothesis with an awareness of the possible bias of the source of the hypothesis.

4) Experimental Design
Skills inventory:

- Sampling

- Controls/calibration

- Safety issues

Performance expectations:

- When provided a question concerning a well-defined system, determine what measurable properties are relevant to the answer.

- Given a well-defined system, identify which variables are likely to influence a specific property of the system.

- Using standardized reagents, calibrate an analytical instrument or technique.

- Anticipate, recognize, and respond properly to hazards of chemical manipulations.

5) Systems Modeling
Skills inventory:

- Molecular and mathematical modeling

- Data analysis

- Graphing

- Word processing

- Spreadsheets

Performance expectations:

- Use computer modeling to visualize three-dimensional molecular structures as a tool in understanding chemical properties.

- Generate graphical representations of data designed to illustrate trends and support a scientific hypothesis.

- Use computer spreadsheets to organize and quantitatively present data, perform linear regression, and evaluate the uncertainty of derived quantities.

- Use computer software to prepare visually appealing reports and documents.

6) Accessing Information
Skills inventory:

- Computer/library searching

- Use of standard references

- Access scientific data over the Internet

- Evaluation of reliability of information

Performance expectations:

- Use search engines, databases, and computer networks to access chemical information.

- Use scientific journal citations to locate articles in the chemistry library.

- Understand the organization of scientific journals and journal articles and be able to efficiently extract information from individual articles.

- Be aware of the utility of standard references in chemistry (e.g., CRC Handbook, Merck Manual, Spectral Atlases) and efficiently use them to extract specific information.

7) Communicating Results
Skills inventory:

- Written

- Visual

- Teamwork

- Lab notebook

Performance expectations:

- Write complete, logical prose that effectively conveys understanding of concepts, new results, and conclusions drawn from data to a general technical audience.

- Draw diagrams and figures that graphically summarize data or complex three-dimensional structures (e.g., molecular geometries, configurations of experimental apparatus).

- Organize a large task among the members of a team, communicate results among team members, and arrive at a consensus conclusion or result.

- Keep legible and complete experimental records in a laboratory journal.

3.1.2 Level 16 (Baccalaureate/Senior Year)

1) Critical Thinking and Problem Solving
Skills inventory:

- Categorizing

- Recognizing trends

- Deduction

- Inference

- Interpreting and using algorithms

- Dealing with ambiguity
- Analogical reasoning
- Formulating questions
- Order of magnitude estimation

Performance expectations:

- Explain new concepts by analogy with the properties or behavior of well-understood systems.
- Distinguish data extraneous to the solution of a problem and avoid confusion due to ambiguity.

2) Laboratory Procedures

Skills inventory:

- Advanced synthetic and analytical methods
- Modern instrumental techniques (theory and practice)
- Understanding of chemical safety

Performance expectations:

- Use vacuum techniques for inorganic synthesis.
- Use sophisticated separation and purification tools in synthetic procedures (e.g., preparative column chromatography).
- Understand principles of safe storage of chemicals and disposal of chemical wastes.
- Know how to use MSDS sheets, OSHA guidelines, and online chemical safety resources.
- Predict possible hazardous products or outcomes of chemical reactions.
- Design electronic circuits using basic electronic components, operational amplifiers, and digital logic for use in data acquisition and signal modification.
- Understand the operational principles and utility, detection limits, and relative expense of modern chemical instruments (e.g., NMR, IR, UV-VIS, AA spectroscopic instruments, electrochemical instrumentation).
- Understand simple concepts of computer-automated data acquisition, computer interfaces, and data structures.

3) Experimental Design
Skills inventory:

- Formulating problems
- Use of the literature for planning
- Sampling
- Decision-making
- Instrumentation
- Controls/calibration
- Safety issues

Performance expectations:

- Independently formulate an experimental approach to test a fundamental hypothesis or address an important societal issue.
- Make critical use of the scientific literature to evaluate the utility of experimental strategies and obtain information relevant to an experimental problem.
- Identify or formulate calibration procedures for instruments or experimental techniques.
- Identify complicating variables that must be controlled in the design of an experimental measurement.

4) Systems Modeling
Skills inventory:

- Molecular and mathematical modeling
- Data analysis
- Graphing
- Word processing
- Spreadsheets

Performance expectations:

- Predict physical and chemical properties of substances using molecular modeling software (e.g., dipole moments, energy levels, spectra, polarizability, structure).
- Perform significance testing and t-testing and assign confidence limits to experimental measurements. Recognize extraneous or invalid data.

3.2 Content Standards

3.2.1 Level 14

1) Particulate Nature of Matter

Knowledge inventory:

- Subatomic particles (protons, neutrons, electrons)
- Structure of atoms and atomic ions
- Structure of molecules and molecular ions
- Stoichiometry and the mole concept

Performance expectations:

- Explain that some atomic nuclei are unstable and decay to produce the nuclei of other elements and ionizing radiation and how useful energy can be extracted from this phenomenon.
- Explain why the planetary model of the atom does not adequately predict detailed behavior of atoms in substances.
- Explain why each atom forms a characteristic geometrical configuration of bonds in molecules.
- Use the balanced equation and the mole concept in a variety of contexts, for example:
  - ~ Determine the mass of product obtained upon reaction of a limited quantity of reactants.
  - ~ Determine the number of solute particles in a given volume of solution with a known concentration.

2) Atomic Structure and Periodic Properties

Knowledge inventory:

- Intramolecular forces (electromagnetic, nuclear)
- Orbitals
- Electron configurations
- Common oxidation states
- Radii
- Electron affinity and ionization potential

Performance expectations:

- Quantitatively calculate the Coulombic attractive force between charged particles (e.g., between a proton and electron in the hydrogen atom).

- Explain the difference between the motion of the earth about the sun and the motion of an electron about the nucleus of an atom.

- Give the occupancy of electrons among the quantum mechanical orbitals of an atom.

- Use the concepts of electron affinity and ionization potential to predict the common oxidation states of elements.

- Predict the trends in size of atoms and atomic ions using the quantum model of the atom.

3) Interaction of Light With Matter
Knowledge inventory:

- Electromagnetic radiation

- Absorption and emission

Performance expectations:

- Given the quantum energy levels of a substance, compute the wavelengths of light that can be absorbed and emitted.

- Explain the relationship between photon energy, wavelength of light, and frequency of light.

4) Molecular Structure and Bonding
Knowledge inventory:

- Ionic/covalent/metallic bonding

- Lewis dot structures

- Formal charge

- Oxidation state

- Bonding theories (valence bond, molecular orbital, delocalized bonding, etc.)

- Bond lengths and energies

- Molecular geometry

- Polarity

- Isomers

- Isomerism

- Functional groups
- Polymers
- Stereochemistry
- Chirality
- Nomenclature

Performance expectations:

- Explain how multiple, distinct molecular structures can be consistent with a single chemical formula.
- Use the concept of formal charge and oxidation state to predict the overall dipole moment of a molecule.
- Determine bond orders between atoms in molecules and use bond orders to predict trends in bond lengths and bond energies.
- Use the concept of orbital hybridization to predict and rationalize the bonding geometry about a central atom in a molecule.
- Predict the conformational rigidity of a molecule resulting from the type of bonds it contains.
- Use the concept of formal charge to predict the most important resonance structures in the distribution of delocalized electrons in a molecule.
- Name molecules according to the IUPAC scheme.
- Recognize important functional groups.

5) States of Matter
Knowledge inventory:
- Gases
- Gas laws
- Solids (amorphous and crystalline)
- Intermolecular forces
- Liquids
- Solutions
- Phase relations
- Postulates of kinetic molecular theory

Performance expectations:

- Explain the relationships among pressure, volume, temperature, and quantity in a sample of a gas.

- Explain why the properties of real gases are distinct from those of the hypothetical ideal gas.

- Use equations of state to calculate properties of real gases.

- Given critical pressures and temperatures, sketch a phase diagram for a substance.

- Give examples of how solutions and mixtures can be separated into their components using both chemical and physical transformations.

- Assess the intermolecular forces that will predominate for a given type of molecule and estimate the resulting physical properties of a bulk sample of that substance.

6) Thermodynamics
Knowledge inventory:

- Conservation of energy

- Enthalpies of formation

- Heats of reaction

- Heat capacity

- Entropy

- Increase in disorder

- Free energy

- Nuclear energetics

Performance expectations:

- Given bond energies, estimate heats of formation for a substance.

- Given heats of formation, compute the exo- or endo-thermicity of a chemical reaction.

- Construct a thermochemical cycle involving known reactions to compute the heat of reaction for a reaction for which no data is provided.

- Know how to use calorimetry to measure the heat of reaction.

- Use the concept of entropy to explain why endothermic reactions can occur spontaneously.

- Classify economically significant energy sources. Analyze a source according to the origin and type of energy, whether it is renewable, and the environmental and political consequences of its exploitation.

7) Equilibrium

Knowledge inventory:

- Le Chatelier's principle
- Gas equilibria
- Solubility and distribution equilibria
- Acids and bases
- Buffers
- Redox reactions

Performance expectations:

- Describe the self-ionization of water in terms of equilibrium solution chemistry.
- Quantify the equilibrium state of a solution using the pH system.
- Explain how buffer compounds are used to maintain the pH of a solution upon the addition of limited quantities of an acid or base.
- Provide methods for altering the balance between reactants and products in a reversible chemical reaction.

8) Dynamics

Knowledge inventory:

- Molecular motions
- Transport phenomena
- Molecular collisions/interactions
- Reaction rates
- Catalysis

Performance expectations:

- Explain how molecular motion in a sample depends upon temperature.
- Explain the factors that influence the rates of chemical reactions (e.g., physical state, temperature, molecular size, diffusion control).
- Explain how catalysis accelerates chemical reactions and give significant applications in industrial processes and biological systems.

9) Electrochemistry

Knowledge inventory:

- Reducing and oxidizing agents
- Half-cell reactions
- Electrochemical cells
- Cell EMF
- Electrolysis
- Corrosion

Performance expectations:

- Identify the oxidizing and reducing reagents in redox reactions and be able to decompose redox reactions into half-cell components.
- Explain the transformations of chemical and electrical energy in electrochemical cells and batteries.
- Describe modern industrial and technological applications (e.g., fuel cells, industrial plating, corrosion prevention).

10) Reactivity

Knowledge inventory:

- Common types of chemical reactions
- Functional group reactivity
- Reaction types
- Nucleophiles
- Electrophiles
- Mechanisms
- Intermediates
- Stereo and regio-selectivity

Performance expectations:

- Given a set of reactants and products, categorize the type of chemical reaction (e.g., redox, metathesis, acid-base).
- Distinguish and describe the characteristic reactivity and properties of the major functional groups of organic molecules.
- Propose a plausible stepwise reaction mechanism to explain the observed products of a chemical reaction. Extrapolate this mechanism to predict the products of similar reactions.

11) Synthesis
Knowledge inventory:

- Synthetic strategies

- Retrosynthetic analysis

Performance expectations:

- Use appropriate reagents, catalysts, and reaction conditions to devise a synthetic procedure for a target molecule. Be able to suggest alternative synthetic schemes.

12) Structure Determination Using Spectroscopic Methods
Knowledge inventory:

- Ultraviolet/visible electronic spectroscopy

- Infrared vibrational spectroscopy

- Radio frequency nuclear magnetic resonance spectroscopy

Performance expectations:

- Identify likely functional groups in a molecule from an IR spectrum.

- Use proton and 13C NMR spectroscopy as an aid in establishing the structure and atomic connectivity in a molecule.

13) Bioorganic Chemistry
Knowledge inventory:

- Simple sugars

- Carbohydrates

- Lipids

- Amino acids

- Proteins

- Nucleic acids

- DNA

Performance expectations:

- Explain the fundamental concatenating reactions that form biopolymers (carbohydrates, proteins, DNA).

- Know the roles of important biomolecules in living systems.

- Explain the primary, secondary, and tertiary structure of biopolymers and why this is important in the operation of the most fundamental biological processes (biological structural materials, protein active sites, DNA transcription, etc.).

14) Analytical Chemistry
Knowledge inventory:

- Distinction between qualitative and quantitative goals of determinations
- Statistical methods for evaluating and interpreting data
- Sources of error in chemical and instrumental analysis
- Exposure to computer-based data acquisition systems
- Fundamental concepts of instrument calibration
- Basic concepts of stoichiometry and chemical reactions involving analytes and ordinary reagents
- Quantization of equilibrium and kinetic aspects of chemistry
- Availability and evaluation of analytical standards
- Standardization methodology

3.2.2 Level 16 (Baccalaureate/Senior Year)
Note: This section is only a beginning

1) Molecular Structure and Bonding
Knowledge inventory:

- Expanded octets/Lewis dot structures
- VSEPR theory, strain, distortions
- Symmetry and group theory
- Structures of solids
- Valence bond theory
- Crystal field theory
- Molecular orbital theory

Performance expectations:

- Ability to deduce structure of simple molecules, predict approximate bond angles and distortions.
- Assign point groups, determine symmetry of molecular vibrations, and derive simple M.O. diagrams.

- Knowledge of unit cells and packing.

- Knowledge of coordination modes and transition metal geometry.

- Distinguish between tenets of valence bond theory, crystal field theory, and M.O. theory for bonding in transition metal complexes. Knowledge of d-orbital splitting diagrams, spectrochemical series, and pi-bonding in octahedral complexes. Assignment of d-d transitions.

- Count electrons in organometallic chemistry. Utilization of the 18 electron rule to formulate complexes. Understanding of backbonding and metal-ligand orbital interactions. Application of organometallic reactions to devise a catalytic cycle.

2) Reactivity
Knowledge inventory:

- Acid/base theory (Lewis acids, hard/soft)

3) Spectroscopy

4) Magnetic Properties (Transitional Metal Chemistry)

5) Organometallic Chemistry

6) Bioinorganic Chemistry

7) Dynamics
Knowledge inventory:

- Transition-state theory

- Statistical mechanics

8) Instrumental methods
Knowledge inventory:

- Comparison and critical selection of methods for elemental and molecular analyses

- Knowledge of sampling methods for all states of matter

- Validation of data and experimental design

- Sources of error in chemical and instrumental analysis

- Theory and operational principles of analytical instruments, including electronic components

- Design of computer-based data acquisition systems

- Principles and operation of instruments for atomic, molecular, and mass spectrometry; magnetic resonance spectroscopy, chromatography and other methods of separation, electroanalytical methods, and thermal methods

Resources

We acknowledge the following organizations for material used in assembling this document:

The Modular CHEM Consortium, University of California–Berkeley
Process and content standards:
http://mc2.cchem.berkeley.edu/
http://mc2.cchem.berkeley.edu/modules/index.html

ChemLinks Coalition, Beloit College
Process and content standards:
http://chemlinks.beloit.edu/summary.html
http://chemistry.beloit.edu/modules.html

American Chemical Society
Committee on Professional Training, topical supplements to *Undergraduate Professional Education in Chemistry: Guidelines and Evaluation Procedures:*
http://www.chemistry.org/portal/a/c/s/1/acsdisplay.html?DOC=education\cpt\guidelines.html

English

Learning Outcomes, Level 16
Towson University Bachelor of English

The undergraduate program in English at Towson University (TU) is designed to achieve a number of learning outcomes. Upon graduation, the successful degree candidate will have developed qualities and skills listed below with knowledge and abilities specific to the discipline.

General Outcomes

Upon graduation, TU English majors can:

- Use their strong communication and organizational skills to compete successfully for professional careers and further academic pursuits, social development, and personal satisfaction.

- Employ the rhetorical principles necessary to adapt their communicative skills to the changing demands of an information-driven society and workplace.

- Be reflective and lifelong learners.

- Experience the intrinsic wonder and delight of imaginative literature and experiment with writing it.

- Interpret written text and, thus, learn about themselves, the text, and the culture it reflects while applying their interpretations to the world beyond the text.

- Communicate a critical perspective drawn from informed choices among a diversity of opinions and interpretations.

- Move from being novice to expert learners and develop an identity within communities of learners.

- Make connections among ideas and fields of knowledge.

- Learn from, and contribute to, their culture.

Knowledge

Upon graduation, English majors will have a demonstrably broad and deep knowledge of the principal areas of the discipline and their terminology:

- ~ Criticism: principal schools and history

- ~ Literature: genres and history

- ~ Rhetoric and writing: conventions, genres, and history

~ Language and linguistics: awareness of the structure, organic nature, and social implications of language

- English majors can also demonstrate knowledge of the historical, social, and psychological contexts (as well as the cultural implications) of the discipline, including awareness of race, class, and gender.

Abilities

Upon graduation, English majors demonstrate instrumental knowledge of reading and writing in the discipline. They can:

- Grasp and interpret metaphor.

- Conduct purposeful analysis of literary discourse, including discussion of the history, forms, and conventions of the different periods and genres.

- Read literary works with understanding of their background, structure, meanings, implications, and relevance.

- Read scholarly works with an understanding of their contexts, concerns, and terminology.

- Interpret written materials flexibly, understanding how multiple meanings are possible and, conversely, how individual interpretations sometimes can be wrong.

- Understand and use evidence to support interpretations.

They can use their understanding of the discipline and its contexts to:

- Apply knowledge of the history, theory, and methodologies of the discipline and its contexts in thoughtful discourse.

- Apply to everyday life knowledge gained from literary, rhetorical, and linguistic study.

- Integrate or synthesize knowledge from a range of disciplines as a means to interpret the text.

- Communicate effectively in speech and writing.

- Speak and write academic discourse competently.

- Recognize a range of social, academic, and professional situations and adapt language accordingly.

- Write in a variety of forms (expository, argumentative, imaginative, academic, business/technical, literary, etc.) as appropriate to audience, purpose, and occasion.

- Comprehend the grammatical and syntactical patterns of the English language and use them as a tool in writing and revising.

They can also:

- Use traditional and electronic research methods competently.

- Use information technology effectively, understand the history of technology in relation to the discipline, and recognize how technology changes English studies.

- Pursue scholarship and other intellectual activities both collaboratively and individually.

- Apply ways of understanding within the discipline (e.g., sensitivity to metaphor, interpretation of symbols, awareness of thematic development and of underlying structures) to other media (e.g., film, television, news, advertising, and the like).

- Ask informed questions about language, literature, and rhetoric.

History ────────────────────────────────────

California State University–Long Beach and Long Beach City College
Draft of Skills and Content Standards for United States Survey Courses Levels 13 and 14

The draft standards below represent the results of discussions that took place among faculty at California State University–Long Beach (CSULB) and Long Beach City College (LBCC) between July and December 2000. Both institutions teach a United States History survey course over two semesters. The State of California requires all students to complete three units of U.S. History, and the survey course taken at either institution fulfills this requirement.

We intended to create standards that reflect what faculty would like students to know and be able to do at the start of their upper-division coursework. As might be expected, the working group was able to agree rather easily on standards for historical understanding (Section I) and historical skills (Section II). Content standards obviously were more problematic and represent the results of strenuous discussion. The skills and content standards are the same for both history and non-history majors.

The CSULB/LBCC working group (Craig Hendricks, Wendy Hornsby, Troy Johnson, Tim Keirn, Lezlie Knox, Dave Lehman, Brett Mizelle, Lisa Orr, and Steve Wallech) acknowledges our debt to standards created by Troy Johnson for the CSULB Integrated Teacher Education Program United States History Survey classes; Tim Keirn for the CSULB Social Science Credential Capstone Course; and particularly the standards compiled by the National Center for History in the Schools (nchs.ucla.edu/standards/us-standards5-12.html and the History-Social Studies Content Standards for California Public Schools (www.cde.ca.gov/re/pn/fd/documents/histsocsci-stnd.pdf) which served as important starting points for our discussions.

I. Historical Understanding (for History 172/173 at CSULB and History 10/11 at LBCC)

- Students will be able to explain and analyze the processes of historical change. Students will distinguish cause from effect and recognize that elements of historical causation are myriad, complex, and often interdependent.

- Students will be able to identify, understand, and explore the connections among cultural, social, economic, political, and environmental developments.

- Students will recognize and analyze how concepts such as race, class, gender, freedom, and rights are historical constructs that change over time.

- Students will recognize the concept of *agency*. Individuals, groups, and communities were not simply "acted upon" but exercised historical agency by the choices they made and the actions they took either individually or collectively.

II. Historical Skills (for History 172/173 at CSULB and History 10/11 at LBCC)

- Students will practice serious historical thinking by building on their knowledge of facts, dates, names, places, events, and ideas in order to ask historical questions and assemble solid evidence in support of their answers.

- Students will read and comprehend various forms of historical literature. They also will recognize the differences among these literatures, including distinctions between primary sources, secondary sources, and textbooks.

- Students will formulate historical arguments that express ideas with clarity and coherence. They may demonstrate this skill through in-class writing, short papers, and short answer and/or essay exams.

- Students will examine historical evidence in order to make inferences, form generalizations, and draw conclusions from it. In addition to written sources, they will interpret non-written sources (e.g., images, maps, graphs, charts, and other types of quantitative resources).

III. Content Knowledge: United States History From the Eve of European Contact Through Reconstruction (for History 172 at CSULB and History 10 at LBCC)

- Students will discuss the spatial diversity in North America of indigenous cultures, economy, and society on the eve of European contact.

- Students will analyze how early European exploration and colonization resulted in cultural and ecological interactions among previously unconnected peoples.

- Students will account for and discuss the motives and patterns of African and European migration to North America and the Caribbean and relate these migrations to the regional development of early British America.

- Students will compare and contrast the origins, character, and impact of slavery in the British Caribbean, Chesapeake, Carolinas, and northern urban centers prior to 1775.

- Students will compare and contrast the social, cultural, and economic development of New England, the Middle Colonies, and the South by 1775.

- Students will analyze the causes of the American Revolution, the challenges involved in forging a revolutionary movement, the reasons for its outcomes, and its varying effects on diverse American cultural groups.

- Students will understand how institutions of and ideas about government created during the revolutionary struggle were incorporated into a political system centered on the United States Constitution and Bill of Rights and how Americans continued to struggle over the organization and extension of political democracy into the 19th century.

- Students will analyze the process of and motivations behind United States territorial expansion between 1801 and 1861. They will explain how expansion affected Native American, Hispanic, and Asian peoples and how these groups responded with accommodation and resistance.

- Students will account for how urbanization and industrialization, the transportation and market revolutions, increasing immigration, the rapid expansion of slavery, and the westward movement changed the lives of Americans. They will also understand the sources and character of Americans' responses to these changes through cultural and social reform movements.

- Students will understand the sectional tension between the North and South and how slavery, politics, and competing ideologies led to the Civil War. They also will analyze the course and character of the Civil War on the battlefield and the home front while examining its effects on the American people.

- Students will understand the different political approaches to national reconciliation. Students will analyze the success and failures of Reconstruction for African Americans and on American social and racial democratization.

IV. Content Knowledge: United States History From Reconstruction Through the Present Day (for History 173 at CSULB and History 11 at LBCC)

- Students will analyze the social and economic changes created by the development of industrial technology after 1870 and its effects on corporate structures and organizations up to 1930. Student also will explain the significance of the United States to the growing world economy.

- Students will assess the social, political and economic impact of population growth, movement, and immigration after 1870.

- Key elements of social and cultural changes, such as race relationships, gender roles, urbanization, technological innovation, consumerism, and progressivism will be evaluated in light of the rapidly changing United States society after 1890.

- Students will evaluate changing political culture, party alignments, and reform movements from the local to federal levels between 1870 and 1930.

- Students will analyze the nature of American imperialism in both domestic and global spheres including federal Indian policy, United States involvement in World War I, and the changing role of the United States in world affairs through 1930.

- Students will analyze the causes of the Great Depression and its effect on American society. They also will examine how the New Deal addressed the problems of the Depression, initiated the welfare state, and resulted in the transformation of American politics and society.

- Students will explore the causes and course of American involvement in World War II, its domestic impact, and its importance in reshaping the United States' role in world affairs.

- Students will examine the economic boom, demographic change, and the social and political transformation of the postwar United States, including the struggle for racial and gender equality and the extension of civil liberties.

- Students will analyze how the Cold War influenced international and domestic politics, including the conflicts in Korea and Vietnam.

- Students will examine developments since 1968 in foreign policy and domestic politics. They will also trace economic, social, and cultural developments in the contemporary United States.

Mathematics _____

Mathematics Standards
Content and Performance
(After Two Years of College)

Notice that communicating and applying mathematics are not separate content areas, but rather are threads integrated throughout the performance descriptors.

1. Number Sense

- Students will perform arithmetic operations, using appropriate technology.

- Students will interpret numerical information and communicate their interpretation clearly.

- Students will estimate reliably and appropriately, judge the reasonableness of numerical results, and communicate their estimates and judgments.

- Students will think proportionally.

2. Algebra

- Students will clearly and consistently define, verbally and in writing, the significant variables in an application.

- Students will identify, verbally and in writing, any restrictions, assumptions, relationships, and characteristics of variables germane to the problem.

- Students will identify an appropriate equation, the solution of which will provide a solution to the problem.

- Students will solve equations by an appropriate combination of graphical, numerical, technological, and algebraic methods.

3. Geometry

- Students will apply analytic geometry in problem solving.

4. Function

- Students will translate functional relationships represented in graphical, numeric, or symbolic form into another form.

- Students will be able to evaluate functions presented graphically, numerically, or symbolically.

- Students will use functions to solve mathematical problems.

5. Continuous Mathematics

(Intended for math [or math intensive?] majors.)

5.1. Derivatives

5.2. Integrals

6. Discrete Mathematics

- Students will use appropriate discrete mathematical algorithms in order to solve problems of finite character.

- Students will apply combinatorial abilities in order to enumerate sets without direct counting.

7. Probability and Statistics

- Students will gather data using a variety of means, including published sources.

- Students will organize, display, and summarize data.

8. Deductive Reasoning and Proof

- Students will draw conclusions or make predictions from the data and assess the chances of certain events happening.

Appendix C

Scoring rubrics are guidelines used to evaluate student responses to specific assignments. Shared—and perhaps developed—with students before they respond to an assignment, these rubrics make the rating criteria explicit and transparent. To the extent they do so, they help demystify the evaluation process, evoke higher levels of student performance, and ensure more consistent evaluation of student work. Since they take time and effort to create, they are most appropriate for high-stakes assignments (e.g., senior theses, term papers, papers in a senior seminar, etc.).

Scoring rubrics are designed to help students produce better work and should:

- Be distributed with the assignment
- Refer specifically to the assignment
- Unambiguously address one or more of the department's content standards
- Clearly define the performance targets for the assignment

Scoring rubrics should not be narrowly prescriptive. Instead, they should achieve a careful balance between providing clear guidelines and leaving as much room as possible for student creativity. As they struggle to maintain this balance, scoring rubrics may specifically address a range of topics including but not limited to:

- The kind or amount of content expected
- The processes used to address the assignment

- The crosscutting competencies appropriate to the assignment

Scoring rubrics define at least three levels of performance including:

- *Expert proficiency.* Expert performance is reserved for those few who demonstrate performance that exceeds the expectations for proficient performance. For this performance level, the description of student work should be based on the best possible responses to the assessment or task.

- *Minimal proficiency.* Minimal performance is the lowest acceptable level of proficiency. Performance at this level clearly indicates that a student has mastered the basic knowledge and skills required by the content standard(s).

- *Non-proficiency.* Descriptions of non-proficient performance identify some of the most common ways in which student work falls short of minimal proficiency.

Whenever possible, anchor papers or annotated examples of student responses at each level of performance should be used to illustrate and support the performance levels described in the scoring rubric.

Worksheet for Drafting a Scoring Rubric

Content standard:

_____

Targeted criteria from the performance standard:

_____

_____

_____

_____

_____

_____

Criterion	Content Targets	Qualitative Targets

Appendix D

Publications

Albertine, S., & Henry, R. J. (2004, Summer). Quality in Undergraduate Education: A collaborative project. *Liberal Education, 90*(3), 46–53.

Henry, R. J. (2000, Winter). A standards-based approach to curricular planning. *Peer Review, 2*(2), 19–20.

Keirn, T. (1999, November). Starting small: The creation of a year fourteen history standard. *Organization of American Historians Newsletter, 27*(4), 9–10.

Conference Presentations

Ahnert, E., Bevis, J., & Henderson, S. (2000, November). *Quality in Undergraduate Education (QUE): Standards and articulation.* Paper presented at the 26th annual conference of the American Mathematical Association of Two-Year Colleges, Chicago, IL.

Albertine, S. (2000, October). *Transferable skills.* Paper presented at the regional conference of Temple University and Maryland Community College, Philadelphia, PA.

Albertine, S., Henry, R. J., & Brown, B. (2002, June). *Quality in Undergraduate Education—standards for learning.* Paper presented at the annual assessment conference of the American Association for Higher Education, Boston, MA.

Albertine, S., Henry, R. J., & Brown, B. (2003, January). *Quality in Undergraduate Education—standards for learning in the disciplines.* Paper presented at the 89th annual meeting of the Association of American Colleges and Universities, Seattle, WA.

Henry, R. J. (2000, February). *Academic standards for transfer students.* Paper presented at the 87th annual meeting of the Association of American Colleges and Universities, San Antonio, TX.

Henry, R. J. (2000, July). *What are we learning from initiatives moving from Carnegie units to standards for the college major?* Paper presented at the NASH/Ed Trust State Teams K–16 Summer Institute, Park City, UT.

Henry, R. J. (2001, June). *Teaching and assessment in a standards-based environment: QUE and STEP.* Paper presented at the University of Georgia Standards-Based Workshop, Atlanta, GA.

Henry, R. J. (2001, July). *Creating state policy on-ramps to aligning standards K–16.* Paper presented at the NASH/Ed Trust State Teams K–16 Summer Institute, Fish Camp, CA.

Henry, R. J. (2002, July). *What about the value added by higher education? College faculty's role within the P–16 context.* Paper presented at the NASH/Ed Trust State Teams K–16 Summer Institute, Denver, CO.

Henry, R. J. (2002, October). *A role for college faculty in a P–16 context: Engaging faculty in looking closely at standards and practice in entry-level courses—what are we learning about changing faculty culture?* Paper presented at the meeting of the Georgia P–16 Network, Atlanta, GA.

Henry, R. J. (2002, October). *Assessing students' learning and increasing institutional accountability: Lessons from college-level science and mathematics programs.* Paper presented at the 6th annual Grantmakers for Education Conference, Denver, CO.

Henry, R. J. (2003, June). *State policies that promote and constrain effective practices.* Paper presented at the National Governors' Association Center for Best Practices, Accountability for Student Learning Workshop, Salt Lake City, UT.

Henry, R. J., & Brown, B. (2002, October). *QUE—standards for learning.* Paper presented at the Making a Difference through Teacher Education Summit, Birmingham, AL.

Henry, R. J., Howard, C., & John, G. (2001, June). *Quality in Undergraduate Education—standards for learning.* Paper presented at the annual assessment conference of the American Association for Higher Education, Denver, CO.

Henry, R. J., Miller, V., & John, G. (2002, January). *The Quality in Undergraduate Education (QUE) initiative.* Paper presented at the annual Faculty Roles and Rewards Conference of the American Association for Higher Education, Phoenix, AZ.

Hetzler, S. M., & Tardiff, R. M. (2001, January). *QUE: How standards and assessment might improve undergraduate education.* Panel discussion presented at the national conference of the American Mathematical Society/Mathematical Association of America, New Orleans, LA.

Mahaffy, J., & Cathey, W. (2002, June). *Pressure + support = change.* Paper presented at the annual assessment conference of the American Association for Higher Education, Boston, MA.

Mahaffy, J., Cathey, W., & Howard, C. (2002, May). *Effectively engaging faculty in assessing learning outcomes: Lessons learned (and still learning!).* Paper presented at the 3rd annual Pacific Planning, Assessment and Institutional Research (PacPAIR) Conference, Honolulu, HI.

Tardiff, R. M., & Kimmel, K. (2003, January). *Quality in Undergraduate Education—history discipline.* Paper presented at the 13th annual conference of the Association of Faculties for Advancement of Community College Teaching, Wye Mills, MD.

White, C., Henry, R. J., Rhodes, T., Riordan, T., & Martin-Erschnig, J. (2003, January). *Building portable and credible documentation of student learning.* Paper presented at the 89th annual meeting of the Association of American Colleges and Universities, Seattle, WA.

Appendix E

Cluster Coordinators

Dorothy Abrahamse, Kathleen DiVito
California State University–Long Beach

Nancy Fitch
California State University–Fullerton

Michael Price
Armstrong Atlantic State University

Valerie Miller
Georgia State University

John Rhodes
Fort Valley State University

Jane Kinney
Valdosta State University

Kent Kimmel, Robert Tardiff
Salisbury University

Beverly Leetch
Towson University

John Mahaffy
University of Nevada–Reno

Cofounders of QUE

Ronald J. Henry
Georgia State University

Ruth Mitchell, Patte Barth
Education Trust, Inc.

Janis Somerville
National Association of System Heads

Staff

Susan Albertine, project director
Gloria John, communications facilitator

Evaluators

Leslie Anderson, Eileen O'Brien, Karen Walking Eagle, Dwayne Smith
Policy Studies Associates

Consultants

Biology
Spencer Benson, CASTL scholar
Department of Cell Biology and Molecular Genetics, University of Maryland–
College Park

Gordon Uno
Department of Botany/Microbiology, University of Oklahoma

Jay Labov
Center for Education, National Research Council

Virginia Anderson
Department of Biology, Towson University

Chemistry
Jerry Sarquis
Department of Chemistry and Biochemistry, Miami University of Ohio

English
Susan Albertine, project director for QUE
Dean of the School of Culture and Society, The College of New Jersey

Paul Bodmer
Associate Executive Director of the National Council of Teachers of English

History
Lendol Calder, CASTL scholar
Department of History, Augustana College

Mills Kelly, CASTL scholar
Coordinator of Western Civilization Programs, George Mason University

James Roth
Department of History, Alverno College

Noralee Frankel
Assistant Director of the American Historical Association

Mathematics
Susan Ganter
Director of the Centers for Ocean Sciences Education Excellence at the Consortium for Oceanographic Research and Education

Bernard Madison
Department of Mathematics, University of Arkansas

Index